Sustaining Abundance

The ultimate goal of environmental policy is reducing pollution. Attention to environmental problems in the social sciences has brought some bold generalizations about causes of good results but almost no systematic cross-national studies that flesh out major theoretical arguments and test those claims with data. This study makes a seminal contribution to that effort in two ways. First, by taking environmental outcomes over the past thirty years as the central dependent variable, it provides a basis for evaluating national performance in reducing environmental problems. Second, by developing a data set including performance in a number of countries and elaborating on major explanations of environmental performance found in the literature, this study provides the most rigorous available analysis of the determinants of environmental performance. In so doing, it challenges what is probably the conventional wisdom in the social sciences. This book will help to place the study of environmental politics on par with other comparative studies such as Gosta Esping-Andersen's *Three Worlds of Welfare Capitalism*, Arend Lijphart's *Democracies*, and G. Bingham Powell's *Contemporary Democracies*.

Lyle Scruggs is Assistant Professor of Political Science at the University of Connecticut. His research and teaching interests are in the areas of comparative political economy and environmental policy. His articles have appeared in the *British Journal of Political Science*, *Ecological Economics*, the *Journal of Politics*, and *Political Research Quarterly*. He is currently working on a project examining changes in welfare state programs since the 1960s among twenty-one OECD countries.

Cambridge Studies in Comparative Politics

General Editor
Margaret Levi *University of Washington, Seattle*

Associate Editors
Robert H. Bates *Harvard University*
Susan Stokes *University of Chicago*
Peter Hall *Harvard University*
Frances Rosenbluth *Yale University*
Helen Milner *Columbia University*
Stephen Hanson *University of Washington, Seattle*
Sidney Tarrow *Cornell University*
Peter Lange *Duke University*

Other Books in the Series

List of books in series continues after the Index

Sustaining Abundance

ENVIRONMENTAL
PERFORMANCE IN
INDUSTRIAL DEMOCRACIES

LYLE SCRUGGS

University of Connecticut

CAMBRIDGE
UNIVERSITY PRESS

PUBLISHED BY THE PRESS SYNDICATE OF THE UNIVERSITY OF CAMBRIDGE
The Pitt Building, Trumpington Street, Cambridge, United Kingdom

CAMBRIDGE UNIVERSITY PRESS
The Edinburgh Building, Cambridge CB2 2RU, UK
40 West 20th Street, New York, NY 10011-4211, USA
477 Williamstown Road, Port Melbourne, VIC 3207, Australia
Ruiz de Alarcón 13, 28014 Madrid, Spain
Dock House, The Waterfront, Cape Town 8001, South Africa

http://www.cambridge.org

First published 2003

Printed in the United States of America

Typeface Janson Text Roman 10/13 pt.   *System* LaTeX 2$_\varepsilon$ [TB]

A catalog record for this book is available from the British Library.

Library of Congress Cataloging in Publication data

Scruggs, Lyle, 1968–
    Sustaining abundance : environmental performance in industrial democracies /
    Lyle Scruggs.
        p.   cm. – (Cambridge studies in comparative politics)
    Includes bibliographical references and index.
    ISBN 0-521-81672-6 – ISBN 0-521-01692-4 (pb.)
    1. Environmental policy.   2. Sustainable development.   3. Environmental economics.
    I. Title.   II. Series.
    HC79.E5 S29245   2002
    363.73′5–dc21   2002067712

ISBN 0 521 81672 6 hardback
ISBN 0 521 01692 4 paperback

For Laura

Contents

Figures and Tables

Figures

Figures and Tables

Tables

Preface

The seed for this book was planted in 1993 while I was working as a research assistant for Margaret McKean at Duke University. What was initially envisaged as a large-scale collaborative project on cross-national energy policy was narrowed into a dissertation investigating correlates of environmental performance among the advanced industrial democracies. When I arrived at the University of Connecticut in 1998, I put the just completed dissertation on a bookshelf and turned my attention to some other ideas. This was done on the advice of some senior colleagues, who suggested that the break would do me good. It was useful advice. Although I did look anxiously at the binder on my bookshelf a few times in the ensuing twelve months, the time off was refreshing. Ultimately, I think it has made the book a better one.

Meg McKean provided great encouragement and helpful criticism (and copious comments) throughout this project, particularly as it developed as my doctoral dissertation. I have not given (and probably cannot give) her enough credit. Others were also kind enough to read and comment on various aspects of the project along the way. David Vogel read a very early version of the manuscript. His comments provided great encouragement. Michael Skou Andersen, Pete Andrews, Peter Munk Christiansen, Robert Keohane, Michael Munger, Sonja Walti, and Albert Weale have all provided very intelligent and helpful advice. To the extent that what follows does not reflect the intelligence of all of these people, it is not for their lack of effort: the responsibility is entirely my own. The political science editor at Cambridge University Press, Lewis Bateman, has been both extremely encouraging and helpful throughout the process. Last but not least, Margaret Levi was very kind to put this book in the Cambridge Studies in Comparative Politics series.

This project would probably not have been possible without the encouraging help from many public officials who provided bits of information, whether in the form of insight into their national regulatory process or details on the pollution problems assessed in this book. On the whole, the experience has reinforced in me the conviction that the inherent ambiguities surrounding social data necessitate fuller, not more circumscribed, comparisons, be they of individuals or countries. Richard Lewis and Wolfgang Gaede provided helpful and friendly support in introducing me to some of these national officials. I also thank the Center for International Studies at Duke University and the Research Foundation at the University of Connecticut for financial support on this project. I would also like to thank my colleagues in the Departments of Political Science at both institutions.

I owe a special credit to Peter Lange, my dissertation advisor and a frequent collaborator. He was the one who encouraged me to work on other things upon arriving in Storrs. Peter has provided invaluable advice on this project and beyond. He is a unique and wonderful person and a great friend. Those familiar with Peter's work will probably find his influences all too easily.

Finally, I would like to thank Scott de Marchi and Layna Mosley for their intangible professional and moral support in seeing the project along. Their contributions have been greater than any of us might have realized at the time.

1

Introduction

This book examines the success of seventeen Western nations in reducing environmental pollution since the early 1970s. Environmental conditions play an increasingly important role in the politics of advanced democracies. Increased human expansion has placed unprecedented strains on the resource base upon which the economy depends. Holes in the ozone layer, global warming, and the loss of biodiversity are only a few of the best-known problems connected with the environmental crisis. Also important are problems less global in scope, like acid rain or the disposal of wastes. Few dispute that historic trends in environmental degradation could hinder the ability to provide increasing levels of well-being into the next century. Current problems stem first and foremost from a failure to use natural resources effectively and from the implications of that failure on historic development paths.

The public has begun to recognize some of the environmental problems confronting the physical and economic sustainability of modern societies. Opinion polls since the 1960s show that large majorities in most economically advanced countries have consistently supported increased public action to ensure the protection of ecosystems and to reduce pollution. Policy makers have responded both to the growing evidence of long-term threats and growing public opposition to past practices by creating a variety of reforms to control environmental degradation. Today, most Western democracies have a wide array of measures to limit pollution and other forms of environmental degradation.

Public policies are essential to resolving many environmental problems because environmental quality is a collective good and thus will tend to be underprovided by the market alone. Even when market-type solutions can be relied on, they will require that political authorities set the appropriate

1

incentives or levels of acceptable pollution. But official public policies, such as product bans or pollution taxes, are not the only way to change behavior for the better. Environmental pollution is ultimately the outcome of individual actions and decisions that are themselves affected by economic choice and social behavior, in addition to government policy.

Understanding the relatively recent salience of environmental protection in politics is a large and complex task. The current literature has no shortage of explanations for growing environmental interest, nor is there a shortage of prescriptions for reforms to address environmental problems more efficiently or effectively. What has been largely absent, however, is an empirical assessment linking explanations and actual changes in environmental pollution. In other words, the impact of various explanations of environmental reform has not been investigated with regard to environmental outcomes.

A main purpose of this study is to provide such an analysis. In so doing, I hope to provide answers to the following questions:

- What is the role of wealth and economic structural change on environmental performance?
- Do cross-national differences in public concern about environmental problems and environmental values explain differences in environmental performance?
- Do strong organizations of economic interest groups operating in close cooperation with the government suppress or facilitate effective environmental reforms?
- What is the influence of basic democratic political institutions on the ability of societies to overcome concentrated interests in order to secure the diffuse benefits of environmental protection?

In answering these questions, this study fills several lacunae in the study of comparative politics generally and comparative environmental policy more specifically. First, the majority of the literature in comparative and environmental politics has focused either on the emergence of environmental pollution as a popular political issue (e.g., Dalton 1994; Dalton and Kuechler 1990; Hofrichter and Reif 1990; Lowe and Rüdig 1986; Rohrschneider 1988, 1990) or on analyzing official environmental policy outputs (e.g., Kamieniecki and Sanasarian 1990; Strom and Swindell 1993; Vail, Hasund, and Drake 1994; Vogel and Kun 1987). An important limitation of these studies is that they tell little about actual pollution outcomes. Indeed, some studies simply *assume* that policy is synonymous with results. This book looks explicitly at progress in environmental outcomes (reductions in environmental pollution), or what I generally refer to as environmental performance, and it assesses the veracity of explanations suggested in the environmental policy and comparative politics literatures in accounting for variations in that performance. Comparing national environmental performance thus adds an important dimension to the understanding of the broader question of how societies deal with environmental challenges.

A second lacuna addressed in this book is the absence of systematic and simultaneous comparison of competing explanations of environmental outcomes. A characteristic of much of the comparative environmental politics literature is that it is limited to individual country studies or comparisons across a few countries in very specific environmental policy areas (Lowe and Rüdig 1986; Vogel and Kun 1987; Strom and Swindell 1993; Andersen 1994; Liefferink 1996). The persuasiveness and generalizability of such studies is severely limited by the existence of more explanations than there are cases under study (Lijphart 1971). Choosing among competing explanations in these kinds of studies is perilous, if not logically impossible. This study attempts to overcome some of these difficulties by conducting a comparison of a relatively large number of countries (seventeen), carefully laying out hypotheses found in the literature, developing a measure of environmental performance, and subjecting various explanations to multivariate statistical analysis. This approach allows for a more systematic comparison of competing explanations than has been done in previous studies and consequently permits more general claims about the determinants of environmental performance. Despite some inevitable compromises of detail, including the experience of as many countries as possible also permits an evaluation of competing explanations.

A third contribution of this book is to expand the understanding of national performance in the comparative politics of industrial societies. Comparative politics has long attempted to explain how societies address highly salient social problems directly. Powell (1982), for example, examined how political institutions affect regime stability and political violence. Others have examined the impact of a variety of structural, cultural, and institutional factors on national economic performance, particularly in Europe, North America, and Asia (e.g., Lijphart 1999; Garrett 1998). Still others have examined how industrial societies affect welfare outcomes and what things shape such outcomes (Esping-Andersen 1990; Hicks 1999). Curiously, however, comparative politics has not placed *environmental* performance alongside economic or political performance as a central topic of comparative government, even though environmental protection is widely considered to be an essential government function that is inherently connected with long-term political stability and economic prosperity. Conversely, policy studies seldom utilize general insights from comparative politics in trying to understand environmental policy (Jahn 1998; Jänicke, Mönch, and Binder 1997; Jänicke and Weidner 1993; Strom and Swindell 1993; Kamieniecki and Sanasarian 1990). By systematically examining the variations in and determinants of environmental performance, I hope this book makes a lasting contribution to our understanding of comparative government and places the study of environment into the center of studies of national performance.

What Is Good Environmental Performance?

Good environmental performance can be defined as progress toward or achievement of a situation in which societal withdrawals from the stock of natural resources do not prevent future generations from having an equivalent stock. This is the conventional definition of sustainability provided by the environmental community (Pearce, Markandya, and Barbier 1989; WCED 1987). One might, for example, evaluate environmental performance much the same way as one would evaluate economic performance. One problem with this approach is that this idealized sustainable state is a moving target.

Carrying capacities in nature are not fixed, static, or simple relations. They are contingent on technology, preferences, and the structure of production and consumption. They are also contingent on the ever-changing state of interactions between the physical and biotic environments. A single number for carrying capacity would be meaningless because the consequences for both human innovation and biological evolution are inherently unknowable. (Arrow et al. 1995: 620–21)

Moreover, sustainability is, in a highly interconnected world of global culture, trade, and production, a slippery concept. British coal use may seem much more sustainable to Britain than to the nations downwind. Moreover, the ability to export (or import) goods across borders complicates comparisons of countries' environmental progress.

In this study I define environmental performance as *evidence of reductions in a variety of common and pervasive pollutants.* The "pollutants" considered are human emissions of sulfur dioxide and nitrogen oxides, the generation

4

of municipal waste, fertilizer use, glass recycling rates, and the proportion of the population covered by wastewater treatment facilities. Reductions in the first four indicators and increases in the latter two imply direct reductions in the pressure placed on the ecosystem at large by human activity. These measures are meant to be indicative of overall national success in solving various pollution problems; they are obviously not an exhaustive list of environmental problems facing these countries. Chapter 2 provides more details about the selection of these particular indicators.

Identifying progress in environmental protection requires not simply a measure of pollution at a single point in time but also changes over time. Although the problems associated with environmental pollution policy date back many decades, most studies place special emphasis on the period since the late 1960s and early 1970s, when public concern and policy initiatives proliferated internationally, especially among countries in North America, Western Europe, and Japan. Thus, wherever possible, measures of environmental progress used in this book are based on changes in pollution indicators using data from the early 1970s to the mid-1990s.

This analysis is presented in Chapter 2. In summary, it suggests that there are considerable differences in the progress made among the advanced democracies, although there has been solid progress across the board (Ireland and Spain being possible exceptions). Thus, we can consider the first decades of the environmental era as a limited success, although some countries seem to have enjoyed greater success than others.

Explaining Performance

Students of environmental policy make two major claims about general, cross-national trends in environmental performance. First, studies of environmental policy often suggest that there has been a pronounced trend toward *convergence* in national environmental performance (e.g., Hoberg 1986; Knoepfel et al. 1987; Kopp, Portney, and DeWitt 1990; Vogel 1995). This argument tends to follow from the observation that national standards and policies have converged. Studies typically point to international treaties and the convergence of standards – due to the international epistemic communities, international coordination in organizations like the Organization for Economic Cooperation and Development (OECD), or pooled sovereignty in bodies like the European Union – as evidence for this trend in standards. Convergent performance follows from the presumption that "laggard" countries catch up to the "pioneers" as the former enact and implement standards more closely resembling the standards of the "pioneer" countries (Andersen and Liefferink 1997).

The main problem with this claim is that it has been empirically evaluated only for policy standards, not for actual outcomes. Because the true test of environmental policy lies in the outcomes, convergent standards may tell us little. Indeed, the evidence presented in Chapter 2 sharply contradicts the convergence claim. Although most countries did experience considerable improvement in environmental performance along many dimensions that I measure, I also find considerable divergence in comparative environmental performance among these developed countries.

A second claim suggested in the literature is that countries do not perform consistently in different areas of environmental policy; although countries may effectively tackle some problems, they perform poorly on others. On the contrary, I find that there is considerable consistency across the measures assessed in this study. Countries that do relatively well on one measure tend to do relatively well on others. Because the measures discussed here represent a wide diversity of environmental problems – point and nonpoint pollution, multiple media (air, land-soil, water), and spatial effect (local, national, regional) – the evidence suggests that different national performance outcomes (at least those I look at) are consistent.

The empirical analysis in this book relies on a multidimensional indicator of good environmental performance, which makes the analysis less vulnerable to the challenge that the factors associated with performance are idiosyncratic. Whereas countries may do well in one or two particular areas because of "natural" or accidental advantages in that area (e.g., starting off with particularly wasteful or pollution-intensive energy sectors), it is unlikely that countries would do consistently well in six areas for those reasons. Thus, the multidimensional indicator increases the validity of my contention that environmental performance is *systematically* related to structural, cultural, and institutional differences emphasized throughout this book.

Of course, the ultimate aim of environmental policy, and one of the aims of environmental policy research, is not simply to describe and analyze broad pollution trends but to explain them. The numerous explanations in the literature can be grouped into three broad categories of comparative politics: structural, cultural, and institutional.[1] Such categories of explanation

---

[1] The distinction is inspired by the approach in Lichbach and Zuckerman (1997).

are admittedly imprecise and are often simply analytical distinctions. At the margins (and sometimes more centrally) the categories fuse. My purpose is not to engage in turf battles over what is properly considered a structural, cultural, or institutional explanation; I am more interested in the substantive relationships.

Structural Change

Changes in the structure of societies, particularly the structure of economic demand and production, are often considered sufficient to explain environmental reform. Particular emphasis, for example, has been placed on the role of rising per capita income and the shift from industrial to a more service-oriented economy. Associated changes – from less pollution-intensive light industry (assembly and foodstuffs) to highly pollution-intensive heavy industry (steel and bulk chemicals) and then to "inherently" lower pollution-intensive high-technology industry (computers and pharmaceuticals) – have been found to be associated with lower pollution intensity (Hettige, Lucas, and Wheeler 1992). Such explanations are particularly prevalent in economics, where economic development is generically assumed to follow the trajectory of the first industrial nations. However, the importance of economic development also features in some political or sociological accounts of environmental policy performance (Jänicke 1992; Inglehart 1990).

There are two often diametrically opposed views about the role of rising incomes and changing economic structure on environmental quality. "Limits-to-growth" proponents tend to view rising income, as measured by gross domestic product (GDP), as part of the problem rather than the solution to environmental problems. The limits-to-growth view correctly points out that attention to the changing share of economic sectors obscures the fact that absolute production in most economic sectors continues to grow even as relative shares change. Environmental problems are sensitive to total pollution. The issue, as Daly (1991) has pointed out, is economic scale relative to natural systems and not the relative shares of activity within sectors of the economy.

In contrast to this "antigrowth" view is one that claims that economic development may be a sufficient condition for eventual improvements in environmental protection (Beckerman 1992). Rising income, so the argument goes, may initially damage the environment, but higher incomes increase the demand for environmental quality due to a decreasing marginal utility for private goods (and income more generally) (Baumol and Oates 1988). As incomes continue to increase, there are absolute decreases in the negative environmental effects of production, because of a relatively greater willingness and ability to pay for environmental protection. Thus, pollution declines even though production increases.

Recent research has suggested that the link between income and environmental quality is in fact not linear but U-shaped (Grossman and Krueger 1995; Shafik 1994; cf. Harbaugh, Levinson, and Wilson 2002). Environmental quality declines as development proceeds from low-agricultural to moderate-industrial levels of development but later improves as middle-income countries grow faster. This U-shaped relationship is sometimes referred to as the environmental Kuznets curve (EKC).[2] The underlying explanations for the EKC suggest two means by which income affects environmental quality: through structure of production and through the structure of demand. Both explanations predict reinforcing effects in economically advanced countries: production structure shifts toward less polluting production *and* consumers shift toward demanding improved environmental quality.

One of the main problems with the EKC thesis is that empirical trends in particular measures of environmental quality vary considerably in their functional form. For some environmental indicators, such as the quality of drinking water, quality improves in line with rising income. Other indicators, such as carbon dioxide emissions, deteriorate as national income increases. Still others do indeed follow the U-shaped pattern suggested by the Kuznets curve.

Another objection to the EKC thesis is that many causes of environmental destruction are independent of income and ultimately institutional or cultural in origin. Such objections imply that higher income is at best a necessary condition for reductions in environmental pollution. The ultimate mechanism for good performance then is appropriate institutions (Arrow et al. 1995). A third problem with the EKC literature is that the results showing a Kuznets curve with "maximum" pollution at middle incomes also find a second inflection point at very high levels of income (Grossman and Krueger 1995: 366; Shafik 1994). In other words, beyond a certain point (just below the income level in the United States, Canada, and Switzerland), more wealth is indeed bad for the environment.

---

[2] The Kuznets curve was a popular observation about the U-shaped relationship between average income and income equality in the United States (Kuznets 1955).

Introduction

An examination of the relationship between environmental performance and wealth in Chapter 3 of this book suggests that the effects of income and economic structure are important. First, the level of income per capita is associated with increased aggregate environmental performance, but only up to a point. After that, greater wealth is associated with worsening environmental performance. This implies that the limits-to-growth pessimists are not necessarily incorrect in claiming that all rich, Western countries are "overdeveloped." Even at very high levels of income – equivalent to the incomes in Italy or the Netherlands – my analysis suggests that more per capita income has improved environmental performance in the first three decades of the modern environmental era. On the other hand, beyond a certain income (less than that in the United States), relative environmental performance declines as income increases. This finding is thus consistent with results elsewhere and suggests that there could indeed be some practical limits to growth. Chapter 3 also examines the relationship between economic structural change and environmental performance. The results suggest that, while structural change is associated with changes in per capita income, it is not associated with differences in environmental performance, at least among developed democracies.

In addition to the effects of income and economic structure on environmental performance, several other structural factors have been put forth as plausible explanations of differences in national environmental performance. Perhaps the most important of these are geographic size and population density. Country size is often suggested as an explanation for differences in environmental performance because larger countries have large "pollution sinks" that effectively obscure (or mitigate) pollution problems. Of course, using country size to account for environmental performance does not take into consideration the population inhabiting the space in question. Perhaps for this reason population density, rather than country size, has been suggested as an explanation for differences in environmental performance. Crowded countries, no matter their absolute size, are considered more likely to address environmental pollution problems because larger proportions of their populations confront a given environmental insult. These additional structural characteristics of countries are also examined in Chapter 3. The evidence suggests that neither factor matters much individually, but the combined effect of size and population density is important in helping to account for differences in environmental performance. Small, densely populated countries tend to have better performance than large, sparsely populated ones.

Public Opinion and Environmental Mobilization

Many view structural factors as unconvincing explanations for change in environmental pollution. Even if structural factors enhance or retard environmental performance, society itself (or more properly individuals composing society) acts to cause or correct pollution problems. Perhaps for this reason many social scientists studying environmental politics and policy focus on expressed social concerns about environmental protection.

In all Western industrial democracies, there is clear evidence from various surveys of popular opinion that public support for environmental protection has increased since the late 1960s. There are two closely related explanations for this public support. The first is an extension of the income thesis just discussed: as wealth increases, the demand for quality-of-life issues like a clean environment increases relative to the demand for material goods. For instance, Inglehart's explanation of "postmaterialist" culture, which claims to be closely associated with greater demand for higher environmental quality, is rooted in the economic principle of "diminishing marginal utility of income" (1997: 33). According to the postmaterialism thesis, environmental concern has grown in the West because the long-term material prosperity since World War II has led subsequent generations to take material abundance for granted.

A second explanation of public support for environmentalism also focuses on the underlying values of mass publics and elites but explains demand for environmental quality as the result of a more general social learning process (Dunlap and Mertig 1995; Jamison, Eyerman, and Cramer 1990; Milbraith 1984; Paehlke 1997). In this explanation – sometimes referred to as the "new environmental paradigm" greater knowledge about environmental processes, not economic security, has transformed people's understanding of human interaction with the environment, thus altering the nature and extent of the traditional economic development process.

The distinction between these economic-resource and knowledge-learning explanations is not always clear. For instance, evidence to distinguish clearly between their effects is not readily available. Cross-nationally comparable surveys of citizen attitudes, values, and preferences are insufficient to distinguish between attitudes reflecting a new paradigm or simply the indirect effects of prosperity. Moreover, at a conceptual level, distinguishing cultural change (in economics the equivalent of a change in preference) from a simple income effect is fraught with

10

difficulty. Values and preferences are interrelated; thus, economic and sociological-anthropological explanations for increasing environmental concern are not easily disentangled.

Finally, postmaterialism and the new environmental paradigm suggest that environmental opinion and environmental performance should be related. Few would argue that the relationship is direct and instantaneous: we are unlikely to find that a small change in opinion immediately translates into changes in environmental quality. Viewed over a reasonable amount of time, however, both value-based explanations of environmentalism suggest a strong correlation between opinion and basic values and national environmental performance. This argument has been made perhaps most forcefully in connection with Inglehart's postmaterialism thesis (Dalton 1994; Hofrichter and Reif 1990; Inglehart 1990, 1997; but cf. Dunlap and Mertig 1995). According to its proponents, the growth of environmental-postmaterialist values transcends institutional and structural differences between advanced industrial countries in the West.

The forces that gave rise to the Ecologists and the National Front in France, or the Greens and Republikaner in Germany, cannot give rise to similar parties in a society like the United States, because of institutional constraints that make it difficult for new parties to emerge here – even though the same forces are clearly present. . . . But a less obvious change has taken place: the issues underlying US politics have changed profoundly with the old parties adopting the same new agenda as in other advanced industrial societies. (Inglehart 1997: 331)

Although recent work may fundamentally challenge the theoretical foundations of postmaterialism (Clarke et al. 1999), it remains essential to examine the impact of indisputable changes in public attitudes, whatever their cause, and the rise of environmental organizations and parties (as expressions of environmental concerns) and comparative environmental performance.

While the connections between opinion and environmental performance do not rest on a solid empirical foundation, the general argument is, in fact, quite defensible, at least for democratic societies. Stimson, MacKuen, and Erikson (1995), for example, provide empirical evidence that government policy in the United States has reflected shifts in public mood. Two other pieces of evidence often cited in the study of the history of environmental protection policy also support the association between opinion and performance. First, the flood of government environmental policy in the 1970s followed the growth of popular environmental awareness. This is true not only in the United States but also in other advanced democracies. Second, many firms seek to capitalize on the public's desire for environmental quality by "green marketing."[3]

Finally, it is important to stress that differences in public opinion are not simply cited as reasons for differences in likely performance in rich or poor countries in the world. Although most would agree that support for environmental protection is higher in the rich countries than in poorer countries, differences *among* industrial countries are often invoked to explain differences in policy outputs or outcomes within rich countries themselves. In Europe, for example, British, French, or Italian lackluster environmental records are often explained by the fact that the public "does not care" about environmental issues.

The analysis in Chapter 4 focuses on the role of differences in the level of public support for and commitment to environmental protection (what I refer to as environmental mobilization) in accounting for national variations in environmental performance. The evidence I use is drawn primarily from cross-national social surveys (Eurobarometer and the World Values Surveys), as well as electoral data for environmental parties. The results suggest that environmental mobilization is weakly associated with environmental performance. Indeed, the bulk of the evidence (once one controls for structural and institutional factors) suggests that mobilization is *negatively* associated with subsequent environmental performance. This somewhat counterintuitive result obviously contradicts the bulk of scholarship on environmental opinion. This effect is probably just an artifact of studying only wealthy, relatively mobilized countries. Thus, I conclude that, although mobilization probably does not hinder performance generally, differences in mobilization among wealthy democracies do not give us much leverage on explaining differences in performance.

Economic and Political Institutions

Another source of explanations for environmental performance lies not in differences in economic or geographic structure or cultural values and mobilization around environmental issues but in institutional differences

---

[3] Environmentalists often take a dim view of such efforts, perhaps too dim. While it is obvious that profit, not environmentalism, drives businesses to "green" their image, it is not obvious that they can get away with simply lying about how "green" they really are. If consumers are sincere in their demands and can monitor producer behavior to some extent, the market can be a means for consumers to redirect production.

among advanced countries. In the area of environmental protection, where collective action problems are pervasive, effective solutions to environmental problems require a great deal of coordination among social actors. This makes environmental policy a domain in which institutions should matter profoundly.

In Chapters 5 and 6, I consider two sets of institutional differences among advanced democracies that have figured prominently in comparative politics as explanations of social outcomes: socioeconomic and political institutions. By *socioeconomic institutions*, I mean the organization of producer and environmental interest groups, their relationship to state institutions, and their role in making and implementing policy. By *political institutions*, I refer to the more-or-less formal rules of representative democracy. The purpose of these chapters is to establish how and why these institutional features should matter and to show how they do.

Most accounts in the environmental politics literature rely (implicitly or explicitly) on a model of interest group interaction that stresses virtues of extensive pluralism. Because environmental concern is a relatively new policy area that conflicts with established issues like economic production and distribution, it is perhaps natural to assume that greater pluralism enhances the space for environmental interests to emerge and affect policy. Pluralism has long been argued to offer a structure (or absence of structure) that is hospitable to the consideration of new issues. Moreover, interest group pluralism, by promoting competition among similar established groups, is often expected to place such interests in a less "institutionally entrenched" position from which to oppose stringent environmental policies. Finally, more pluralist institutions are considered conducive to environmental reforms because the government has fewer ties with economic groups and is thus presumed to be willing to impose costs on such groups.

An alternative view highlights the environmental benefits of institutions that produce more negotiated solutions to environmental problems and that include an active role for strong groups, including major economic interest groups and the government. In comparative politics this is sometimes referred to as *neocorporatism*.[4] In contrast to the criticisms often

---

[4] It is important to distinguish between the neocorporatism referred to here (and in much of the contemporary literature on comparative political economy in Western Europe) and more traditional uses of the term (see Wiarda 1997 for a discussion of many of the distinctions). As further discussed in Chapter 6, neocorporatism describes a generalized system of making and implementing public policy in formalized consultation between state and interest groups.

leveled against them, neocorporatist institutions in advanced democracies have several features that can be expected to facilitate national environmental performance. First, such institutions facilitate economic structural change. They have well-established procedures for compensating distributional losers from conflicts over policy change. Such conflicts are potential deal breakers in enacting many environmental policies because losers typically have a concentrated interest in opposing regulation, whereas beneficiaries reap small and diffuse benefits. This confronts society with a classic problem of achieving Pareto-improving outcomes for society that are likely to be blocked by particularistic interests. Pluralist institutions may be ineffective in such situations because losing groups have every incentive to dig in their heels. Corporatist institutions, on the other hand, may help to alleviate such conflicts by providing a forum for credible commitments of compensation for the distributional losers in exchange for implementing socially beneficial reforms.

Second, highly organized interest organizations (a characteristic of corporatism) reduce the prospects of free-riding behavior among regulated interests. The large peak interest groups characteristic of neocorporatist countries tend to encompass large portions of both the winners and losers from environmental policy change. The principle guiding the choice of environmental policies by such encompassing groups is likely to be similar to that suggested by Olson (1982) for economic public goods: maximize public benefits, not individual rents.

A third argument in favor of neocorporatist institutions is that peak interest groups are more likely to pick up on and communicate to their members the benefits of strong environmental policies, not just the costs, as they build consensus. This fact helps to expose many of the misconceptions surrounding the compatibility of macroenvironmental and macroeconomic goals, facilitating environmental protection in the long run.

Finally, neocorporatist institutions appear to facilitate good performance by creating "organizational imperatives" among environmental interests to compete with strong economic groups, making such an institutional arrangement more conducive to long-run environmental improvements: effective organization and a broad interest in reconciling economic and environmental issues. Neocorporatist institutions may thus facilitate the representation of otherwise diffuse interests for environmental protection within peak groups.

It is interesting that, despite generally being studied and portrayed as a policy field that is sui generis, the analysis of the environmental

14

policy-making institutions of individual countries closely resembles policy institutions in other arenas. Countries with more pluralist economic policy institutions also tend to have pluralist environmental policy institutions, whereas those with more neocorporatist institutions dominating economic policy also have more neocorporatist environmental policies. This close correlation across issue areas is not really surprising and has been observed in many other policy areas (Soysal 1994; Lehmbruch 1984). Close correlation between traditional policy institutions and environmental ones might also be expected because environmental policy involves transforming the views and behavior of producers and consumers. One could go so far as to say that successful environmental regulation *requires* the active cooperation of traditional economic groups and their self-transformation.

Of course, whether this transformation is ultimately best achieved under more pluralist or corporatist arrangements is at some level an empirical question. Evidence presented in Chapter 5 provides strong support for the neocorporatist perspective. Countries with encompassing economic interest groups and neocorporatist institutions have had better environmental performance than countries with more pluralist arrangements. This association is robust to different measures of corporatism and to the introduction of controls for other explanations (e.g., income, geography, environmental mobilization).

The results in Chapter 5 suggest that the decline of neocorporatist institutions for economic policy making in the late 1980s and 1990s may be a mixed blessing. Such changes may unravel cooperation in the area of environmental policy that has improved environmental performance during the first twenty years of the modern environmental era. Although environmental policy may not be the cause of declining neocorporatist institutions, the evidence in this study suggests that the desire for an environmental policy may be a reason not to dismantle neocorporatist institutions.

A second set of institutional factors that have also been argued to affect environmental reform as well as many other substantive policy areas is the *formal political structures of representative government*. Electoral laws, the power of executives vis-à-vis legislatures, and the division of authority between national and subnational political entities can all affect the prospects of environmental reform (Vogel 1993). Although such institutions might not be expected to impact systematically the day-to-day regulation of specific environmental pollution problems, by influencing the ability of politicians to aggregrate diffuse environmental interests against concentrated opposition, such institutions may have long-term effects on environmental performance that are important to understand.

Chapter 6 analyzes the impact of several types of political institutions. Drawing on Arend Lijphart's work on the varieties of democratic institutions as well as other work on the implications of political institutions on policy making, I isolate five critical and distinctive aspects of democracy likely to affect environmental performance: the frequency of coalition government (coalition dominance); the relative power of the executive and legislative branches (executive dominance); divisions in the legislature (bicameralism); geographical separation of power (federalism); and the openness of the electoral system to "new issue" parties (electoral proportionality). Other institutional differences in democratic societies might also matter for environmental policy performance, but these five are generally considered important in comparative politics. They are a natural starting point for considering the effects of democratic institutions on performance. As detailed in Chapter 6, these differences have also been considered important in many existing studies of environmental policy.

Whether these political institutions promote or hinder performance is controversial. For each argument in favor of a particular arrangement along each of the five dimensions of democratic institutions mentioned, there are opposing explanations. I lay out the arguments and assess them against the data. The results of the empirical investigation support the contention that configurations of democratic institutions that concentrate political power experience better environmental performance. In contrast, greater separation of powers tends to be associated with poorer national performance.

Case Selection and Methodological Approach

The bulk of this study relies on an analysis of a multidimensional indicator of environmental performance among seventeen industrial democracies. The countries considered are Austria, Belgium, Canada, Denmark, Finland, France, Germany, Ireland, Italy, Japan, the Netherlands, Norway, Spain, Sweden, Switzerland, the United Kingdom, and the United States.[5] Chapter 2 addresses issues related to the selection of the environmental

---

[5] Generally speaking, Germany refers to the western part of the country. Thus, the measured improvements in Germany are not due to improving Eastern Germany's poor environmental conditions and infrastructure.

performance indicator; however, the limitation to advanced industrial democracies merits some explanation.

Industrial countries were selected primarily because they are the countries that have attempted to address the large environmental problems created in the process of industrialization for a considerable period. This makes them distinct from countries that have (at best) only recently made serious efforts to clean up or protect their environments. In this regard, one might argue that the "sample" of countries is biased by effort. As explained in Chapter 3, this is clearly true. Insofar as the experiences of these countries serve as models, understanding their relative success can improve the prospects for better performance in all countries in the future.

The high-pollution industrial countries of Eastern Europe and of Asia (such as Korea, Taiwan, Singapore) were excluded for several reasons. First, they have a shorter history of dealing with environmental problems. Second, they were not democracies for most of the period under study. Given the fact that the literature I examine presumes well-established democratic governance, including these countries, most of which are very new democracies, would not be an appropriate test of most of the hypotheses examined. The final reason for excluding these countries is practical. Given the available data, including these countries would have made developing a comprehensive indicator of environmental improvement over a long period impossible.

Some established industrial democracies – for example, Australia, Greece, Iceland, New Zealand, and Portugal – were excluded due to a lack of data over a sufficient period of time. Although the absence of data for these countries might imply that there is something systematically different about their environmental performance compared with that of the countries included, I have found no such indication. Moreover, these countries vary considerably from each other on many of the main explanatory variables I examine, and it is unlikely that excluding them affects the variation in the explanatory variables.

The empirical results here are based on a "truncated " sample of countries, that is, wealthy, postindustrial democracies. Such restrictions on the range of cases increase the uncertainty in inferring that the results apply to the broader universe of nation-states. Nevertheless, it is important to bear in mind that this general set of conditions typifies what most countries aspire to. Given this fact, what we can say about determinants of environmental performance in wealthy, postindustrial democracies should have implications for other countries as they develop.

This book treats environmental performance in a "large-n" statistical analysis.[6] Conducting such analysis with seventeen cases (sometimes fewer) has limitations, but there are several reasons why such an approach is valuable. First, comparative environmental politics and policy studies have focused almost exclusively on a case study approach that places severe limits on the types of inferences that can be drawn. In particular, such studies make it extremely difficult to test competing hypotheses reliably. While the larger data set used here does not overcome all of these problems, it does provide a worthwhile complement to most prior work.

Second, the comparative case studies to date have concentrated on a small subset of advanced democracies – primarily the United States, Germany, the United Kingdom, the Netherlands, and Sweden. By including countries that are not normally considered in comparative analysis, the approach used in this book expands the "population" of cases compared and provides a better test of the explanatory power of the explanations of environmental performance in the literature.

Finally, the statistical analysis throughout the book is technically cross-sectional. However, the dependent variable captures a cross section of changes in environmental performance. The main reason for opting for cross-sectional analysis of change over pooled cross-sectional time series is fourfold. First, the environmental data do not provide complete time series for most pollution indicators in most countries, which makes a true pooled time series design impossible. Second (as Chapter 2 makes clear), the aggregate measure of performance is not amenable to being broken down into yearly changes. Third, many of the explanatory variables do not change very much, if at all, over time. This tends to make the results of a pooled analysis similar to simple cross-sectional analysis because most variation is captured by those factors that do not vary over time. Fourth, social science theories about environmental outcomes are not so exact as to allow us to specify fully the complexity implied in a pooled time series model.[7]

---

[6] Of course, "large-n" is a relative term. Relative to the comparative politics literature generally, and environmental policy studies more specifically, the appellation "large-n" seems justified.

[7] Indeed, if the last two points are valid, many uses of pooled time series in comparative politics are misleading. Pooling may technically increase the number of observations on which statistical estimates are made ($N \times T$ as opposed to N), but whether observations are reasonably considered random draws from an underlying population is not clear. Moreover, insofar as most explained variance in a model is captured by a pure cross-sectional effect (i.e., a variable that does not change over time in a particular country), pooling "artificially" deflates standard errors.

2

Measuring National Environmental Performance

Historically, a major reason that previous work did not directly investigate environmental outcomes was the lack of data with which to make comparisons (Hoberg 1986; Strom and Swindell 1993; Vogel 1986). The statistical abstracts of most national governments have only recently included environmental data alongside the economic, social, and political data collected for decades. In a few countries, the amount of environmental data is impressive but often of rather limited duration and not comparable across countries. Evidence from a few countries over short periods may be useful for various purposes but does not permit the evaluation of existing explanations for long-term environmental outcomes within countries. The reason is that short-term fluctuations in economic, social, or environmental conditions may mask long-term trends of man-made environmental impacts. Still, the paucity of empirical studies of outcomes is puzzling, given the stakes involved. For instance, even in the United States the first major empirical work on political determinants of environmental outcomes was not published until the 1990s (Ringquist 1993).

The environmental data in this study come primarily from the OECD's *Environmental Data Compendium*. It represents the best source from which to ascertain general trends within and across countries in the OECD.[1] This

---

[1] Some of the earliest work on comparative environmental performance was conducted at the Free University in Berlin (Jänicke et al. 1989; Jänicke, Mönch, and Bindar 1993). More recent literature that does analyze performance data more systematically is Jänicke (1992), Andersen (1994), and Jahn (1998, 1999). Portions of the OECD data have been used in other studies comparing environmental pollution performance (e.g., Crepaz 1995; Davies and Mazurek 1998; Jahn 1998; Scruggs 1999, 2001; World Economic Forum 2001). My use of comparative trends is a more conservative approach than several other studies of comparative environmental performance – e.g., World Economic Forum et al. (2001), Crepaz, Davies, and Mazurek – that generally compare pollution levels that may not be directly comparable.

19

volume has been published biannually since 1985. The data are collected on the basis of a questionnaire coadministered with Eurostat and sent to the member states of the OECD. The compendium provides data on a variety of pollution issues common to OECD countries. The questionnaire was developed by the OECD Group on the State of the Environment, which has increasingly tried to assure the quality and maximize the comparability of the data reported. The resulting data are subjected to an internal and external quality assurance process to assure accuracy and harmonized by the OECD Group on the State of the Environment to enhance cross-national comparability. Although different national definitions limit the comparability of some of the data at a given point in time, by comparing pollution trends across countries, I have avoided some of the comparability problems. I have also checked the OECD data against a variety of other sources. I note these sources in the extended discussion of each measure later in the chapter. Where there is evidence that the OECD does not appear to report a consistent series – for example, due to a reported break in the series – I note how I resolved the issue.

My evaluation of comparative performance covers the period from 1970 to 1995, the first twenty-five years of the modern environmental era. It may seem contentious to assign the same period (circa 1970) as the beginning of an "era" in different societies. The early 1970s, however, marks what is generally regarded as an international recognition of environmental problems among the relatively advanced industrial countries examined here (Weale 1992). This period coincides with the first major international conference on the environment (Stockholm) and the nongovernmental Earth Day celebration (Caldwell 1996). The period between the late 1960s and early 1970s is also marked by a flurry of national legislative and administrative reforms around that time in all of these countries, dwarfing efforts theretofore. For instance, all of the countries considered in this study had established a national environmental authority or ministry between 1968 and 1974 (Jänicke 1992). For all of these reasons, using the early 1970s as a common starting point from which to judge environmental performance is justifiable.

What Is Environmental Performance?

The term "national performance" is often used by social scientists comparing political systems. Many studies of the political economy of industrial societies focus on explaining economic or social outcomes, and not simply policy outputs. Common examples are the study of unemployment, inflation, economic growth, the "decommodification" of labor, government stability, and political violence (Powell 1982; Esping-Andersen 1990; Lijphart 1999). Most studies of comparative *environmental* politics, however, have focused almost exclusively on environmental policy outputs. Although the attention paid to policy outputs is not necessarily wrong, this book's attention on *outcomes* is more in keeping with major questions motivating comparative study of political economy.

When scholars focus on social outcomes like unemployment, economic growth, or pollution, there are implicit or explicit reasons for the choice of any particular idea of performance. Even when they are not acknowledged as such, all performance indicators are imbued with fundamentally normative judgments or assumptions. Often it is the assumption that performance in a particular area is simply of wide interest (e.g., unemployment). This is a necessary part of practicing social science.

Performance measures also have important practical implications (Hammond et al. 1995). They summarize information and communicate it to decision makers whether they be citizens as voters or consumers, or elites as public or corporate policy makers. Environmental performance indicators can also have important practical feedback effects on polities.

The importance of a particular indicator depends on a number of factors. Public interest about the problem is often an important one for democratic and market societies, but not always. Environmental performance, as used here, is founded on the same basis as most performance indicators. First, it implies a general normative assumption: less pollution is better than more. It also implies and requires that environmental performance is something that is not fully encompassed by government policy and should be measured directly. As becomes clear in later chapters, environmental performance is affected by more than government policy, just as economic performance is caused by factors other than economic policy.

Second, environmental performance implies addressing a wide range of pollution problems. The indicators used here encompass six environmental problem areas that have been identified as important across all industrial countries, thus making them candidates for remedial action by business, government, and the public. By examining changes in multiple indicators, we can better judge overall successes much more effectively than if we just look at one specific pollutant in making general claims. Third, environmental performance is evaluated here at the national level. Although this distinction is somewhat arbitrary, given the transboundary nature of many pollution problems, several arguments justify this usage here. Nation-states remain the primary repository of authority over environmental issues. In most countries, nation-states also maintain a great deal of authority over environmental policy goals and are ultimately responsible for implementing international policies.

An important issue for fourteen of the seventeen European countries in this study is the effect of European integration on national environmental policy. Although the European Union (EU) increasingly affects national policy, its impact is not considered at length in this book for several reasons.[2] First, EU environmental policy has been, for most of the period considered here, relatively weak. The EU's "environmental ministry" – Directorate General XI – remains poorly staffed and funded, and the rules of the game continue to prevent it from having much control over implementation of directives and regulations. The EU policy process may keep environmental issues higher on some national agendas than would otherwise be the case but does not necessarily eliminate national diversity of most aspects of policy within the EU. Substantial room for differentiation in environmental performance based on national institutions or contexts remains (e.g., Aguilar 1993; Aguilar Fernandez 1994). The empirical data here suggest little convergence in environmental outcomes in Europe. Thus, whereas implications of European integration on environmental *policy* are present and arguably increasing, those effects do not appear to have led to a convergence in EU environmental *performance*.

The broad definition of environmental performance used here is essential to capture the ostensible purpose of environmental concerns and environmental actions: reduced environmental damage. The more traditional methods of assessing outcomes – spending more money, levying higher fines, or increasing legal compliance rates – overlook the fact that spending and the law are means to an end. If environmental quality is costly, and it usually is, spending less for a given quality level is the ideal. Moreover, if environmental concerns are truly "norm-alized," that is, they are internalized in people's day-to-day decision making, then there is need for fewer formal environmental policy outputs. Finally, while specialized government organizations devoted to environmental protection issues are important, *integrating environmental policy into traditional "sectors"*

---

[2] I use EC (European Community) and EU (European Union) more or less interchangeably in the book, despite the fact that the latter appellation did not apply until 1992.

of government or production is now seen as vital for effective environmental governance. In all of these instances, what is normally taken to be evidence of effective policy may be inversely, or simply not, related to good outcomes.

The final advantage of using changes in pollution outcomes as indicators of performance is that it goes some way toward integrating environmental policy into the field of comparative political economy. Focusing on environmental outcomes complements the overwhelming attention on outputs in the environmental policy literature; and it supplements the focus in comparative political economy on economic outcomes.

Environmental Performance Compared

The rest of this chapter examines pollution trends across seventeen OECD countries in six areas: sulfur dioxide emissions, nitrogen oxide emissions, municipal waste generation, glass recycling, apparent fertilizer consumption, and coverage of wastewater treatment facilities. I divide the performance indicators into three broad categories based on the receiving environmental medium: air, water, and soil. I present data over as long a time period as possible, generally encompassing the period from 1970 to 1995.

The following analytical presentation of the data accomplishes two objectives. First, it allows me to evaluate two general propositions about the pattern of environmental outcomes that are common in the comparative environmental policy literature:

Proposition 1. National environmental policies have failed to reduce targeted pollution problems appreciably.

Proposition 2. Environmental performance is converging among advanced industrial countries as environmental attitudes and policies have diffused, and as countries have adopted similar standards and regulations.

I evaluate these propositions by examining cross-national trends in the reduction of pollution and the degree of convergence in pollution reduction among countries. Second, the presentation forms the basis for developing a multidimensional measure of environmental performance that incorporates comparison across countries, time, and types of pollution. Unless otherwise stated, this measure is used as the indicator of environmental performance in later chapters.

Ambient Quality versus Emissions as Measures of Performance

Before evaluating the data, it is important to mention the two main classes of environmental degradation measures that might be used as indicators of environmental performance: *ambient quality* and *total emissions*. While both approaches to evaluating performance have value (and are thus examined to some degree in this chapter), this section explains why emissions are ultimately a more basic and useful measure on which to base a national performance measure.

Ambient quality refers to pollution at particular locations. It is usually measured by pollution concentration levels (e.g., parts per million). The rationale for using ambient measures in assessing environmental quality is that most pollutants are dangerous only when concentrated, and the concentration, more than the mere existence of a pollutant, constitutes a human health or ecosystem risk. The advantages of ambient quality standards lie in their incorporation of a spatial aspect of pollution and their potential to result in a more "efficient" pollution abatement effort. By focusing on areas with the highest pollution concentrations, the efficiency of pollution cleanup can be enhanced. The classic example of the latter is the use of inexpensive dispersal methods (e.g., taller smokestacks) to alleviate local ambient quality problems. Because of altitude and winds, the use of taller stacks "dilutes" the concentration of the pollutant in a given problem area.

The major problems with relying on ambient quality in the evaluation of national environmental performance are threefold. First, in a world in which polluting activity is increasing, dispersing pollution either delays the day of reckoning or transfers it to someone else. For example, the "tall stacks" strategy used in countries like the United States, United Kingdom, and Germany may have alleviated adverse health effects locally but caused other problems (e.g., acid rain) and transferred pollution problems to other areas and to the broader ecosystem. At some point, one that many suggest is approaching rapidly, when there is no longer space to disperse pollution, pollution sources (i.e., emissions from stacks) must be reduced.

Second, many pollutants do not really become less harmful if less concentrated. Concentrating some pollutants may pose fewer risks than dispersing them. Other pollutants tend to persist and accumulate in indirect ways. For example, one of the main environmental problems with DDT was that it remained in the bodies of the animals that consumed it, so a person eating contaminated fish would get higher and higher concentrations of the chemical in his body. Dispersing the chemical widely in the ecosystem still tended to produce noticeable effects at the upper end of the food chain.

Third, determining a sufficiently concentrated threat is often difficult and contentious. It may even be more difficult practically speaking than simply eliminating a pollutant altogether. Such a statement may seem paradoxical. However, if one assumes that banning a chemical results in a more immediate search for (or uptake of) more benign substitutes, bans or direct limits may be practically superior to other forms of regulation.

A second, more fundamental measure of environmental performance – and the one that I rely on in the aggregate performance measure – is emission reduction, which means reducing overall quantities of the pollutant. Lower concentrations of pollution in a fixed area require lower emissions from some pollution sources. Given the extent of environmental problems by the 1970s and the transboundary problems associated with shifting the problem across jurisdictions by dispersal, there is simply not much continued credibility in the claim that the "larger" ecosystem can process pollution if it is simply dispersed.[3]

Figure 2.1 presents a stylized representation of ambient concentration and emissions. In panel a, there is a concentrated area of pollution where ambient standards are established. Panel b shows the emission reduction strategy from the same initial condition. Both approaches result in the same reduction in pollution from the concentrated areas (small circles), but the ambient approach promotes a major transfer to surrounding areas.

Several other factors limit the wisdom of relying on concentrations as an indicator of environmental performance and justify the use of emissions reduction. First, pollution emissions that are dispersed to other jurisdictions typically exacerbate the cost of good performance by increasing the number of affected parties and by moving the problem from areas of better (local firm or national jurisdiction) to less well defined (community or international) property rights. Second, because dispersal occurs over time as well as space, it passes the adjustment problem on to future generations. Moreover, if overall emissions continue to grow globally, dispersal may mean that

---

[3] The major shortcoming of emission reduction is the inverse of the advantage of ambient standards; it ignores the fact that concentrations may increase despite reduced emissions, resulting in more health problems in the area of concentration. Thus, emission reductions may be less expedient. Another potential shortcoming of emission reductions arises if emission limits are imposed on individual pollution sources. This is not a problem for this study, because it looks at aggregate emissions.

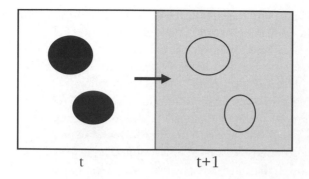

a- Ambient Concentration Reduction

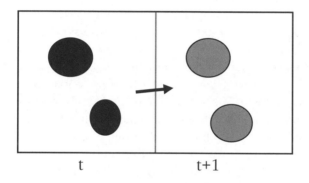

b- Emission Reduction

Figure 2.1   Spatial Effects of Ambient versus Emission Reductions

the whole system eventually faces high pollution concentrations. In short, dispersal risks globalizing an initially localized problem.

Finally, ambient concentration data introduce another level of complexity in evaluating *national* performance: a country may have little influence on its own concentration levels if pollution crosses boundaries. The alternative, emissions data, does not penalize countries whose ambient pollution is imported nor does it reward countries that simply export their problems to others.[4] Thus, overall, emissions data seem

---

[4] Pollution transfers can still occur, for example, if trade patterns result in exporting high-polluting processes and then importing the finished products.

26

a better, if still imperfect, basis for comparing national environmental performance.

Levels or Changes?

In attempting to judge nations with the best environmental performance, I rely primarily on percentage changes in emissions over long periods of time. Several reasons justify the use of changes rather than direct comparison of pollution levels at a given point in time. First, OECD sources suggest that comparative interpretations should generally be made on trends, not specific levels, because measurement methods vary to some degree. In other words, one can be more confident comparing percentage reductions of a pollutant across countries than comparing pollution levels.

The following example explains the importance of evaluating changes in pollution over time as opposed to pollution levels. In 1995, the United Kingdom had almost 20 times more total sulfur oxide emissions than Denmark (2.4 million metric tons to .15 metric tons). Even if one controls for different populations, emissions in the United Kingdom were much higher (about 40 kg/person versus about 30 kg/person). If we judge only by their emissions in 1990, we might conclude that the United Kingdom performed considerably worse. Yet the differences in 1990 might be attributed to a number of factors that *preceded* 1990. For instance, if the United Kingdom emitted 100 times more sulfur in the 1970s when environmental policies took off in the West, its performance between 1970 and 1990 would probably be judged to have been comparatively more successful. Closing the gap would require that they cut a much larger percentage of their emissions in the same period. Only by examining the evolution of emissions since the beginning of what I call the "environmental era" (basically since 1970) can we ascertain responsiveness in the period.[5] (As it turns out, the Danes, not the British, appear more responsive in this period. Given their starting point in 1970, the Danes cut emissions by 74 percent, the British by only 64 percent.)

Second, using percentage changes helps to reduce the influence of the "preenvironmental era" on the period being considered and allows us to gauge performance since the beginning of the environmental era. Many

---

[5] The recent publication of several environmental quality indexes – like the *Environmental Sustainability Index* (World Economic Forum et al. 2001) – present only a contemporary national snapshot, not progress over time.

of the harms of environmental degradation were not considered important public policy concerns until the late 1960s and 1970s (Weale 1992). Because pollution levels in 1970 or 1975 could vary greatly as a result of decisions undertaken before concerted action was under way, comparing pollution levels may conflate a country's effective response to the environmental crisis (1970–95) with "precrisis" behavior (in the 1950s or 1960s). Measuring percentage pollution reductions since the early to mid-1970s allows one to control somewhat for this problem.

One might argue that differences in the beginning level of pollution will dictate how much countries actually reduce. For example, in two otherwise identical countries with different beginning pollution levels (measured over some common denominator like population), the country with less pollution will achieve the same level of environmental quality with fewer emission reductions compared with the second country. To "reward" the second country for a higher initial pollution level would seem invalid. Relying on *percentage* reductions, however, captures some of the initial magnitude differences. For example, a country starting with lower emissions needs to reduce emissions less in absolute terms to get the same percentage change compared with a country with an initially higher level of emissions. The same percentage reduction is more likely to reflect a similar measure of successful performance, even if it does not directly measure "environmental quality."[6] The statistical analysis in later chapters also controls for factors, such as income or size of the manufacturing sector, that might make it relatively "cheaper" to reduce pollution.

The approach used here does not directly evaluate countries based on their current level of environmental quality, something that might be considered important for contemporary policy making. This objection is addressed directly to some extent in Chapter 7, but it is also essential to bear in mind that relying on a cross section of data on contemporary conditions (especially if not really comparable) does not shed much light on what factors produce improvements (changes) in performance.[7]

[6] The measures used here also do not calculate national marginal abatement costs. Attempting to do so would have severely limited the number of countries and pollutants that could be considered (if it could be done at all). Instead, I assume that for each country, the range of pollution levels observed in the period is higher than the optimum level.

[7] It is also true that some might object that the past experiences of these countries are a poor guide to confronting current problems in any country. This is a difficult charge to refute a priori and leads one to question on what basis one can suggest any course of action with empirical support (which must be based on past events). It does, however, suggest using some caution in interpreting the results.

The Measures

The pollution measures dealt with in this section were chosen on the basis of environmental importance and for their availability across countries and time. Some may have greater salience in particular countries, but all of the environmental problems investigated here are considered to be important. (The OECD's first round of national environmental performance reviews encouraged action on all of the measures analyzed here.) After briefly discussing why the particular measures are important environmental indicators, I assess if there is evidence of widespread success or failure among these countries in dealing with the problem and if there appears to be convergence in pollution levels across countries.

Sulfur Oxides

Sulfur oxide emissions, primarily sulfur dioxide, are responsible for a number of adverse human health and ecosystem effects. They are the primary ingredients of acid rain, which causes premature erosion of human structures and the eutrophication of lakes and ponds. Sulfur oxides also damage plant growth and have been linked to declining forest health in some areas. The primary sources of sulfur oxide emissions are fossil fuel combustion in industry, electricity generation, and, to a lesser extent, automobile exhaust.

Sulfur oxides were one of the first air pollution problems (compared with, e.g., carbon dioxide, chloroflourocarbons [CFCs], or nitrogen oxides) to attract widespread policy attention. The threat to forests and freshwater sources in Scandinavia, North America, and Germany prompted demands for rigorous action. The 1972 UN Stockholm Conference was instigated in no small part as an attempt to attract attention to SO_x pollution problems in Scandinavia. SO_x were also the first pollutants targeted by the Long Range Transboundary Air Pollution Treaty (LTRAP), to which most Western democracies are signatories (Levy 1993).

National trends in the emissions of sulfur oxides are presented in Table 2.1.[8] The first thing to note from the table is that there have been dramatic reductions in most countries since 1970. Only during the oil

---

[8] These figures have been checked against those reported by the United Nations Economic Commission, for Europe (UNECE), the Environmental Protection Agency, and the European Environmental Agency (also see Scruggs 2001). Although different definitions sometimes resulted in discrepancies in the levels of reported pollution, trends are virtually identical.

Table 2.1. *Total SO$_x$ Emissions, 1970–1995*

Country	Emissions (1,000 tonnes)						Change (%)		
	1970	1975	1980	1985	1990	1995	1970–80	1980–95	1970–95
Austria	*484*	*408*	400	195	91	52	−17.4	−87.0	−89.3
Belgium	*1,002*	*844*	828	400	320	245	−17.4	−70.4	−75.5
Canada	*6,677*	*5,319*	4,643	3,178	3,305	2,805	−30.5	−39.6	−58.0
Denmark	*574*	*420*	454	363	217	150	−20.9	−67.0	−73.9
Finland	*515*	*535*	584	382	260	96	13.4	−83.6	−81.4
France	*2,966*	*3,328*	3,348	1,451	1,252	959	12.9	−71.4	−67.7
W. Germany[a]	*3,708*	*3,303*	3,164	2,367	880	604	−14.7	−80.9	−83.7
Ireland	*159*	*188*	222	141	178	161	39.9	−27.5	1.5
Italy[b]	*3,081*	*3,626*	3,757	1,901	1,651	1,322	21.9	−64.8	−57.1
Japan[c]	*5,028*	*2,615*	1,277	835	876	903	−74.6	−29.3	−82.0
Netherlands	*786*	*416*	495	254	202	145	−37.0	−70.7	−81.6
Norway	*170*	*136*	137	98	53	34	−19.3	−75.2	−80.0
Spain[d]	*2,428*	*2,732*	3,073	2,574	2,266	1,927	26.5	−37.3	−20.6
Sweden	*966*	*717*	508	266	136	94	−47.4	−81.5	−90.3
Switzerland	*115*	*100*	116	76	43	34	0.8	−70.7	−70.5
United Kingdom	*6,634*	*5,543*	4,894	3,759	3,764	2,360	−26.2	−51.8	−64.4
United States[e]	*28,420*	*25,510*	23,501	21,074	20,973	16,860	−17.3	−28.3	−40.7

Note: Figures in italics are estimated endpoints (see Appendix I).

[a] 1995 refers to 1994.
[b] 1970 and 1975 estimated from a superseded series.
[c] 1995 refers to 1992.
[d] 1975 estimated from superseded series.
[e] 1990 and 1995 exclude "nonroad diesel" engines to be consistent with data for 1970–85.

Source: OECD (1999).

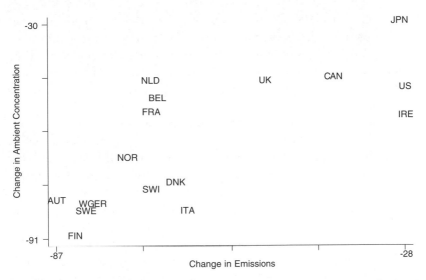

Figure 2.2 Ambient Concentration and Total Emission Reductions, SO_x (1980–1995)

crisis (1975–80) did most countries *not* reduce emissions. In that period, a bare majority (eight of fifteen) had emission increases. These increases are primarily attributable to the sudden decision of countries like Denmark, Finland, and Spain to switch from oil to coal as major sources of electricity. (Coal has a higher sulfur content.) Between 1975 and 1980, for instance, Denmark went from using 2 million tonnes of oil equivalent (MTOE) (11.5 percent of total energy consumption) of coal to using 5.9 MTOE (30.2 percent). Its SO_x emissions rose about 7 percent in that period. In the next five-year period, coal consumption continued to rise dramatically (by 26 percent in MTOE and up to 38 percent of total energy consumption), but, due to the implementation of environmental controls, such as flue gas desulfurization and energy conservation measures, sulfur dioxide emissions declined by 24 percent.

Data on ambient concentrations (taken from national monitoring networks) also show marked declines in SO_2 concentrations. The relationship between the changes in concentration levels and total emissions between 1980 and 1995 is seen in Figure 2.2.[9] (Ambient concentration

[9] Spain is excluded from Figure 2.2 because it did not report ambient pollution data for most of the 1980s. Ambient concentration data measure only SO_2, not other SO_x's, but can be considered closely representative of SO_x concentrations.

data are unavailable for many countries before 1980, so it is not possible to show the full 1970–95 changes.) The two are closely correlated (.74, n = 16), which is consistent with the intuition that emission reductions enhance ambient quality.[10] As noted previously, data on emission levels may not be strictly comparable, so these results should be taken as suggestive.

Although the overall trends clearly suggest lower sulfur dioxide pollution in all countries but Ireland, what can we say about convergence over time? Convergence implies that rates of change move differently and that laggards catch up to environmental leaders. A primary argument for convergence is that the effort required to reduce emissions is increasing as the level of emission declines. Other reasons for convergence might stem either from international commitments or harmonization (Vogel 1995). In order to determine if convergence is occurring, we need information on pollution levels, not just changes. If convergence is occurring, countries with higher pollution levels at the beginning of the period (normalized on a per capita basis) should experience larger reductions than countries with lower pollution levels in 1970.

The empirical evidence suggests that there has *not* been convergence among these countries. If there were, we should see a downward sloping line from left to right. Figure 2.3 suggests, if anything, divergence. For instance, West Germany's emissions per capita were among the lowest in 1970, but its SO_x emissions declined 84 percent between 1970 and 1995. The United States, with the second highest emissions per capita in 1970, reduced its total emissions by only 41 percent in the same period.[11] Even if we ignore the United States and Canada – attributing their poor performance to a combination of low population density and vast land area – there is not much evidence of convergence among the other countries.

Although there is not convergence in all seventeen countries, might there be convergence among the European Union countries? Many suggest that the influence of the process of European integration is causing environmental pollution to converge among those countries (Sbragia 1996). Yet,

---

[10] Countries deviating significantly from a perfect correspondence between emission and ambient quality reductions are those without national monitoring networks. Thus, their ambient quality reductions are based on measures for only one (Denmark and Italy), two (Austria, Finland, and Ireland), or three (Sweden and Switzerland) major cities.

[11] Alternative manipulations of the data – logging per capita emissions, using data for the 1980–95 period, or using land area (rather than population) as the denominator – also do not indicate convergence.

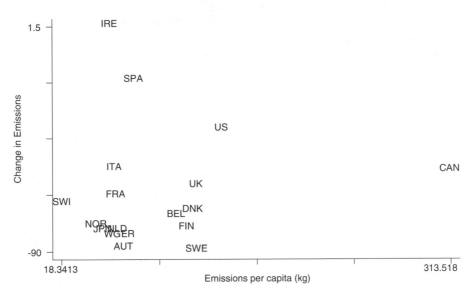

Figure 2.3 SO$_x$ Emission per Capita (1970) and Changes in Total Emissions (1970–1995)

if only EU members are considered (those who were members before the 1990s), there is no evidence of convergence.[12]

Nitrogen Oxides

Nitrogen oxide emissions are another pervasive air pollution problem facing many industrial countries. NO$_x$ are the by-products of high-temperature combustion of fossil fuels and leaching of nitrogen from unstable chemical compounds. They are produced by industrial processes, car exhaust, fossil-fuel-fired electricity generation, and the use of nitrogen-based fertilizer. Effects on humans come primarily through nitrous oxides' contribution to photochemical smog, but nitrogen compounds also contribute to "acid rain" and the greenhouse effect. International agreements for action on nitrous oxides began later than those for sulfur oxides, but the LRTAP in

[12] The number of members of the European Union in my sample changes from five in 1970 (Belgium, France, Germany, Italy, and the Netherlands) to eight in 1972 (Denmark, Ireland, United Kingdom) to nine in 1985 (Spain) to eleven in 1995 (Austria, Finland, Sweden). The last three countries are not counted here as part of the EU because they are not bound by EU environmental policies for all but the last year of the period under consideration.

1989 included provisions for reducing these emissions. One of the major political distinctions between regulation of NO_x and SO_x is the role of automobiles in generating significant emissions of the former (Boehmer-Christiansen 1995).

Table 2.2 shows national trends in NO_x emissions.[13] Widespread reductions in NO_x do not begin until the 1980s. Only Japan reduced emissions during the 1970s. In fact, emissions of NO_x increased 25 percent or more during the 1970s in six of the eleven countries for which there are data. In the 1980s, however, most countries reduced emissions, although the reductions were generally small. Substantial reductions (more than 10 percent) were registered in only four countries in the period between 1980 and 1995 (Austria, Belgium, Sweden, and West Germany). In that more recent period, emissions increased substantially in five countries (United Kingdom, Norway, Italy, Spain, and Ireland). Over the entire period from 1970 to 1995, only Japan, Germany, and the United Kingdom reduced emissions below initial levels. Figure 2.4 plots emission reductions and against changes in ambient concentration between 1980 and 1995. As with SO_x, change in emissions is positively correlated with change in ambient concentration (.48, n = 14).

Despite a slow international response, it is hard to say that no significant progress has been made in reducing NO_x. This is certainly not true for Japan or for several countries since the 1980s – the United States, Germany, France, Austria, Sweden, the Netherlands, and Belgium. Moreover, if either emission reductions or ambient quality improvement in the 1980–95 period is taken as a measure of progress, then ten countries show improvement in one of these measures, and eight of these ten experienced progress in both.

Are NO_x emissions converging? As with SO_x we can evaluate this question by looking at the correlation between higher levels of emissions at the beginning of the period and subsequent reductions. The results in Figure 2.5 indicate there is no convergence. Countries with more NO_x pollution per capita in 1980 are no more likely to have had greater emission reductions over the next fifteen years. However, there is evidence of convergence if only the EU countries are considered.

The convergence effect in the EU is probably attributable to EU environmental policy. One of the most relevant EU policies for NO_x reductions – the Car Directive – required almost all cars to install

---

[13] As with sulfur emissions, these have been checked against figures reported by UNECE, EPA, and EEA sources (see n. 12).

Table 2.2. Total NO_x Emissions, 1970–1995

Country	Emissions (1,000 tonnes)						Change (%)		
	1970	1975	1980	1985	1990	1995	1970–80	1980–95	1975–95
Austria		*195*	231	220	194	170		−26.4	−12.6
Belgium		372	442	325	343	341		−22.4	−8.4
Canada	1,364	1,756	1,959	2,044	2,106	1,999	43.6	7.5	13.8
Denmark		197	273	298	282	252		3.3	27.9
Finland		179	295	275	300	258		1.7	44.1
France[a]	1,676	2,038	2,087	1,776	1,886	1,729	24.5	−9.6	−15.2
W. Germany[b]	2,085	2,249	2,617	2,540	2,018	1,606	25.5	−22.9	−28.6
Ireland		70	83	85	116	115		39.8	64.5
Italy[c]	1,457	1,580	1,638	1,614	1,938	1,768	12.4	7.9	11.9
Japan[d]	1,913	2,065	1,622	1,322	1,476	1,409	−15.2	−9.0	−31.8
Netherlands	466	492	584	581	579	498	25.2	−0.9	1.2
Norway	161	181	188	210	218	212	16.8	16.0	17.1
Spain		624	945	849	1,176	1,223		24.4	95.9
Sweden	319	325	448		388	354	40.4	−13.4	8.8
Switzerland	129	141	170	179	166	136	31.5	−2.4	−3.2
United Kingdom[c]	2,386	2,336	2,460	2,398	2,752	2,145	3.1	11.9	−8.2
United States	19,214	20,982	22,558	21,302	20,900	21,561	17.4	−7.3	2.8

Note: Figures in italics are estimated end points (see Appendix I).
[a] Pre-1990 data are based on growth rates.
[b] 1995 refers to 1994.
[c] 1970 and 1975 estimated from superseded series.
[d] 1995 refers to 1992.

Source: OECD (1999).

35

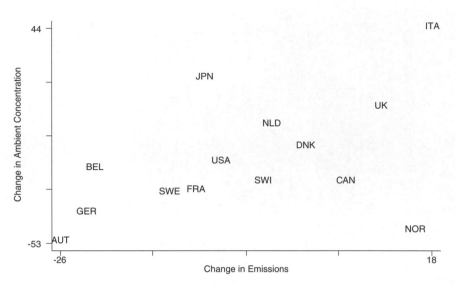

Figure 2.4 Ambient Concentration and Total Emission Reductions, NO$_x$ (1980–1995)

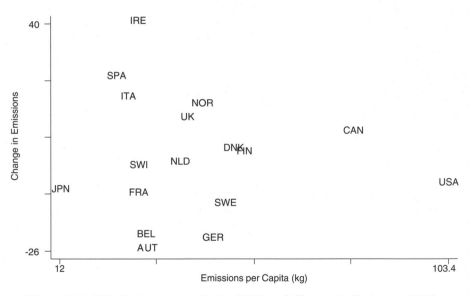

Figure 2.5 NO$_x$ Emissions per Capita (1980) and Changes in Emissions (1980–1995)

catalytic converters. It was proposed in 1987 and passed in 1989, yet full implementation was not required until 1992. Delays were due to strong resistance from "laggard" member states. By 1995 the EU countries that had been historically opposed to the directive – France, Italy, Spain, and the United Kingdom – had only 10, 16, 13, and 22 percent (respectively) of the car fleets equipped. This compares with 35, 32, 55, and 40 percent in the same year for those EU countries that were the historical proponents of the directive (Denmark, Germany, and the Netherlands) (EEA, 1998). Whether the existence of the EU can be considered responsible for "racheting up" standards in laggard countries is hard to assess. Some accounts suggest that governments in these countries did not want to seem "antienvironment" at the time, although that desire seems directly related to domestic, not EU, political incentives. However, the "pro-directive" coalition of the three Northern European countries was prepared to act unilaterally to create stringent requirements *sooner* in the absence of the EU process (Dearing 1992; Boehmer-Christiansen 1995).[14]

Municipal Waste

The creation and disposal of waste creates various types of environmental problems.[15] All disposal methods, including burial in landfills and incineration, have some negative environmental consequences. The material that becomes "waste" must be created, transported, collected after use, and disposed of. Even recycling requires the use of resources to collect and reprocess discarded material back into usable form. In addition to the ultimate disposal problems, material discarded as waste often contains non-renewable resources. Attempts to reduce the amount of waste generated by society, no matter what the ultimate destination of the discarded material, are considered effective strategies for increasing long-term sustainability (Rathje and Murphy 1991).[16] Source reduction reduces pollutants, saves

---

[14] It is true that the EU regulations will probably force the United Kingdom, a country with high per capita NO_x emissions, to reduce emissions more than it appeared inclined to do. But the point remains that empirically this "EU effect" is not observed in the period considered here.

[15] Industrial waste streams are also an important part of the waste problem. However, the available data preclude a comparison of trends.

[16] Rathje's unique research on the "archeology of garbage" reveals many popular misconceptions surrounding the "waste crisis" in the United States and other advanced countries. Nevertheless, he is a strong and consistent advocate of source reduction and recycling in solid waste policy.

Table 2.3. *Generation of Municipal Waste per Capita, 1975–1995*

Country	Per Capita Waste Generated (kg/person)					Change (%)	
	1975	1980	1985	1990	1995	1980–95	1975–95
Austria[a]	185	220	230	320	330	50.0	78.4
Belgium	300	310		350	480	54.8	60.0
Canada[b]	*475*	510			630	23.5	*32.6*
Denmark	370	400	480		430	7.5	*16.2*
Finland[c]	*430*	*460*	510	624	460	0.0	*7.0*
France[a]	270	310	340	350	350	12.9	29.6
W. Germany[a,d]	330	350	320	340	325	−7.1	−1.5
Ireland	175	190	310		560	194.7	220.0
Italy[e]	260	250	260	350	430	72.0	65.4
Japan[f]	380	380	360	410	400	5.3	5.3
Netherlands[g]	*445*	500	440	500	580	16.0	*30.3*
Norway	425	420	460	530	620	47.6	45.9
Spain	225	270	280	320	380	40.7	68.9
Sweden[e]	290	300	320	370	360	20.0	24.1
Switzerland[b]	*365*	440	520	610	600	36.4	64.4
United Kingdom	325	310	340	350	*415*	33.9	27.7
United States[i]	540	600	630	740	730	21.7	35.2

Note: Figures in italics are estimated end points (see Appendix I).
[a] Household waste only.
[b] 1995 refers to 1992; includes all waste disposed of.
[c] 1995 estimated from Ministry of Environment data.
[d] 1995 refers to 1993; includes 5 million tonnes collected under the Duales system.
[e] 1995 refers to 1996 figure given in Fischer and Crowe, table 10.
[f] 1995 refers to 1994.
[g] Includes solid waste from sewerage and a small amount of demolition waste.
[h] 1975 figure based on growth rate in household waste series (+17%).
[i] 1990 data from U.S. Environmental Protection Agency.
Sources: OECD (1997a, 1999); Finnish Ministry of Environment (2000); Fischer and Crew (2000); and own calculations (see Appendix I).

energy, conserves resources, and reduces the need for new landfills and combustors (EPA 2000). Virtually all OECD countries have adopted a waste reduction hierarchy that uses (in order of decreasing emphasis) source reduction, reuse, recycling, and disposal (OECD 1998b).

Municipal waste is typically defined as the waste collected by (or on the order of) municipalities; it includes household and commercial waste but generally not waste from major industries and construction or demolition sites (OECD 1999). Table 2.3 shows trends in the generation of per capita municipal waste in seventeen nations between 1975 and 1995. The calculation of waste generation differs among countries, and comparative statistics have been the subject of great scrutiny in recent years, particularly in Europe (Fischer and Crew 2000). The results reported in Table 2.3 attempt to provide consistent trends within countries over time. Due to differences in definition, comparing waste levels at particular points in time for the other figures is particularly problematic. Further details about the data in Table 2.3 are provided in Appendix I.

The data in Table 2.3 suggest that there has been little progress in reducing waste during this twenty-year period. Only Germany experienced an overall decline in waste generated between 1980 and 1995. This trend is probably attributable to its adoption of a stringent packaging law in 1991, an innovation that has recently been adopted by the EU, though in a considerably moderated form.[17]

Waste generation is generally held to follow trends in the economy (Christiansen and Fischer 1999). The widespread economic expansion in the mid- to late 1980s appears to have substantially increased waste generated everywhere but Norway. Moreover, if we look at waste and economic growth in the 1980–85 period, countries with higher GDP growth (United States, Sweden, United Kingdom, Switzerland, Ireland, and Denmark) did have higher growth in waste generation than did countries that grew more slowly (Austria, France, Germany, Italy, and the Netherlands). Waste generation between 1990 and 1995 dropped in countries like Finland, Japan, and Sweden, that experienced their most severe economic downturns since the depression.

It is extremely hard to gauge whether there is cross-national convergence in waste generation. The correlation between starting levels of waste per capita and change is not appropriate here because changes are computed from very different bases (e.g., household rather than municipal waste).[18] However, given the fact that there has been convergence in gross domestic product among the OECD countries studied here (especially in Europe)

---

[17] Criticisms of the static economic inefficiency of setting up Germany's packaging law (Duales System) generally overlook powerful incentives it provides to producers to limit packaging and, by extension, packaging waste. Indeed, waste industry trade journals criticize the system for increasing unit costs due to "lower disposal quantities" and the high start-up costs of switching to a new system of sorting waste (Schroll and Staudt 1999). More sympathetic voices point to the obvious reductions in packaging waste produced and stress dynamic rather than static efficiency (Motavalli 1997).

[18] It is important to emphasize that despite noncomparable waste bases (i.e., household and municipal), comparing trends is reasonable as long as there are not differences in the rate of change in the component waste streams.

and that most countries instituting stringent waste reduction strategies have been wealthier European countries (Germany, Sweden, Denmark, and, to a lesser extent, the United States), there is a case to be made for convergence in per capita waste generation.

Recycling

A great deal of waste is not buried or burned; it is recycled. While recycling is generally considered a second best solution (reduction being first), it is still a step in the direction of sustainability.[19] Materials made from recycled products usually require less energy to produce and use smaller amounts of other natural resources.[20] Moreover, by reducing levels of waste for burning or burial, recycling contributes to reducing air, land, and water contamination. These factors make national recycling rates an important measure of environmental performance. Finally, because high levels of recycling require activity and awareness at "grass-roots" levels of society (production, retailing, household consumption), recycling rates may also be considered indicative of the integration of the economy and an environmental ethic that is necessary for long-term sustainability.[21]

Table 2.4 shows recycling rates for glass and paper and cardboard, two important materials requiring considerable environmental expense to produce and dispose of. For example, in the United States they constitute more than 40 percent of municipal waste (EPA 1999). European data suggest similar proportions. Although paper is the more significant landfill problem, energy savings from glass recycling is higher than that for paper.

Although these data do reveal significant scope for improvement in many countries, it is hard to deny that significant progress has been made in almost all countries. The average level of paper and cardboard recycling has gone from 30 to 45 percent for paper between 1980 and 1995. Glass recycling increased more dramatically from 16 to 55 percent in the same period.[22] Several countries – Austria, Finland, Japan, the Netherlands, Sweden, and

[19] High recycling *rates* and waste reduction are not mutually exclusive. One can recycle all waste (or none or anything in between), regardless of how much is generated.
[20] Some definitions of recycling include "energy recovery" (incineration). The data discussed in this section do not count incinerated waste as recycled.
[21] This point should not be exaggerated. The popularity of recycling may be unrelated to other environmental habits and may even operate *against* ultimate environmental and economic sense (cf. Rathje and Murphy 1992).
[22] Replacing missing values for Norway and Sweden with a reasonable range of estimates does not significantly affect these averages.

Table 2.4. *Recycling Rates for Paper and Glass*

Country	Paper Recycling						Glass Recycling				
	1970	1975	1980	1985	1990	1995	1975	1980	1985	1990	1995
Austria			30	38	52	66		20[a]	38	60	76
Belgium	15	15	15[a]	14	13[b]	12		33[a]	42	55	67
Canada[c]			20	23	28	33[c]		12	12		17[c]
Denmark	18	28	26	31	35	44		8[a]	19	35[b]	63
Finland		29	35	39	43	57		10	21	36	50
France	28	28	30	35	34	39		20[a]	26	41[b]	50
W. Germany[d]	30	35	34	43	44	67	8	23	43	54	75
Ireland[e]			9	10	10	11		8	7	23	39
Italy			34[a]	25	27	28		20	25	53[b]	53
Japan			48	50	50	51		35	47	48	56[c]
Netherlands	34	44	46	50	50	65	3	17	49	67	80
Norway		24	17	16	20	37		5		22	75
Spain	28	32	39	44	39	41		8	26	27	32
Sweden		30	34	40	46	59		9	20	44	61
Switzerland			35	39	49	61		36[a]	46	65[b]	85
United Kingdom	29	28	32	28	33	35		5	12	21	26
United States	19		21	21	28	40	3	5	8	20	24

Note: Figures in italics are estimates (see Appendix I).
[a] 1980 refers to 1981.
[b] 1990 refers to 1991.
[c] For paper and glass 1995 data refer to 1992.
[d] 1995 refers to united Germany.
[e] 1980 refers to 1983, 1990 refers to 1989.
Source: OECD (1999).

Switzerland – recycled most of their paper and glass by the mid-1990s. The only truly poor progress occurs in Ireland and Belgium (paper recycling) and Canada (glass recycling). Belgium is the only country where the recycling effort has stagnated or declined.

One way to measure convergence among the countries, similar to the method used in the prior sections, is to see if the change in the percentage of material recycled is negatively correlated with the initial recycling rate. The starting date is 1980, as there are too many missing values for earlier years. Despite the fact that the statistical test is biased toward finding convergence (because the maximum recycling rate is 100 percent), the correlation co-efficients are actually positive, though not statistically different from zero – .13 (for paper) and .24 (for glass). If one looks solely at the European Union countries, there is also no evidence of convergence.

Wastewater Treatment

The third environmental medium covered in the environmental performance indicators is water pollution. Industrial processes and human sewage have long been considered the primary water pollution control problems. Efforts have been undertaken to control these processes, usually by filtering out or chemically treating polluting discharges. Investments in water treatment plants in industrial countries increased markedly in an effort to keep up with the increasing amounts of waste literally washed down the drain in the last half of the twentieth century. Regulations and, in some cases, effluent charges have also been established for industry discharges in all industrial countries.

Recently, two facts have become obvious about treatment. First, other "peripheral" processes contribute significantly to water pollution. Sometimes called nonpoint pollution, these diffuse sources of pollution enter waterways as water travels on its natural course from air to the soil and into oceans, lakes, and streams. The natural hydrological process often concentrates nonpoint pollutants, creating both acute and long-term environmental or human health problems. Much nonpoint pollution, such as the runoff of animal waste, fertilizer, and other chemicals in agriculture, is now viewed as a major water pollution problem (Vail et al. 1994; EPA 1998). Another problem that became apparent in the 1970s and 1980s was that treatment, while important, was only a limited solution. Treatment creates its own forms of waste that may be as dangerous as the originally polluted water because it contains levels of concentrated pollutants like nitrates, phosphates, or heavy metals. Ultimately, source reduction is the only truly sustainable solution.

The first indicator of water pollution performance examined here is the proportion of the population served by wastewater treatment. As mentioned, although treatment is not a permanent solution to the problem of increasing water pollution, it is vital to alleviating environmental harms. Even with great reductions in the amount of wastewater that must be treated, the population covered by treatment facilities will remain important for preventing many environmental and health problems.

Table 2.5 displays cross-national trends in the percentage of the population served by wastewater treatment facilities.[23] There are three categories

---

[23] Population coverage is not a perfect measure of wastewater treatment because it does not necessarily map precisely with effluent discharged. However, comparative indicators of absolute effluent discharges (or proportions that are treated) are not available.

Table 2.5. *Population Served by Wastewater Treatment*

Country	% Served (total and secondary-tertiary)											
	1970		1975		1980		1985		1990		1995	
Austria	17	5	27		38	28	65	58	72	67	75	73
Belgium	4	4	6	6	23	23					27	27
Canada	30		57		64	50	63	63	70	57	78	59
Denmark	54	22	70	42			91	63	98	71	99	85
Finland	27	22	51	47	65	63	72	72	76	76	77	77
France	19		40		62		64		69		77	
W. Germany[a]	62	41	75	56	80	70	85	77	86	79	89	85
Ireland	5				11	11			44	21	61	26
Italy	14	6	22		30				61		71	
Japan	16	16	23	23	30	30	36	36	44	44	50	55
Netherlands	50		52	37	73	64	87	79	93	92	96	92
Norway	21	20	27	25	34	27	42	34	57	44	67	52
Spain	9		14	7	18	9	29	16	42	31	48	38
Sweden	63	53	81		82	81	94	93	94	94	93	93
Switzerland	35	35	55	55	73	73	84	84	90	90	94	94
United Kingdom	60				82	76	83	77	84	75	86	79
United States	42	40	67	44	70	50	72	57	71	62	73	64

Note: Figures in italics are estimates (see Appendix I).
[a] Data for 1990 and 1995 for united Germany.
Source: OECD (1999) and national sources (see text and Appendix I).

of treatment: primary, secondary, and tertiary. Primary treatment involves filtering wastewater with screens or gravity (i.e., allowing sediments to sink in a sedimentation chamber). Secondary treatment uses microbial processes to remove organic matter from the effluent after primary treatment. Water may subsequently be disinfected (e.g., with chlorine) after either primary or secondary treatment. Tertiary treatment uses biological or chemical processes to remove other potentially harmful substances (like phosphorus) from water. Where available, the table presents data for total coverage and coverage using secondary or tertiary treatment methods only.

Overall, the data suggest a great deal of improvement over time. The average degree of coverage and stringency measured by the level of secondary or better coverage increases steadily between 1970 and 1995 in almost every country. Some countries with relatively low coverage in 1970 (e.g., Austria and France) have high coverage in 1995. Furthermore, with the exception of Italy and Ireland recently and the United States in the early 1970s, virtually all improvement has come from expanding secondary and tertiary

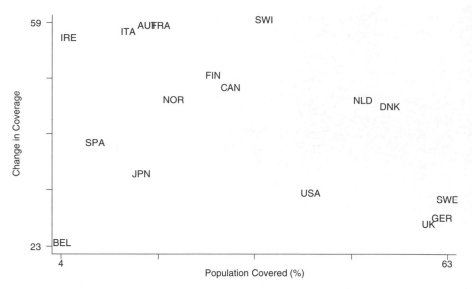

Figure 2.6 Water Treatment Coverage (1970) and Change in Coverage (1970–1995)

treatment coverage.[24] Both the level and quality of water treatment appear to be improving.

Along with this general improvement, there is some evidence of convergence. Figure 2.6 shows a scatterplot of beginning coverage and change over time. The correlation between starting levels and absolute change is around −.40. The pattern suggests a relatively clear downward sloping pattern. The one outlier is Belgium, which has worse-than-expected performance, given its low level of treatment coverage in 1970. If Belgium is excluded the correlation is −.63. As with recycling rates, however, because the test is biased toward finding convergence, this statistic should be treated with caution.

Fertilizer Use

The second indicator of water pollution performance is total fertilizer use. While fertilizer use within certain limits is beneficial, intensive use, as has

---

[24] There are no data for secondary and tertiary treatment in Italy, so we cannot be certain that it falls into the same category as Ireland. However, two facts are suggestive. First, Italy had not implemented the EU Directive on wastewater treatment as of 1998. Second, Milan, Italy's second largest city, had no secondary treatment plant as of 2002.

Table 2.6. *Apparent Fertilizer Use*

Country	Fertilizer Use per 10,000 ha of Arable Land						% Change in Absolute Usage	
	1970	1975	1980	1985	1990	1995	1970–95	1980–95
Austria	2.4	1.9	2.5	2.5	2.0	1.6	−41.9	−41.8
Belgium	5.1	4.5	5.8	5.4	4.9	3.8	−40.6	−31.4
Canada	.2	.3	.4	.5	.5	.6	220.1	32.5
Denmark	2.2	2.4	2.4	2.4	2.5	1.9	−26.7	−30.2
Finland	1.8	2.1	2.1	2.2	1.9	1.6	−30.0	−30.5
France	2.4	2.5	3.0	3.0	3.0	2.5	5.7	−12.4
W. Germany[a]	3.5	3.4	3.7	3.3	2.2	2.2	−31.0	−38.0
Ireland	3.1	3.5	5.4	6.0	5.5	5.6	76.7	24.5
Italy	.9	1.2	1.7	1.7	1.6	1.7	39.4	−11.6
Japan	3.4	.9	3.3	4.3	4.0	3.3	−16.0	−9.6
Netherlands	7.5	8.0	8.3	8.2	6.1	5.8	−17.6	−21.2
Norway	2.4	2.9	3.2	2.8	2.3	2.1	5.5	−19.0
Spain	.6	.7	.8	.8	1.0	1.0	53.7	12.4
Sweden	1.6	1.7	1.6	1.4	1.2	1.1	−41.6	−39.4
Switzerland	3.8	3.6	4.4	4.4	4.1	3.0	−8.5	−25.5
United Kingdom	2.6	2.6	2.9	3.6	3.6	3.7	15.7	6.7
United States	.8	1.0	1.1	.9	1.0	1.1	29.0	−6.7

Note: Fertilizer use refers to apparent consumption of commercial fertilizer (NPK).
[a] 1995 estimated from data for unified Germany.
Source: Food and Agriculture Organization (2001).

been the case in industrial countries over the past fifty years, can have negative environmental impacts. Fertilizer runoff is an excellent example of nonpoint pollution. Much of the plant nutrient in applied fertilizer is washed into bodies of water or leaches into the atmosphere. The excessive use of fertilizer associated with overcultivation contributes to phosphate and nitrate buildup in soil and rivers with detrimental effects on flora and fauna. Fertilizer and other agricultural compounds can also toxify drinking water. Reducing fertilizer use is important in reducing these negative impacts, and countries have undertaken efforts to reduce fertilizer use since the 1970s.

Table 2.6 shows that trends in the intensity of fertilizer use – measured by total apparent consumption of commercial (NPK) fertilizer per unit of arable and permanent cropland – have varied dramatically.[25] These data are

[25] Although there is a tendency for fertilizer use to fluctuate from year to year, these figures are more or less indicative trends in all countries.

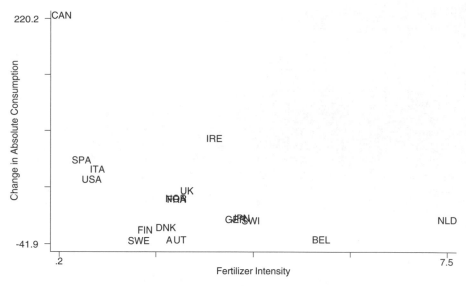

Figure 2.7 Intensity of Fertilizer Use (1970) and Change (1970–1995)

taken directly from the Food and Agriculture Organization's statistical data base.[26] In most of the Northern European countries, which were relatively intensive users of fertilizer, consumption declined from peaks in the late 1970s and early 1980s. Only in Sweden does it peak earlier, in 1975. In those countries with relatively low fertilizer usage rates – Canada, the United States, Spain, and Italy – consumption increased into the early 1980s but appears to have leveled off since then.

The last two columns of Table 2.6 show percentage changes in absolute fertilizer use (rather than changes in intensities). This latter measure of change can be considered more directly relevant to the total environmental burden.[27] Between the general peak around 1980 and 1995, absolute fertilizer consumption declined by 25 percent or more in Austria, Belgium, Denmark, Finland, Germany, the Netherlands, Norway, and

[26] These data are almost identical to those reported in the OECD data. The small differences that do exist are probably because the FAO database has the most up-to-date and complete series.

[27] The OECD tables note that the definition of arable and permanent cropland may differ among countries (1999: 266). Thus, using absolute changes in fertilizer use is arguably more comparable than fertilizer use per unit of arable land. Moreover, change in absolute use is closely correlated with change in intensity of use (r = .98; excluding Canada, .93).

Table 2.7. *Progress and Convergence in Environmental Performance*

Indicator	Progress?	Convergence?
SO_x	Yes	No
NO_x	Limited	No
Municipal waste	No	Probably
Recycling	Yes	No
Wastewater treatment	Yes	Yes[a]
Fertilizer use	Limited	Yes

[a] Test biased in favor of finding convergence.

Sweden. In Southern Europe, Britain, and Ireland, the intensity of fertilizer use, and typically the absolute amount, rose steadily in this period. Most of this increase was in the 1970s. In North America fertilizer intensity has been more stable (albeit at different levels in Canada and the United States) since the early 1980s, after growing significantly in the 1970s.

How does absolute consumption correlate with initial levels of use? Figure 2.7 shows 1970 intensities and percentage changes in absolute use between 1970 and 1995. The scatterplot suggests some moderate convergence among the countries. The correlation coefficient is −.54 (n = 17). Excluding the extreme case (Canada) reduces the correlation considerably (−.46). Convergence within the EU appears even more pronounced (−.64, n = 9). However, although it might be tempting to attribute this convergence to the long-standing importance of the Common Agricultural Policy (CAP) in the EU, this explanation is not particularly compelling. The CAP has not historically regulated production inputs like fertilizer use. Moreover, European agroenvironmental policy did not play much of a role in affecting consumption until perhaps the mid-1990s.

Summary

Table 2.7 provides a summary of the results relating to the two hypotheses presented at the beginning of the chapter. In contrast to the pessimism sometimes expressed about efforts to reduce pollution, general progress can be found in five of the six areas. Clear progress has been made with respect to reductions in SO_x emissions and increases in both recycling and wastewater treatment. Progress in reducing NO_x emissions and fertilizer consumption has been more limited, though there have been improvements since 1980.

On the other hand, there has been little progress in controlling waste in any of the countries considered. This overall success does not imply that these or other environmental problems have been solved. Nevertheless, the trends for these six indicators do suggest a degree of progress that may sometimes be overlooked when considering social adaptation to the environmental crisis.

With respect to the question of whether environmental outcomes are converging over time, the evidence is limited. Except for fertilizer use – perhaps the least likely candidate for convergence given the relative political power of farmers and nonpoint nature of the associated environmental problems – there is not unambiguous evidence of convergence. There may also be convergence on water treatment coverage and the generation of municipal waste, although the tests of convergence are problematic. In the cases where one would most expect to find outcome convergence because of greater harmonization of standards, more widespread public attention, and international treaties, such as air pollution, there is no convergence. Finally, with the exception of fertilizer consumption, there is no evidence of convergence in environmental outcomes among the European Union countries.

Overall, these findings cast some doubt on two popular claims about environmental performance: progress has in fact been made in many areas, despite claims to the contrary; and whatever the evidence of generally converging policy standards, generally convergent outcomes do not seem to characterize advanced democracies in this period.

Aggregate Environmental Performance

The primary purpose of the remainder of this book is to account for variations in the national environmental outcomes suggested in the preceding pages of this chapter. In the following chapters, I focus less on individual pollution trends and instead seek to account for the relative success or failure of different countries in reducing environmental problems overall. Although one could focus on an explanation of cross-national variations for each of the six indicators discussed here, I am less interested in explaining exactly why SO_x abatement differs across countries. Instead, I want to account for differences in overall performance. This requires a method of aggregating performance in each of the pollution categories discussed. As I show later, countries that do very well (poorly) on some tend to do well (poorly) on the others.

Four of the environmental indicators – SO_x, NO_x, waste, and fertilizer use – are assigned a score between 0 and 100 based on the total percentage change in that pollutant. Scores were assigned based on the following formula (p = pollutant, n = country):

$$\text{Env}_n = \sum_p \left[\frac{(\%\,\text{reduction}_{np} - \text{lowest}\%\,\text{reduction}_p)}{(\text{highest}\%\,\text{reduction}_p - \text{lowest}\%\,\text{reduction}_p)} * 100 \right] \quad (1)$$

Thus, if a country had the lowest percentage reduction (or highest percentage increase) for a particular pollutant, it is scored 0. The country with the highest reduction (or lowest increase) is scored 100 for that pollutant. If the percentage reduction was the midpoint between the highest and lowest national reduction, it is scored 50. Two cases, Canada (fertilizer use) and Ireland (municipal waste), had very extreme values relative to the rest of the group. For this reason, they were assigned a score of 0 for those respective indicators, and scoring of the other sixteen countries proceeded according to the method discussed earlier.[28]

For the two other performance indicators – recycling rates and water treatment – Equation 1 alone is inappropriate because it would severely punish countries that started out with higher recycling rates or water treatment coverage. For instance, a country with a glass recycling rate of 50 percent in 1980 and 80 percent in 1995 would have a "percentage improvement" value (the first term in the numerator of Equation 1) of $(80 - 50) * 100/50 = 60$. Meanwhile, a country with a recycling rate of 10 percent in 1980 and 40 percent in 1995 would have a percentage improvement value of $(40 - 10) * 100/10 = 400$. To compensate for this I used the following formula to compare levels and changes in recycling rates and water treatment:

$$[([\text{ending }\%] - [\text{beginning }\%]) * 100]/(100 - [\text{beginning }\%]) \quad (2)$$

This formula computes progress in closing the "gap" between initial position and 100 percent. Using the previous example, this method gives the first country score of $(80 - 50) * 100/(100 - 50) = 60$, and the second country receives a score of $(40 - 10) * 100/(100 - 10) = 33$. Although this revised measure may seem "biased" against poor initial performers, it is nonetheless more consistent with real "effort expended." Going from a 10 to a

---

[28] In other words, both the worst and second worst performer scored 0.

40 percent recycling rate is "cheaper at the margin" than going from 50 to 80 percent.[29]

Each country's glass and paper recycling and water treatment coverage scores were calculated from Equation 2; to ensure that these scores had the same range (0–100) as the first four, the scores were then scaled using Equation 1.[30] In order not to double count progress in the recycling category, I averaged the paper and glass recycling scores derived from Equation 2 before scaling them. Whether one uses paper or glass alone or an average of the two does not critically change the recycling performance scores; the cross-country correlation between the two measures is .90.

An ideal measure of comparative environmental performance would include data for all countries on all indicators for 1970 and 1995. As the tables presented in the previous section make clear, there are missing data, particularly in the 1970s. Because the existing data do suggest that progress was made in some countries in this decade, it is important to include as much data from the 1970s as possible in order not to bias the results against those countries. The periods used for each measure are SO_x (1970–95), NO_x (1975–95), waste (1975–95), recycling (1980–95), water treatment coverage (1970–95), and fertilizer use (1970–95). Missing values were estimated using procedures that are explained in greater detail in Appendix I. In all cases the overall comparative results are not highly sensitive to estimates in the range of those used.

Table 2.8 shows the country scores on all six performance measures. The sum of scores is the aggregate measure of national environmental performances. Because I am interested in explaining countries' adaptations in the face of environmental problems generally, and not responses to specific pollution problems, this aggregate measure is used as the dependent variable in the remaining chapters. This scoring method assesses each nation's relative success in reducing each pollutant separately. This avoids comparability problems that might emerge from equating percentage point changes across the different pollution measures. In the absence of a clearly superior alternative and the fact that all six of the indicators included here are

---

[29] This is consistent with the idea that there is a rising marginal cost curve. For instance, connecting the 80 percent of the population in cities and suburbs to water treatment plants is cheaper per person than reaching the remaining 20 percent of people who are in rural or isolated areas. The same can be said of recycling.

[30] Using the "raw" scores from Equation 2 produces scores that would implicitly have lower weights than the first four environmental indicators.

Table 2.8. *Comparative Environmental Performance Scores*

Country	SO$_x$	NO$_x$	Waste	Recycling	Fertilizer	Water Treatment	Total
Austria	99	85	0	95	100	62	441
Belgium	84	82	23	36	99	0	324
Canada	65	64	57	21	0	60	268
Denmark	82	53	78	66	87	100	466
Finland	90	41	89	63	90	60	433
France	75	87	61	41	60	65	388
W. Germany	93	98	100	92	91	64	538
Ireland	0	25	0	29	0	47	101
Italy	64	66	16	25	31	57	259
Japan	91	100	92	31	78	22	414
Netherlands	91	74	60	86	80	92	482
Norway	89	62	41	75	60	46	373
Spain	24	0	12	25	19	26	105
Sweden	100	68	68	75	100	77	489
Switzerland	78	78	18	91	72	90	427
United Kingdom	72	82	63	23	51	56	346
United States	46	73	54	37	40	40	291

Source: Tables 2.1–2.6.

generally regarded as important environmental problems in all of the countries considered in the study, all six scores are weighted equally.

The aggregate scores suggest a considerable degree of cross-national
diversity in environmental performance. The score has a maximum of 600
(if a country scored highest on all measures) and a minimum of 0. The
actual maximum is 546; the range, about 445 points; the mean, 361 with a
standard deviation of 127. Statistical tests suggest that the distribution of
scores does not violate normality assumptions – that is, we cannot reject a
null hypothesis that the scores are normally distributed.

Contrary to the suggestion that countries do not consistently perform
well in different areas, there is also a strong intercorrelation between the individual scores within countries. A factor analysis of the individual measures
shows that all load positively on a single common factor.[31] Moreover, the
intercorrelation between such disparate measures of environmental pollution suggests that there is an a priori basis for believing general, "macro"

---

[31] The eigenvalue for the first factor is 3.0; for the second it is .77, well below the standard
cutoff of 1.0. The Cronbach's alpha is .83.

features (not idiosyncratic, pollutant-specific ones) promote environmental performance.

The best performance appears to be clustered among the Northern European countries, particularly Germany, the Netherlands, and Sweden. The (former) West Germans have consistently been the best performers, having scores that are well above average on all six of the indicators, while Sweden and the Netherlands are well above average on five of the six. The scores of Austria, Denmark, Finland, and Switzerland are also above average.

Several results in Table 2.8 may be surprising. In particular, U.S. performance seems surprisingly low (it ranks thirteenth) given the fact that the United States is often considered to have very stringent environmental regulations. The United States scores poorly on four of the six measures. The only category in which it does comparatively well on is NO_x emissions. Here the United States performs well due to its relatively early and stringent regulations of auto exhaust.

Might the United States compare better, for example, if other major indicators of performance were used to evaluate aggregate performance? For instance, the generation and disposal of hazardous chemicals, an important problem in all advanced economies, is not included in the performance measure. The United States might be considered somewhat ahead of most other countries in remediating, rather than simply containing, contamination at abandoned hazardous waste sites through its "Superfund" program (see, e.g., Church and Nakamura 1994). On the other hand, several comparative case studies of overall hazardous waste management policy – including reduction, handling, and disposal of presently generated waste – have indicated that the United States has lagged behind other industrial countries since the 1970s, in particular in areas of reducing and disposing of current hazardous wastes (e.g., Piasecki and Davis, 1987; Mangun 1988; Davies and Mazurek 1998; Jahn 1999).[32] These and other studies suggest that the strongest performers in this area are also those at the top of the aggregate performance index in Table 2.8 (e.g., Austria, Denmark, Finland, Germany, the Netherlands, Norway, and Sweden). Therefore, it is not likely that the

---

[32] Both Jahn and Davies and Mazurek use data on hazardous waste generation per unit of GDP at a single point in time (the early 1990s). Although this measure should favor the much wealthier United States, it is still rated as the worst performer on this measure. Andrews (1999: 281–82) also notes that U.S. performance on toxic chemicals has been inadequate.

absence of a measure of hazardous waste performance would have a large effect on my comparative results.[33]

Alternatively, one could argue that cross-national differences captured here are due to different priorities, measured by still other items. For example, the United States is often seen as a leader in species conservation, a measure not included in the index. Given the diversity of environmental fields and absence of data, it is impossible to discount all of these possibilities. But, if true, it is important that such claims can be supported by comparative outcomes data, and not just evidence of U.S. efforts.

Other cross-national comparisons of environmental performance, using different indicators of performance, generally support these findings for the United States and the other countries (Davies and Mazurek 1998; Jahn 1998, 1999; World Economic Forum 2001). The World Economic Forum's *Environmental Sustainability Index* ranked the United States thirteenth of the seventeen countries considered here.[34] Jahn's results place the United States in sixteenth position and overall are closely correlated with my own (r = .81). Although Davies and Masurek do not use an overall summary measure of performance, they do conclude that the United States has not performed well relative to other developed countries. While all three of these studies use performance indicators in very different ways from the present one, their findings are consistent with my own and suggest that the United States might not perform as well as is often assumed.[35]

---

[33] Hazardous waste outcomes have been excluded from this study because data across a large set of countries and time – both of which are necessary to gauge environmental performance over time – are not available. In addition, the data that do exist are subject to comparability problems, such as large differences in what is classified as hazardous both across countries and within the same country over time.

[34] The best comparative ranking I have seen for the United States is Jänicke (1992), who ranked the United States eighth of the seventeen, relying on some early OECD data on a incomplete set of air and water pollution data. His ranking, based on data through only 1985, was biased heavily toward air pollution (four air pollution versus two water pollution measures and no indicators for solid waste problems). In addition, his data set had an *extraordinarily* large number of missing values for some indicators that he used. For example, for carbon monoxide emissions, fully half (seventeen of thirty-four) of end-point values around 1970 and around 1985 were missing, and there were no data in *any* year for four of the countries included in his rankings! (I have been unable to replicate them.) For these reasons, this ranking seems of doubtful reliability.

[35] The authors of the ESI and Davies and Masurek do not consider pollution performance over time as I do here. Instead, they compare *levels* of environmental sustainability in the mid-1990s. Given some of the problems with comparing levels mentioned earlier, this raises some questions about what they are measuring. Jahn's study shares some of the problems of the other two. Although it does also consider progress over time in some cases, it covers a much shorter period (at best 1980–90).

It is important to emphasize that the performance indices used here assess comparative improvements in environmental performance (while trying to take into account country starting points), not the state of national environmental quality. In this regard, one should not interpret these results (e.g., low scores for the United States) as evidence that the absolute level of environmental quality is worse in one country than in another. Such an assessment is very hard to make given the data. Recall the results of most of the measures discussed here suggest overall improvements in most countries (Spain and Ireland being the exceptions.) Poor results should thus not be interpreted as indicating *worsening* conditions. The measures here are instead intended to ascertain relative improvement. Can we explain the observed differences in these trends systematically? This question is the subject of the rest of this book.

3

Economic Development, Geographic Advantage, and Environmental Performance

In this chapter, I evaluate economic and structural explanations of national environmental performance. One of the most prominent explanations for differing commitments to environmental quality in the contemporary literature is national income and economic development. Conventional wisdom (and many studies) suggests that higher incomes increase people's attention to environmental problems and willingness to pay for environmental improvements (Baumol and Oates 1988; Grossman and Krueger 1995; Inglehart 1977, 1990; Jänicke 1992). Often associated with increased wealth are broader structural changes in the economy that, according to many, should reduce environmental pressures by shifting production and consumption away from pollution-intensive goods toward less polluting services. Without necessarily rejecting such explanations, others suggest that general physical and demographic features of a society help to explain differences in the salience of environmental performance and scope for better environmental quality (Cropper and Griffiths 1994; Kitschelt 1989).

These factors – national wealth, the structure of production, demographics, and geography – can all be considered structural explanations of environmental performance in the sense that they cannot be easily changed, or if they can be (as in the case of wealth or population density), they can change only very slowly.[1] For instance, increasing population density is not a conscious strategy of trying to augment concern for the environment;

---

[1] In a sense one could argue that there is almost no such thing as a feature that is not changeable. Indeed, environmental issues generally concern the effects that society has on what have been taken as structures. This might be a reason that environmental issues remain difficult to fit into conventional frameworks. Nevertheless, even if the distinction made is ultimately only analytical, it is a common one. The analysis presented remains worthwhile insofar as it can cast light on the veracity of existing distinctions.

and, practically speaking, there is little that a democratic country can do in the short run to alter its population density.

In this chapter, the empirical relationship between income or economic structure and the aggregate environmental performance measure is shown to be consistent with many existing empirical findings, although with something of a twist. After a brief overview of recent studies that actually do look at national environmental outcomes, I find that my environmental performance indicator increases with per capita income in my group of seventeen advanced democracies as generally predicted; however, I also find that, beyond a certain point, income becomes associated with *worse* performance, something also found, but dismissed, in previous studies.

Next, I explore some of the underlying mechanisms linking income and environmental performance. Despite some well-publicized cases consistent with the hypothesis that increasing (decreasing) industrialization is associated with worse (better) environmental performance (e.g., Ireland and Sweden, respectively), this is not borne out in a larger sample of countries . Finally, I examine whether differences in country size and population density, collectively referred to as "geographical advantages," help to account for differences in environmental performance. I find that they do, but only to a limited degree. By revealing the limited explanatory power of the socioeconomic structure in explaining differences in environmental performance in advanced democracies, I lay the groundwork for the examination of cultural-attitudinal and institutional explanations of environmental performance that follow in subsequent chapters.

Income Growth and Environmental Protection

Although there were precursors (e.g., Boulding 1966; Commoner 1963), the most intense debate concerning the effects of human economic expansion on environmental quality was launched with the Club of Rome report, *Limits to Growth* (Meadows 1972). Based on what were at the time sophisticated computer models of environmental systems, *Limits to Growth* became the quintessence of the Cassandran doomsaying about the environment. The study suggested that humanity would face ecological collapse as a result, according to the model, of continuing growth in population and consumption on a planet with inherent resource limits. This report was perhaps the most popular work at the time, although not the only one calling into question the ecological sustainability of modern societies (Council on Environmental Quality 1982).

56

Some were quick to leap to the defense of economic expansion. They pointed out numerous errors contained in the *Limits* models. Most notable was the absence of a role for the price system in signaling and moderating the impact of resource scarcity. Critics also suggested that the negative effects of growth could be compensated, if not rendered irrelevant, by substituting abundant for scarce resources and increased technological know-how (Simon and Kahn 1984).

The views of the optimists appeared to prevail in subsequent years as many of the predictions in the *Limits to Growth* and works making similar arguments came and went without ecological collapse. By some indications, many resources have become more abundant over the years. Coupled with a greater understanding of how the market might sometimes be made to work effectively to protect the environment, faith in markets and technological innovation to reduce the negative effects of scarcity has been bolstered.

For their part, adherents to limits-to-growth arguments correctly pointed out that their "deadlines" for catastrophe often went unmet because of policy efforts taken to address problems in the market (Meadows, Meadows, and Rander 1992). Recent developments, they have argued, provide hope but not reason for relief: the catastrophic effects of growth have only been delayed or simply transferred.

The continuing conflict over the compatibility of economic expansion and environmental quality can be seen in a recent explosion of controversy about the effects of income growth on pollution. In the 1990s a number of studies of ambient environmental quality reported evidence of a curvilinear relationship between per capita income and some common pollutants (Grossman and Krueger 1989, 1995; Panatoyou 1993; Seldon and Song 1994; Shafik 1994; Stern, Common, and Barbier 1996). For countries with low or moderate income (lower than those in my sample), increasing wealth was associated with increasing pollution. At higher levels of income, however, more wealth was associated with improvements in environmental quality.[2]

This finding led some to conclude that there was a "Kuznets curve" for pollution.[3] Although many "environmental Kuznets curve" (EKC) studies cautioned against interpreting their results as proof that economic growth

[2] Grossman and Krueger, Shafik, and Panatoyou use ambient pollution measures rather than emissions. The previous chapter explained why such measures are only partially adequate as a measure of environmental performance.

[3] The Kuznets curve refers to Simon Kuznets's observation that income inequality increased dramatically during industrialization but then decreased as growth continued.

solves environmental problems, others interpreted the results as suggesting that the best policy of environmental protection was increased economic growth (Beckerman 1992). Even more cautious conclusions have tended to infer causation, if not reasons for complacency, from the correlation between environmental quality and income (e.g., Portney 2000).

The Grossman and Krueger study has come came under considerable scrutiny in environmental economics and policy analysis (Harbaugh, Levinson, and Wilson, 2002; Hettige, Mani, and Wheeler 1998). An ensuing debate "as heated as that provoked by the Club of Rome Report some twenty-five years ago" (*Environment and Development Economics* 1996) cast some doubt on the generalizability of Grossman and Krueger's findings for other pollution problems such as deforestation, municipal waste generation, and carbon dioxide (Shafik and Bandyopadhyay 1992). For some pollutants there does appear to be a curvilinear relationship as Grossman and Krueger suggest; for others, there is a linear relationship. Whether that linear effect is positive or negative (i.e., whether income growth is correlated with increasing or decreasing pollution levels) also depends on the pollutant in question.

The empirical debate has prompted noted ecologists and economists to lay out main points of their interdisciplinary agreement (Arrow et al. 1995). Their statement underscored doubts about both the sufficiency of economic growth as a solution to environmental problems as well as an inherent incompatibility between these two goals. The authors emphasize that institutions (legislation, regulation, etc.), not income, are the keys to resolving economic and environmental issues.

We conclude that economic liberalization and other policies that promote gross national product growth are not a substitute for environmental policy. On the contrary, it may well be desirable that they are accompanied by stricter policy reforms.... Economic growth is not a panacea for environmental quality; indeed it is not even the main issue. What matters is the content of growth.... This content is determined by, among other things, the economic institutions within which human activities are conducted. (1995: 521)

Here I evaluate the EKC thesis using data developed in Chapter 2. The analysis makes three important contributions to this literature. First, it tests the income argument against cross-national changes in pollution. Existing studies have focused on pollution concentration levels. Examining changes captures the process implied by the theories underlying EKC studies: countries with higher incomes are more willing and able to reduce unhealthy levels of pollution in some cases. Second, by using an indicator of environmental emissions rather than ambient concentrations, my results should provide some idea of the robustness of earlier findings. One advantage of the emission data is that ambient concentration data in the Grossman and Krueger and similar studies deal mostly with urban pollution. Although the bulk of "economic value" is likely to be included here, such measures overlook human or ecological effects that occur at points without monitoring stations. Third, using an aggregate environmental performance indicator permits an assessment of whether higher income in a country results in general national environmental performance across pollutants.[4] Previous studies only look at pollutants individually, making it more difficult to make statements about the effects of wealth on overall performance.

Restricting the sample of countries to only wealthy ones does not pose a major inference problem due to selection bias. All of the countries in this sample have incomes above the point at which greater income is associated with declining performance.[5] Thus, we are dealing with a subset of countries in the curvilinear results in the EKC literature that fall on one side of the inflection point. Figure 3.1 demonstrates the point graphically. Whereas the EKC literature found curvilinear relationships across all countries, confining the analysis to rich countries amounts to examining only data after the inflection point. The EKC literature clearly suggests that for that subset of countries there should be a negative relationship between income and pollution.

Studies claiming that economic growth is good for the environment based on the empirical relationship between per capita income and environmental quality measures suggest a relatively simple (reduced form) model, such as

$$\text{ENV} = b_0 + b_1 \ln(\text{Income}) + b_2 \ln(\text{Income})^2 + b_k X_k + e \qquad (1)$$

ENV is the aggregate environmental performance measure developed at the end of Chapter 2, *Income* is starting real per capita income at purchasing

---

[4] The existing EKC results rely largely on individual pollution measures. Inferences about the general relationship between environmental quality and income are subject to the fallacy of composition: a positive correlation on each of their individual measures of environmental performance does not necessarily mean that rich countries do better across numerous different pollutants. Given the fact that the EKC models are reduced form, it is arguably more appropriate to use a more general measure on the left-hand side.

[5] It includes almost all of those countries on the "downside" of the curvilinear relationship in the existing EKC literature.

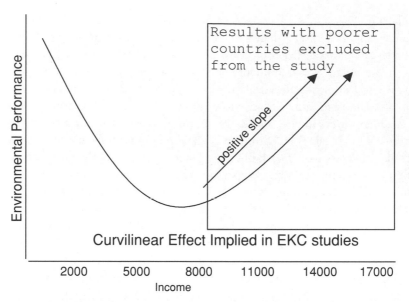

Figure 3.1 Results in the EKC Literature versus Expected Results in This Study

power parity (Summers and Heston 1991), and X_k is a vector of "control" variables. I take the level of income in the year corresponding to the average beginning period used for environmental performance measures (ca. 1975).[6] This avoids bias in the coefficient estimates if income growth is "endogenous" – that is, if income growth is negatively (or positively) affected by improved environmental performance.

Based on the EKC studies, we should see a strong linear relationship among the seventeen advanced countries considered here. However, the empirical relationship in the figure resembles an inverted U as seen in Figure 3.2.[7] For all countries, income and performance are positively related up to an income (in 1975) of about $11,000 and negatively related after that. However, there is evidence, albeit weaker, that income is linearly related to environmental performance. The bivariate correlation is .46 (p < .06).

This evidence of a linear relationship can be explained by the fact that two countries, Spain and Ireland, have much lower incomes and environmental

---

[6] Recall that the start year for three measures is 1970; for two measures, 1975; and for one measure, 1980.

[7] Using an alternative operationalization of wealth (e.g., per capita income in 1970 or the average of 1970–95) does not change the result much.

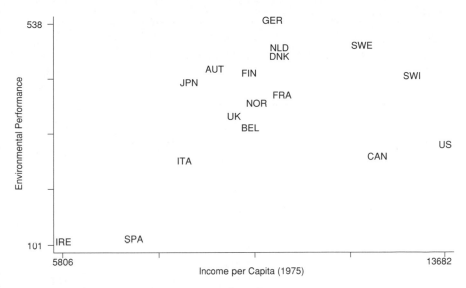

Figure 3.2 Income and Environmental Performance

performance than the others. For instance, if Spain and Ireland are excluded form the calculations, the correlation between income and environmental performance is close to zero (−.08), *but the U-shaped relationship between income and performance remains,* with a turning point at around $11,000.

Interestingly, the observed U-shaped relationship seen in Figure 3.2 is consistent with some of the empirical results from EKC studies. Both Grossman and Krueger and Shafik found a similar effect – lower environmental quality among the very rich countries compared with "moderately rich" ones, as did some specifications in Harbaugh, Levinson, and Wilson. They dismissed the finding as based on too few cases to be reliable.[8] As Figure 3.2 suggests, the relationship is influenced by the two richest countries, Canada and the United States. In replicating the finding that very rich countries do a little worse than moderately rich ones, these results provide some support for claims that some countries may be "unsustainably rich." Because the performance measure used here is quite different from the one used in the EKC literature, such a confirmation suggests considerable evidence of a general effect.

---

[8] These authors estimate environmental quality as a *cubic* function for their larger sample of countries, which corresponds to the estimate for the income-squared term here.

Even if there are reasons to doubt that very high incomes do worsen environmental performance, these results demonstrate that income is not a robust *linear* explanation of environmental quality once countries reach very high living standards. This perhaps more cautious conclusion is echoed by several recent "revisionist" studies of the EKC: pollution levels off at moderate to high levels of income (Hettige et al. 1998; Harbaugh, Levinson, and Wilson 2002). Thus, the findings here and in the EKC literature generally underscore the importance of looking at additional factors in explaining cross-national environmental performance for higher levels of development.

In summary, the evidence that income matters for environmental performance is seemingly contradictory. Consistent with prevailing explanations that wealth is good for environmental performance, the relative poverty of countries like Spain and Ireland goes some way toward explaining why their environmental performance is so poor. But contrary to the same explanation, the relative wealth of the United States, Canada, and Switzerland also seems to account for their relatively poor performance. In order to get more leverage on the problem, we need to look a bit further into the income-environment relationship as well as at alternative explanations of environmental performance.

Structural Economic Change and Environmental Performance

The reasons why environmental quality improves with increased income are not well established theoretically. Some economists maintain that the demand for environmental quality increases with (or even faster than) income, and that this rising demand explains rising environmental quality in societies with very high per capita income (e.g., Baumol and Oates 1988). On the other hand, most environmental economists and many environmentalists also consider the growth of industrial production as a major cause of environmental problems.[9]

For the conventional approach to environmental pollution, the translation of individual interest in environmental protection into social outcomes

---

[9] The range of perspectives on the topic is varied, in ways similar to explanations for such things as the welfare state, or economic and social development. Many hold to an industrialization thesis that focuses on the technology of production rather than its organization per se. Others blame mass production and particularly mass consumption. Still others blame capitalism (or socialism) rather than industrialism or mass consumption. Others go much deeper to blame fundamental religious or spiritual values. Needless to say, this book will not resolve such debates.

is not so simple. Environmental quality is a public good, meaning that individuals have few incentives to contribute to its supply unless some institutions help to overcome associated collective action problems. Second, the societal forces that give rise to excessive pollution may be the result of "path-dependent" choices (Arthur 1994; Goodstein 1995). If wealth is produced by "high-pollution" processes that are too expensive to abandon ex post, incremental technical and economic progress along the path may mean more pollution unless there is some type of unorthodox intervention to change market signals. Values or preferences are still relevant in producing better environmental quality; however, income is not sufficient to produce better environmental performance.

Others have suggested that income matters insofar as it creates changes in basic values that propel entire societies toward "more environmentally friendly" outcomes. Inglehart (1977, 1990, 1997) explains the rise of "postmaterial" values as based on the "decreasing marginal returns" to material consumption. This view is very close to the economist's account of the demand for environmental protection.[10] Inglehart's cultural argument is subject to a number of criticisms. First, environmental quality is in many respects a basic necessity for life. Thus, it is ambiguous whether "valuing" the environment is a postmaterial or basic survival value. The measures most closely corresponding to environmental concerns in Inglehart's empirical analysis suggest that "environmentalism" does not fit clearly into either materialist or postmaterialist values (Inglehart, 1990: chap. 4, 1997: chap. 4). Value change theories also ignore collective action problems associated with the provision of collective goods. How do individuals with pro-environmental values (if one assumes these are increasingly pervasive) come together to affect outcomes? Values may motivate action and help to prevent strategic behavior, but the extent to which they do is an empirical matter. Moreover, the individual level approaches based on microeconomics or individual socialization cannot explain why, at the highest per capita income levels, environmental performance has been worse as national incomes get higher.[11]

In the EKC literature, income is usually offered as a proxy (Grossman and Krueger 1995). Per capita income is supposed to capture aspects of an

[10] Inglehart (1990, chap. 2) argues that as cultures become more postmaterialist, their economic growth rates decline. Economists explain declining growth with increasing income without reference to preference change.

[11] As we will see in the next chapter, these wealthy poor performing countries also have high levels of postmaterialism.

63

evolutionary process that is really a diverse constellation of factors. One of the most commonly cited features, and one suggested to reduce pollution, is changing economic structure.

Per capita income serves to measure directly the relationship between economic growth and environmental quality and measures indirectly the endogenous characteristics of growth. Thus the impacts of rising industrialization and urbanization at middle-income levels and the growing importance of services in high-income economies are typical patterns that are proxied by per capita income. (Shafik 1994: 758–59)

Others provide quite similar rationales for assuming environmental and economic development proceed in a curvilinear fashion:

At low levels of development both the quantity and intensity of environmental degradation is [*sic*] limited to the impacts of subsistence economic activity.... As economic development accelerates with the intensification of agriculture and other resource extraction and then take off into industrialization, the rates of resource depletion begin to exceed the rates of resource regeneration, and waste generation increases in quantity and toxicity. At higher levels of development, structural change towards information intensive industries and services, coupled with increased environmental awareness, enforcement of environmental regulations, better technology and higher environmental expenditures, result in leveling off and gradual decline of environmental degradation. (Panayotou 1993, quoted in Stern et al. 1996)

The alleged relationship between economic expansion and other forms of social development is popular in the so-called modernization theory of social development, with various economic features serving as "preconditions" for various modern institutions – for example, democracy, civil rights, and better regulatory capability (Jänicke 1992; Przeworski and Limongi 1997).

Such "economic determinism" has been thrown into doubt by the study of economic development itself, most recently in studies of economic growth. The nature of social institutions and public expenditures are increasingly seen as factors that affect growth. If social institutions and policy play a role in the determination of economic development (as the endogenous growth literature claims), it seems logical to expect that they will play a role in determining environmental outcomes.

Figure 3.3 reflects the possible causal processes. Although social change may be correlated with environmental change, as in panel a, the effect in this case is spurious as both are "caused" by higher income. By reversing the arrow from society to economic change (panel b), social institutions are only *indirectly* related to environmental outcomes via economic change.

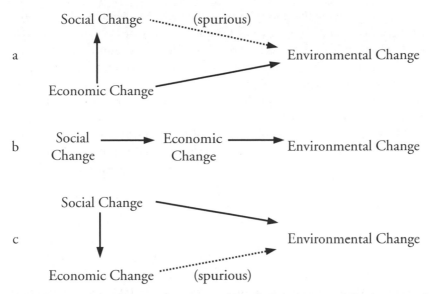

Figure 3.3 Three Relationships among Social, Economic, and Environmental Change

If social change is embodied in economic changes, however, per capita income (or related summaries of economic conditions) will "explain" most empirical variation in social effects. In panels a and b, income either is the underlying determinant of environmental performance or serves as a good proxy for the indirect effects of social institutions. A more society-driven causal path (panel c) suggests that environmental performance and income are *both* produced by independently generated social change. Viewed this way, economic change (to the extent that it is correlated with environmental performance) is a spurious cause. Of course, all three factors are intercorrelated to some degree. To get a better understanding of environmental performance, we may be able to use the mechanisms isolated in the theories to better explain performance.

The Structure of the Economy

The two models of industrial development discussed in the two quotations in the previous section share an underlying assumption: pollution-intensive production rises because of industrialization and then declines due to deindustrialization, some part of which is the result of demands for less pollution. It is the structure of production, not demand for environmental regulation, that is the mechanism by which environmental outcomes change. According to Shafik (1994) and Panatoyou (1993), the relative share of manufacturing versus services is a key mechanism for changing environmental quality. This structural explanation for environmental performance is also popular among many environmentalists, who view a less "productionist" (i.e., less manufacturing-oriented) economy as essential to reduce dangerous pollution.

The structure of production affects pollution in three related ways. One is that the industries associated with full-scale industrialization (such as mining, pulp and paper production, metal products, transportation equipment, and chemicals) are pollution-intensive. Second, although there may be cleaner methods of production, it is usually cheaper, all else equal, to have pollution-intensive goods produced abroad, and to make up for the imports with exports of less pollution-intensive goods. This argument is the basis for a large empirical literature on the comparative advantage effects of environmental protection. Yet this literature generally finds little evidence to support the pollution haven thesis (Jaffe et al. 1995). Third, trade complicates linkages between pollution-intensive production and consumption. The upshot is that structural changes in the economy, which are associated with higher incomes, can result in reduced pollution, *even if individuals in society do not have particularly effective ways collectively to overcome environmental externality problems.*

The explanations offered by more elaborate EKC studies imply that the structure of production is correlated with both income and environmental protection. Thus, the theoretically relevant causal pathways shown in Figure 3.4 are a slight elaboration of those in Figure 3.3. Based on the prevailing descriptions, economic structure should be a key to environmental quality. If so, industrial structure is linked to environmental quality. That is, structure partially mediates (as a sort of transmission belt) the income-environment link.

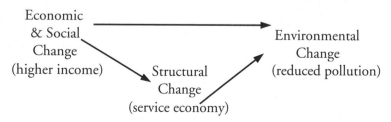

Figure 3.4 Structural Change as a Mechanism for Environmental Change

Table 3.1. *Structural Economic Change and Income*

Country	Heavy Industry (% GDP)			Income per Capita ($ at PPP)	
	1974–75	1994–95	Change	1975	1992
Austria	35.1	23.3	−11.8	8,936	12,955
Belgium	31.0	22.8	−8.2	9,633	13,484
Canada	26.0	21.6	−4.4	12,287	16,362
Denmark	19.5	19.5	0	10,236	14,091
Finland	28.3	25.5	−2.8	9,609	12,000
France	30.2	22.1	−8.1	10,297	13,918
W. Germany	38.7	28.3	−10.4	10,094	14,709
Ireland[a]	22.8	29.1	6.3	5,806	9,637
Italy	32.3	26.3	−6.0	8,282	12,721
Japan	34.3	27.6	−6.7	8,381	15,105
Netherlands	31.3	22.0	−9.3	10,255	13,281
Norway	26.8	26.1	−0.7	9,773	15,518
Spain	30.1	22.7	−7.4	7,238	9,802
Sweden	32.0	21.9	−10.1	11,958	13,986
Switzerland[a]		23.5		12,991	15,587
United Kingdom	31.0	22.9	−8.1	9,312	12,724
United States	28.1	22.7	−5.4	13,682	17,945
Average	29.8	24.0	−5.8		
Coefficient of variation	0.16	0.11			

Note: Heavy industry is manufacturing, mining, and utilities.
[a] Manufacturing sector only.
Source: OECD, national accounts, and OECD *Historical Statistics*, various years; Penn World Table 5.6 (Summers and Heston 1991).

If economic structure is a more proximate cause of environmental performance than income, structural factors could account for the poorer outcomes found among the very wealthy countries. For example, very rich countries may have a great deal of heavy industry compared with the others in my sample. This seems like a promising hypothesis, because both the United States and Canada (both very rich OECD countries with poor environmental performance) have abundant natural resources and associated basic industries.

Structural economic change, according to these accounts, implies a decline in heavy industry as income rises. For the seventeen countries examined here, I measure this change by combining the shares of value added in manufacturing, mining, and utility sectors. Table 3.1 shows this measure for the mid-1970s and the mid-1990s. The final two columns show per capita income in 1975 and 1992.[12] Based on the income-induced structural change thesis, higher income in each period should be associated with lower manufacturing intensity.

During the late 1970s and 1980s, manufacturing declined most rapidly where it was previously the highest (e.g., Austria, Germany, and Sweden). This decline is due *primarily* (though not exclusively) to changes in the manufacturing sector.

From Table 3.1 it appears that, despite the apparent convergence among the advanced democracies toward less heavy industry intensity (as suggested by the decline in the coefficient of variation), there is only limited evidence that income differences have had much to do with this change. The best predictor of economic structural change is a country's 1975 economic structure. Note, however, that economic structure is *not* correlated with income. For instance, Austria had comparatively low income in 1975 (thirteenth of seventeen, $1,000 per person below average), high heavy industry intensity, and the largest decline in heavy manufacturing between 1975 and 1995. Sweden, also high in heavy industry intensity in 1975, experienced a significant decline through 1995 but had *comparatively high income* (fourth of seventeen and $2,000 above average).[13] While there appears to be some statistical correlation between starting income and change in manufacturing, it is due exclusively to a single case: Ireland. If Ireland is excluded, there is no statistical evidence of a relationship.[14]

The weak empirical association between income and economic structural change is not simply the result of looking only at these particular countries. Similar evidence from twenty-four non-OPEC countries with per capita incomes above $7,500 in 1992 (a level above which we would expect a negative relationship between manufacturing and income) suggests that

[12] This was the last year available in the Summers and Heston (1991) data set as of December 2001.

[13] The correlation between income in 1975 and heavy industry in 1975 is 0 (n = 16); for income in 1975 and change in heavy industry from 1975 to 1995, it is −.31 (n = 16), but +.10 if Ireland is excluded.

[14] Is Ireland really an outlier? Perhaps it is actually representative of moderate income countries and seems to be an outlier here only because my sample has only two countries with such low incomes. Probably not. In a sample of seventy-one countries in the period 1975–94, Hettige, Mani, and Wheeler (1998) found that manufacturing intensity peaks at a per capita income of around $5,000 to $6,000. The upper end of this range is Ireland's income level in 1975. Thus, the fact that its manufacturing share and income grew considerably from 1975 and 1995 does make it exceptionaal here.

Table 3.2. *Regression Results: Economic Structure, Income, and Performance*

Independent Variables	1	2	3	4	5
Heavy industry (1975)	10.4 (6.8)	10.4 (6.2)	4.32 (4.94)		
Change in heavy industry				−0.86 (5.78)	
Income		3.0* (1.5)	32.3*** (8.8)	34.0*** (10.0)	
Income squared			−.0015*** (.00044)	−.0016*** (.00049)	
Constant	48.3 (205.1)	−244.1 (238.2)	−1449.4*** (397.9)	−1415.2*** (471.9)	
Observations	16	16	16	16	
Adjusted R^2	0.08	0.24	0.58	0.55	
R^2	0.14	0.34	0.66	0.64	
Turning point[a]			$10,667	$10,625	

Note: Standard errors in parentheses; income estimates in hundreds of dollars.
[a] Point at which relationship turns from positive to negative.
* $p < .10$; ** $p < .05$; *** $p < .01$.

there is also no discernible negative relationship between income and the size of the manufacturing sector.

How can we square these results with the conventional claim that there is a negative relationship between income and economic structure among wealthy countries? Hettige et al. (1998) suggest that it is due to the fact that there is a steep rise in manufacturing intensity as countries industrialize but a much less pronounced decline in manufacturing as development proceeds. This apparent paradox might be explained by the alternative ways to address productivity problems at high-income levels. For example, compare Germany's "diversified quality production" to the "business services revolution" in the United States. Both result in higher productivity, although only the former is consistent with a large manufacturing sector.

Although the idea that structural change explains the correlation between income and environmental performance receives little empirical support, it is certainly plausible that structural change could itself systematically affect comparative environmental performance. Because income and structural change are statistically independent, we can estimate the income and structural effects simultaneously and get reasonable estimates of both. Table 3.2

presents regression estimates using the initial level of heavy industry, the change in heavy industry between 1975 and 1995, income, and income squared as predictors of environmental performance.[15]

All of the estimates presented in Table 3.2 suggest that neither economic structure nor changes in that structure have systematically affected environmental performance. Insofar as change in structure is negatively correlated with initial heavy industry intensity ($r = -.83$), we would expect a positive sign for initial structure and a negative sign for change. None of the heavy industry estimates, however, are close to statistical significance. The estimates for income and its square are consistent with the previous results: there is an inverted-U relationship, there is a turning point at about $10,500, and all estimates are statistically significant.

To summarize, the empirical evidence for advanced democracies does not support the common claim that variations in environmental performance are related to income via changes in economic structure. Income is not negatively associated with the size of the industrial sector as many accounts suggest or with changes in that structure. Moreover, neither the structure of the economy nor changes in that structure away from heavy industry are systematically associated with improvements in environmental performance. This suggests that the reasons that income and performance are related might perhaps be better explained by changes in *demand* for environmental protection rather than by changes in the "pollution intensity" inherent in modern production. The next chapter examines this linkage – between income and the demand for environmental protection policy – in more detail.

Economic Growth

The speed of economic accumulation has been commonly considered a basis for negative environmental performance ever since the *Limits to Growth*. Indeed, empirical work in the EKC literature even suggests a positive short-run relationship between growth and changes in pollution (Harbaugh et al., 2002). A number of factors associated with the rate of increase in economic activity might explain such a relationship. First, higher production levels typically imply greater transformations of matter and energy into satisfying human desires often worsening environmental conditions. This is the standard reason why economic growth is viewed suspiciously

---

[15] Other specifications did not alter the substance or significance of the results reported.

by many environmentalists. Although economists often point out that economic growth implies a growth in human *value* and not necessarily more pollution, that is not completely disarming; that growth *need not* compete with the environment is not the same as saying that it actually *does not*.

Second, although a high level of income may mean that there are more resources to combat environmental problems and more demand to do so, this association does not mean that environmental protection does not reduce growth *subsequent* to achieving a high level of income. This distinction is often made in comparing regulatory policy tools such as market-based incentives and "command and control" regulations. Most discussion in these contexts centers on minimizing environmental protection costs, not eliminating them completely. (Of course, the discussion of protection costs often tends to ignore many estimates of social benefits associated with protection.)

In short, we might expect growth to be related to environmental performance for two contradictory reasons. On one hand, growth generates more pollution. On the other hand, stronger laws against pollution might slow the growth process. Regardless of the direction of the causal arrow, both effects imply a negative correlation between economic growth and environmental performance.

Table 3.3 presents economic growth rates for each of the seventeen countries for the periods 1960–75 and 1975–95. The first period serves as a reference. In the second period, economic growth slowed considerably in all countries except Ireland; and the slowdown was greater in countries that had grown faster in the previous period.

It might be tempting to compare average growth rates in these two periods and conclude that lower growth is linked to improvements in environmental conditions: most of these countries experienced improved environmental conditions in the period of slower growth. However, such an inference is faulty. First, there are no environmental data for the period prior to 1970, so we cannot ascertain whether environmental conditions were really getting worse in that period. Second, even if we had such evidence, there may still be considerable international variation, just as we have found in the period since 1970. We can get a much more accurate appraisal by looking at the growth-performance relationship across countries during a period in which we have data on both growth and environmental quality.

At first glance it appears that higher growth rates have little systematic impact on comparative environmental performance. For instance, above-average growth is associated with both relatively good performance (Norway and Japan) but also poor performance (Ireland, Canada, and the

71

Table 3.3. *GDP Growth Rates*

Country	1961–75	1975–95
Austria	4.8	2.3
Belgium	4.9	1.9
Canada	5.2	2.7
Denmark	4.0	2.1
Finland	4.8	2.1
France	5.2	2.0
W. Germany	4.1	2.2
Ireland	4.4	4.6
Italy	5.2	2.3
Japan	8.9	3.4
Netherlands	4.8	2.2
Norway	4.4	3.4
Spain	7.2	2.2
Sweden	4.1	1.5
Switzerland	4.2	1.0
United Kingdom	2.8	2.0
United States	3.7	2.5
Average	4.9	2.4

Source: OECD, national accounts.

United States). Similarly, if low growth enhanced environmental performance in two of the best performers (Sweden and Switzerland), high growth
did not prevent the Dutch from enjoying the second best environmental
performance.[16]

Because most countries were able to reduce pollution in the 1975–95
period, positive growth is *not* associated with growing pollution. Indeed, if
growth is entered in the regression equation with income (and income
squared), it is not a significant factor in accounting for environmental
performance.

Geographical Advantage

Other important features of countries that might impact their environmental performance are based on demography and geography. Geographic

---

[16] The bivariate correlation between growth and environmental performance is deceptively
high (−.48), solely because Ireland has both poor performance and high growth. If Ireland
is excluded, the correlation is insignificant (−.17) though in the expected direction. If Spain
is also excluded, under the assumption that it and Ireland are not real "high income" cases,
there is likewise no significant correlation (−.24).

features of countries can facilitate or impede efforts to reduce environmental pollution. However, whereas many geographic features of a country might influence particular aspects of "pollution tolerance," others apply only to particular types of pollution and to overall environmental performance.

Consider the claim that in the United Kingdom the "large windswept shoreline" and "rapidly flowing rivers" make the country less subject to environmental pressures than other countries. Although such features would thereby function to make Britain more pollution-intensive, they tend to reflect a very narrow view of environmental protection as limited to human health. More important, however, such claims are often more convenient than true. For instance, the claim that Britain had few eutrophication problems because of its geography is untrue. Most British NO_x pollution falls on Britain. Evidence for the concentrations of pollution in British rivers similarly suggests that the claim of geographic advantage can hardly explain British pollution performance (OECD, 1994c).

Other geographic factors, may have more widespread effects on all or most types of environmental pollution. These factors may make pollution more objectively problematic, more obvious to the public, or more costly to abate. Two such factors are a country's size and its population density. Both have numerous effects on a country's ability to address environmental problems. Size may also be correlated with a host of factors that make pollution problems more expensive to address. For instance, the ability to bury trash "elsewhere" might not affect the cost of reducing waste generation, but vast distances may make it more expensive to collect and transport recycling, create a mass transit network, or police polluter behavior. From a political perspective, then, larger country size or lower population density should make it easier for governments and people to ignore pollution problems or make it harder for those concerned about pollution to mobilize broad enough support for actions to reduce those problems. Looked at from another angle, structural factors such as a high population density will make it more likely that a government will feel compelled to address pollution problems.

Table 3.4 provides the area and population density of each of the seventeen countries considered in this study. Because the United States and Canada are more than an order of magnitude larger than the largest of the remaining countries, I took the natural log of area to make comparison tractable. (The difference between the United States and Canada without using logged values overwhelms any differences among the other countries; this is less of a problem with the logged values.) There is a weak negative correlation between performance and country size. This association

Table 3.4. *Geographical Advantage*

Country	Population Density 1975–92 (persons/km^2)	Log of Area (km^2)	Geographic Advantage[a]
Austria	91	4.43	0.29
Belgium	319	3.43	2.81
Canada	2	9.21	−3.30
Denmark	119	3.76	0.93
Finland	14	5.82	−1.19
France	99	6.31	−0.76
W. Germany	253	5.50	1.03
Ireland	49	4.25	0.04
Italy	189	5.71	0.36
Japan	315	5.94	1.29
Netherlands	343	3.74	2.84
Norway	13	5.78	−1.17
Spain	75	6.23	−0.91
Sweden	19	6.11	−1.32
Switzerland	158	3.71	1.29
United Kingdom	231	5.50	0.84
United States	25	9.14	−3.07
Correlation with environmental performance	0.30	−0.26	0.32

[a] Sum of standardized values for population density and inverse of ln(area).
Sources: OECD; Summers and Heston (1991).

is, however, still dominated by the United States and Canada. Excluding these countries, there is not a clear correlation between country size and performance. For instance, of the six "small" countries (those with an area of less than 100 square kilometers), all but one (Ireland) have above median environmental performance score, but so do four geographically large states, including the second best performer (Sweden).

In contrast to land area, the correlation between population density and performance should be positive. The four worst performers (Canada, Ireland, Spain, and the United States) do have low population density, and some countries with good performance have high population densities (the Netherlands and Germany). However, some of the best performers (Austria, Finland, and Sweden) have quite low population densities, in some cases lower than the population density of poor performers. In short, the evidence for a systematic relationship between population density and environmental performance is also relatively weak.

Table 3.5. *Regression Results: Income, Geographic Advantage, and Performance*

	1	2	3
Income (1975)	34.0***	29.0***	
	(7.8)	(7.8)	
Income squared	−.0015***	−.0013***	
	(.0004)	(.0004)	
Geographical advantage		21.9*	23.0
		(12.7)	(17.6)
Constant	−1389***	−1195***	362***
	(384)	(377)	(30)
Observations	17	17	17
Adjusted R^2	.57	.63	.04
R^2	.63	.70	.10
Turning point[a]	$11,333	$11,153	

Note: Standard errors in parentheses; income estimates in hundreds of dollars.
[a] Point at which relationship turns from positive to negative.
* $p < .10$; ** $p < .05$; *** $p < .01$.

Although neither area nor population density alone explains differences in environmental performance, their combined effects might. The combined effects of large (small) size and low (high) population density can be expected to have a combined effect and more likely to promote poor (good) environmental performance than either factor considered in isolation. To see if this is true, I summed the standardized values of both variables, creating a measure of "geographical advantage." Relatively large and sparsely populated countries (such as Canada) have very low scores, whereas small, densely populated countries (such as the Netherlands) have high scores. The evidence presented in column 3 of Table 3.4 suggests that differences in geographical advantage do not correspond much more closely with differences in environmental performance; the correlation coefficient is .32.

Table 3.5 shows estimates of environmental performance regressed on geographic advantage, income, and income squared.[17] All three variables are substantively significant. Including geographic advantage in the model does not significantly alter the income estimates, but including income considerably improves the precision of estimates for geographic advantage (compare columns 2 and 3).

[17] If growth rate is added as an explanatory variable in the model, it provides no leverage in explaining environmental performance and does not alter the reported results.

Accounting for a country's "geographic advantage" improves the fit of the model slightly. The adjusted R-squared improves from .57 to .63. The estimate implies that a change of one standard deviation in geographical advantage – going from the "average" country in terms of combined size and population density, such as Italy or Ireland, to a country with combined small (large) size and high (low) population density, such as Denmark (France) – results in an expected increase (decrease) in environmental performance of twenty-two points. The residuals suggest that, given income and geographic structure, Belgium (in particular) but also Canada and Spain are "underperformers," whereas Japan, Germany, and Sweden perform better than predicted.[18]

Conclusion

This chapter has shown that, as many other studies have suggested, per capita income is an important determinant of environmental performance. Moreover, like the actual empirical findings of previous studies – but in contrast to their substantive conclusions – the income-performance relationship among these rich countries has an inverted-U shape. For countries with "low" (Ireland and Spain) to "moderate" (Denmark or Germany) income per capita in 1975, more income is associated with better aggregate environmental performance; but for countries with starting per capita incomes around $11,000 (Canada, Sweden, Switzerland, and the United States), higher income is associated with declining performance.[19] This supports, to varying degrees, both the claims of those who maintain that wealth is beneficial for environmental quality and those who suggest that, beyond a certain point, wealth is counterproductive to good environmental performance.

There is no systematic support for the argument that income is related to environmental performance through structural economic change. Among these countries there is no relationship between income and economic structural change, or between economic structure, structural change, and

[18] Belgium is something of an outlier with respect to geographic advantage, performing worse than expected. If it is excluded, the size and precision of the geographic advantage estimate as well as of the model more generally improves considerably.

[19] Another implication of the results is that even controlling for the geographic expansiveness of the United States and Canada, the curvilinear relationship between income and performance remains. The income effect is also robust to a number of other controls as well, such as casewise deletion and elimination of apparently "high leverage" cases.

environmental performance. Furthermore, there does not appear to be a systematic relationship between environmental performance and *economic expansion* (growth rates) in this period. The evidence confirms a common position among many economists and ecologists that, while the *growth* of wealth and pollution is associated with the development of industrial society, neither the decline of industrial society per se nor the growth in per capita wealth independently affects environmental performance.[20]

Finally, the evidence presented in this chapter confirms that certain geographical factors may facilitate good environmental performance. Countries like Canada or the United States with low population density and large land area have somewhat poorer environmental performance, whereas small, densely populated countries like the Netherlands have very good performance. Although the implication of this result is that environmental problems may be easier to ignore (or harder to deal with) for citizens of larger, more sparsely populated countries, the mechanisms underlying such an explanation remain relatively undeveloped and might prove a fruitful avenue of further research.

[20] Given data limitations, it is impossible to tell whether cross-national variations in growth and environmental performance in the early postwar years (say, 1955–75) was more closely related to environmental performance than was the case from 1975 to 1995. This would clearly provide a more complete test.

4

Public Opinion, Environmental Mobilization, and Environmental Performance

A common explanation for environmental protection in advanced democracies is public awareness and concern about environmental problems. Virtually all studies cite, in one form or another, the emergence of environmental preferences among citizens as an important cause of action. According to such arguments, citizens perceive the environmental impact of industrial production as undesirable. Advances in the scientific understanding of the effects of human activity on the natural environment and recognition of the dependence of human society on environmental processes have also helped focus attention on environmental policy reforms. Greater scientific understanding has been ever more widely communicated via the news media, and increases in physical well-being since World War II have increased the salience of environmental protection on the political and social agenda.

Despite the research on increasing environmental concern and its causes, the relationship between mass attitudes and environmental outcomes in comparative politics remains virtually unexplored. This chapter attempts to address this oversight by investigating the relationship between the "mobilization of environmental bias" and environmental performance in advanced democracies. Drawing on several international opinion surveys and electoral data on environmental parties, I assess whether cross-national differences in aggregate support for environmental protection help us to explain cross-national differences in environmental performance in ways commonly assumed. Additionally, I investigate the extent to which cross-national differences in environmental mobilization are related to income. Then, the chapter more systematically evaluates the idea introduced in the preceding chapter that "environmental mobilization" is largely a product of income growth.

After reviewing the literature on public environmental concern (and noting some limitations of this research in addressing the link between opinion and both environmental policy outputs and outcomes), I discuss why (and how) public opinion data might be expected to correlate with environmental performance. I then review the data on public opinion in the advanced democracies between the 1970s and the mid-1990s and test the hypothesized associations using bivariate and multivariate statistical analysis.

Environmental Mobilization

Most empirical work on environmental attitudes in comparative politics concentrates on two central questions: what do people want and why do they want it? Numerous opinion studies demonstrate that environmental concern is high in Western societies. Moreover, they suggest that public attitudes are coherent enough (if not always factually well informed) to justify claims that the public wants action taken on a variety of environmental problems (e.g., Dunlap 1995; Dunlap and Scarce 1991; Erskine 1972; Gilroy and Shapiro 1986; Hofrichter and Reif 1990; Rohrschneider 1988). As Lowe and Rüdig noted in their review of the literature, "despite variations in the degree of concern [across countries], there appears to be relative stability of attitudes to environmental protection" (1986: 514).

Why people are environmentally concerned has also been the subject of considerable argument. Although this important question is secondary to this chapter, it is worth touching on the main explanations. The prevailing claim in the literature is that people want environmental protection because more environmental amenities (like clean air and water) are always better than less. But some, such as Ellis and Thompson (1997), challenge this assumption, maintaining that concern is determined by more fundamental cultural attitudes, which vary both within and between countries (cf. Douglas and Wildavsky 1982). Although the latter assertion has merit, and may account for some differences in the intensity of opinion among different people, it does little to explain the relatively widespread and rapid *change* in public attitudes about the environment that has occurred since the late 1960s. Such change within a generation is something that most cultural accounts typically have difficulty explaining.

Another common claim is that the deterioration of environmental conditions leads to popular concern. This claim is often made implicitly in studies of environmental problems and policy but has not been investigated explicitly (cf. Inglehart 1995). Establishing a causal relationship between an

79

"objective" threat and an attitude is fraught with complications. There is no easy way to establish whether attitudes are constructed by "cultural bias" or "objective threats," especially when these concepts themselves are inter-related. (Such conceptual fuzziness does not make for easy social science, but that does not make the issues less important.)

Perhaps the most popular explanation of environmental concern at-tributes it to widespread cultural change in advanced industrial societies. Broad changes in patterns of living and working have created a space for a new dimension of politics that is distinct from the traditional left-right dichotomy that dominated politics (and political science) throughout most of the twentieth century (Abramson and Inglehart 1994; Dalton and Kuechler 1990; Inglehart 1977, 1990, 1997; Mueller Rommel 1989).[1] An-other, slightly different, suggestion is that the growth of environmental awareness stems less from structural changes (and their cultural products) and more from a change in consciousness, due in part to greater under-standing of the negative impacts of modern human society on the natural environment (Paehlke 1989, 1997). This view tends to stress the growth of knowledge about environmental problems. In both understandings envi-ronmental concerns become important due to a large increase in the por-tion of well-educated, materially secure citizens who are willing and able to address more complex, "higher-order" social problems (Marsh 1981, in Lowe and Rüdig 1986: 516).

Despite the evidence of increasing environmental awareness and the role of such awareness in changing politics in postindustrial societies, ex-isting research has only recently begun to explore the implications of these changes for important social outcomes (e.g., Esping-Andersen 1999; Kitschelt 1994). This study extends such work by investigating the sub-stantive impact of new attitudes and social outcomes for the environment. To do so, I look at how expressed concerns are reflected in actual envi-ronmental performance. In other words, taking opinion or mobilization as given, do differences in public opinion matter for environmental outcomes in advanced democracies?[2]

---

[1] The connection between postmaterialism and environmentalism was first made by Dalton and Hildebrandt (1977) and has been widely accepted, at least at the individual level. The distinctions often made between Douglas and Wildavsky's (1982) "cultural" explanation and that of the new politics–new social movements school are more apparent than real (cf. Ellis and Thompson 1997).

[2] I assume that the true *causes* of concern (new threats, increased knowledge, changes in culture) are not particularly relevant to the likelihood of a response. This need not be true.

At one level the answer might seem obvious. Both environmental concern and environmental protection have increased markedly in the past thirty years. Must we not then attribute increased environmental protection to this concern? This logic has intuitive appeal, and one would be hard-pressed to substantiate a claim that public opinion has nothing to do with increased environmental protection. However, the claim that "public opinion matters" needs to be subjected to a more rigorous cross-national evaluation. For instance, it may well be that policy (and publicity of it) drives opinion rather than the reverse.

The main question addressed in the rest of the chapter is whether differences in the strength of opinion and its activation across industrial democracies matter in explaining differences in national environmental performance.[3] Other tests could examine opinion and performance over time in a given country or across time and space. Given the nature of the data available, however, this is not feasible for most of the countries considered here. Almost all cross-national opinion questions have been asked in only a few questionnaires (and not to the same people), making it impossible to speak of comparative national panels.

Are Opinion and Performance Related?

There are three chief reasons why opinion and environmental outcomes might be related in advanced democracies. Perhaps the most obvious way is through the effect of opinion on public policies. Vote-seeking politicians have electoral incentives to adapt policy to the desires of public opinion. The notion that policy tracks public opinion has been long examined by social scientists (Dahl 1956; Sen 1970), although much of the empirical work on the relationship between opinion and policy (both in general and with respect to environmental issues) comes from the United States (Page and Shapiro 1983; Stimson et al. 1995).

Of course, there are those who suggest that policy bears little relationship with public opinion (Hardin 1982; Olson 1965; Schattschneider 1960).

However, given that democracies have institutions in place to respond to mass concerns and given that most material and technological aspects of human society are essentially a social construction, one could argue that democratic societies respond to the desires of the society (through elections and even the market).

[3] Spain is anomalous because it has been a democracy only since the 1970s. None of the empirical results discussed here depend critically on Spain's inclusion or exclusion from the analysis.

Politicians do not respond to "latent," unorganized interests but to organized ones. Even if government activity reflects electoral incentives to cater to unorganized interests, policy responsiveness can be symbolic rather than substantive (Edelman 1964; Miliband 1969). For instance, politicians may pass laws but provide little by way of enforcement or implementation. Particularly in environmental policy, the process of implementation leaves numerous spaces for subversion by particularistic interests. Despite differences of opinion about the influence of public sentiment on substantive policy issues in democratic countries, environmental policy could provide empirical evidence for one view or the other.

The second way that public attitudes might matter is through the market. Although the market tends to be portrayed by some environmentalists as inherently antithetical to environmental protection, markets have responded to increasing demands for environmental responsibility in both the production process and in the characteristics of the products for sale. Market-based policies – environmental taxes, pollution-permitting systems – are increasingly accepted as vital approaches to reducing pollution, and there is evidence that consumers in many countries select products in part for environmental friendliness. Because employees are citizens and because firms can be considered governance structures that reflect, to some degree at least, opinions of the individuals that compose them, changing public attitudes may thus push along social reforms through "private effort" as well as by official public policy, even if public policy is an essential factor restraining the negative environmental impacts of private behavior.

Of course, the linkage between the market and public opinion should not be taken too far. Several factors limit the market's responsiveness to environmental pollution problems, even in the face of "greening" public opinion. Firms might provide less than honest or complete information about their "green" credentials (Tokar 1997). Moreover, the public-good character of many environmental problems means that the market will provide too little protection in the absence of government intervention or some type of political coordination among market actors be they producers or consumers. The upshot of these important exceptions is that it is at best naive to expect outcomes in the market to reflect public opinion in many cases.

The final means by which opinion may affect environmental outcomes is through individual behaviors at what may be considered a normative-psychological level (Buttel 1987). For example, where collective concern is high, more "environmentally sound behavior" may follow. The aggregate level of environmental concern may even influence individual actions, among those who do not necessarily express those concerns. Take, for example, curbside recycling. The propensity to recycle is almost certainly influenced by the fact that one's neighbors put out their recycling.

Data

In examining survey data on public attitudes about environmental protection and environmental organizations, I rely extensively on the Eurobarometer (EB) surveys of EU member countries and World Values Surveys (WVS). Neither set of surveys is ideal, but both incorporate several desirable features for a comparative study. First, they survey citizens in many countries asking identical or very similar questions. Second, the EB contains environmental questions dating back to the mid-1970s and has several questions that have been asked over a long period of time. Two World Values Surveys are used here (1981, 1990): one includes fifteen of the seventeen countries included in this book; the 1990 version includes sixteen of the seventeen.

I look at several different types of attitudinal indicators. First, I examine simple and intuitively obvious measures of public attitudes in support of environmental protection. These include general concerns about environmental problems and willingness to sacrifice personal or other social goals for environmental protection. Also examined is the extent to which the public supports organizations that "represent" environmental interests. The complexity of environmental issues, the interest group dominance of modern democracies, and modern theories of democracy all provide a basis for the claim that the popular support of "environmental lobbies" might have as important an impact on public responses to environmental problems as the attitudes of individuals. To get at this support, I also use questions from the EB and WVS as well as electoral data on votes for environmental parties.[4] The rest of this section presents a cross-national comparison of these measures of public support for environmental protection. I examine to what extent these indicators explain observed variations in national environmental performance in the subsequent section.

---

[4] Other EB questions ask about particular environmental issues. Because this study is concerned with general attitudes as they relate to national income and national environmental performance, these specific questions are not considered.

General Concern for the Environment

One indication of national attitudes about a problem is a general concern about that problem. Given the large number of public issues, higher concern about the environment does suggest a higher level of social preference for protection and is taken to indicate high salience.[5] Greater concern is also taken to suggest a higher "demand" for environmental protection to which politicians, activists, and/or firms might respond. Two questions asked in EB surveys since the 1970s offer comparative time series evidence regarding general environmental concern.[6] The first questions, used in 1976 (EB6), 1978 (EB10), 1983 (EB20), 1987 (EB 28), and 1991 (EB35.0), asked how important citizens believe fighting pollution is.

Here is a list of problems the people of [country] are more or less interested in. Could you please tell me, for each problem, whether you personally consider it a very important problem, important, of little importance or not at all important?
  – Protecting Nature and Fighting Pollution

A second question used in 1986 (EB 25), 1992 (EB37.0), 1995 (EB43.1BIS), asked a similar but slightly different question:

Many people are concerned about protecting the environment and fighting pollution. In your opinion, is this

  1. An immediate and urgent problem
  2. More a problem for the future
  3. Not really a problem

Responses to these questions make it clear that environmental protection has long been a valence issue – that is, something that no one is or would say they were actually opposed to. Even as far back as 1976, more than 85 percent of respondents in each European Community (EC) country answered "very important" or "somewhat important." (This high level of concern is matched in the United States based on similar surveys.) As a valence issue, there is little variation among countries if both of these categories are considered favorable responses. However, we can get some sense

---

[5] The level of environmental concern does not necessarily indicate a social preference. Society can be concerned about environmental problems, but, when forced to choose, always prefers efforts in other areas (say, reducing unemployment) to protecting the environment.

[6] One question asked in the 1973 EB provides earlier evidence of environmental concern. Unfortunately, this question has a different format from all others and was asked of only 40 to 90 percent of the respondents in different EU countries based on a lead-in question. The responses are broadly in keeping with those reported for 1976.

Table 4.1. *Public Concern about Environmental Problems*

Country	Fighting Pollution Is "Very Important" (%)						Environment an "Immediate and Urgent" Problem (%)		
	1976	1978	1983	1987	*1989*	1991	1986	1992	1995
Belgium	65.4	54.3	46.1	56.8	*75.9*	82.8	62.5	86.9	63.6
Denmark	74.2	64.1	79.4	85.4	*88.8*	90.6	77.4	87.6	86.2
France	70.6	60.8	53	56	*68.4*	84.6	55.6	80.6	78.1
W. Germany	63.7	54.8	63.5	69.1	*82.6*	88.4	80.1	89.6	84.7
Ireland	49.4	46.8	37.4	49	*71.5*	83.4	56.1	72.9	81.6
Italy	67.3	62	57.8	67.9	*84.7*	89.1	84.9	91.4	90.1
Luxembourg	74.5	42.3	66.1	72.9	*78.1*	89.5	83.3	88.1	87.4
Netherlands	67.4	69.6	53.2	61.3	*82.5*	85.1	63	85.9	80.9
United Kingdom	48.0	48.2	48.4	52.5	*75.1*	91.6	66.7	86.2	80.3
Greece		46.7	67.7	66.6	*71.1*	87.3	83.7	97.4	96.9
Portugal				53.3	*78.6*	82.2	70.9	83.2	79.8
Spain				57.9	*74.4*	86.1	72	86.1	83.9
E. Germany						90.5		95.4	89.4
Finland									78.6
Sweden									94.1
Austria									80.4
Norway								81.2	
United States[a]	55	52	54	60	69	68		58[b]	58[c]

Note: Question wording in italics differs slightly from other years.
[a] The figures are percent responding that government environmental spending is "too low."
[b] 1993.
[c] 1996.
Sources: Eurobarometers 6, 10A, 20, 25, 28, 31, 35, 37, 43.1bis; Dunlap and Scarce (1991).

of how intensely the public in EC countries regards environmental protection by considering the percentage of national publics who rate environmental problems as "very important." Table 4.1 shows the percentage of respondents in each country who say that environmental protection is "very important" between 1976 (the first year the question was asked) and 1991, as well as those indicating it as an "urgent and immediate" problem in 1986, 1992, and 1995. (Table 4.1 also includes information from the United States over this period.)

Despite the fact that a majority in every country felt that fighting pollution was a "very important" problem, there is substantial variation across countries and over time. Popular concern was very high throughout continental Europe in the 1970s.[7] Concern was considerably lower in Ireland and the United Kingdom. (The latter perhaps explains the characterization of Britain as the "dirty man of Europe.")

In the late 1970s, however, concern dropped in six of the nine EU members. By 1983, it rebounded in Denmark and Germany but remained more or less stable in the United Kingdom. It continued to fall in Belgium, Ireland, and France and fell precipitously in the Netherlands. In the latter five countries fewer than 50 percent considered pollution a "very important" problem during the early 1980s. From this nadir, the degree of public concern about the environment climbed sharply throughout the EU over the next decade. The leap in concern in the 1987 survey is hardly surprising – the nuclear accident at Chernobyl occurred in May 1986 – but public concern continued to grow even as the memory of that event would have presumably worn off. By 1991 more than 80 percent of the population of *all* EU members was "very concerned" about pollution, an increase of 27 to 46 points compared to the lows of the late 1970s and early 1980s. The rise in concern is particularly dramatic in Ireland and the United Kingdom.

Because the question format was different, responses in the 1986, 1992, and 1995 surveys are not strictly comparable with the others. The general pattern of responses between 1986 and 1992 is similar, however. If we compare the 1992 and 1995 responses, environmental concern appears to have leveled off or declined somewhat in most EU countries. Decline was especially pronounced in Belgium. Nevertheless, it would appear that concern was much higher in all EU countries than it was in the 1970s or 1980s.

A similar pattern exists in North America. Concern in the United States rose sharply in the late 1960s to early 1970s, declined somewhat from the mid-1970s through the early 1980s, and rebounded more significantly through about 1990. After that, it fell in the early part of that decade (Gilroy and Shapiro 1986; Dunlap and Scarce 1991; General Social Survey 1999). As in the EU countries, support for environmental protection in the 1990s was higher than in the early 1970s. More limited evidence for Canada suggests a similar pattern (Doern and Conway 1994: 116–18).

---

[7] Although there are not public opinion series for the early 1970s in Europe, evidence – from surveys in Germany and the Netherlands, the convening of the Stockholm Environmental Conference in 1972, and the EC's designation of 1970 as the Year of Nature Protection – suggests a major surge in EC concern between the late 1960s and early 1970s that mirrors the rise of environmentalism in the United States (Erskine 1972; Cramer 1989: 103–4; Pehle 1997).

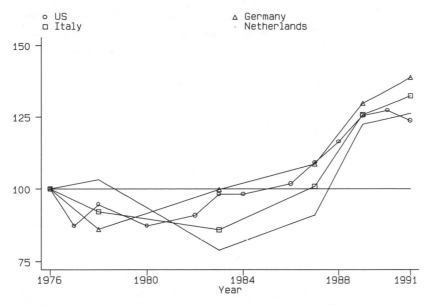

Figure 4.1 Environmental Concern (1976–1991; 1976 = 100)

Figure 4.1 compares trends in concern in the United States with trends for Italy, West Germany, and the Netherlands. Because the wording of the question is different, we cannot compare the levels of support between the United States and the European countries, so the responses are indexed at 100 in 1976.[8] The pattern of opinion is relatively similar over time for all four countries. Explanations for fluctuating environmental concern vary. In the United States, an environmentally insensitive Republican administration is sometimes credited with remobilizing the environmental movement and undermining environmental policy (Andrews 1999). In Europe, rising concern, especially in Germany and the Netherlands, is often viewed as part of the growth of New Social Movements.

Both of these explanations fail to account for common patterns on both sides of the Atlantic based on economic and energy problems.[9] Compare the data in Table 4.1 with the economic cycles in each country. During the

---

[8] The U.S. question asks whether government spending on the environment is "too little," "too much," or "about right."

[9] Nor is it the case that the United States was unique in suffering a political shift to the right in the 1980s. In Denmark (in 1982), Germany (1982), the Netherlands (1982), Norway (1981), the United Kingdom (1979), and Canada (1984) governments shifted from left (or center left) to the right (or center right) for the majority of the decade.

general decline in environmental concern in the late 1970s and early 1980s, Denmark and the United Kingdom, two countries that experienced a *less* drastic economic slowdown in the period, also experienced relatively lower declines in aggregate environmental concern. In countries with larger declines in economic performance – Belgium, the Netherlands, and France – environmental concern declined more precipitously. These are also the only three EU countries in which concern was much lower in 1987 than in 1976. From this, one might argue that changes in concern are explained largely by the economic cycle.

In Germany and Italy changes in concern do not match with economic performance, however. Italy had perhaps the best relative economic performance (growth rates fell only 25 percent), and concern for the environment also fell considerably between 1976 and 1983. In Germany concern between 1976 and 1983 was unchanged (even increasing between 1978 and 1983), although growth rates were much lower than they had been in the late 1960s and early 1970s.[10]

During the 1980s economic recovery might help to explain the increasing level of environmental concerns in the EU through the early 1990s. For instance, the United Kingdom doubled its average growth rate between 1976–83 and 1984–90 and saw environmental concern increase by almost the same proportion. Denmark, whose growth rate changed little between the two periods, saw only a modest level of growth in concern (albeit from a higher base than the other EU countries).

Table 4.2 provides the results of a statistical analysis of the effect of fluctuations in the economy with changes in environmental concern. The data used are the nine countries with data for 1976–91 in Table 4.1.[11] The dependent variable is change (from the preceding survey) in the percentage of respondents reporting that pollution is a "very important" issue. The key independent variable is the recent economic performance of the country, measured by the average growth rate in the year of the survey and the preceding year. Alternative specifications included a time trend; estimated the model, using panel-corrected standard errors (PCSE); and combined PCSE and estimates of separate country intercepts. The results all suggest a

---

[10] On the whole, the economy in the United States performed slightly better in the 1976–83 period, and support declined very marginally. Perhaps a likely explanation for this is the energy crisis and the fact that the United States experienced a much steeper recession (in 1982) than most of Europe did in the period.

[11] These countries are Belgium, Denmark, France, Germany, Ireland, Italy, the Netherlands, the United Kingdom, and the United States.

Table 4.2. *Regression Results: Environmental Concern and Economic Growth*

Independent Variables	OLS	OLS	PCSE	PCSE & Country Intercepts[a]
GDP growth[b]	2.66*	2.83***	2.83**	2.66**
	(1.41)	(1.04)	(1.23)	(1.36)
Time[c]		30.2***	30.2***	30.2***
		(5.0)	(6.0)	(6.1)
Constant	.80	−17.2***	−17.3***	−19.2***
	(4.4)	(4.4)	(5.3)	(7.0)
Observations	45	45	45	45
Adjusted R^2	.06	0.51		
R^2	.08	0.48	0.51	0.56

Note: Standard errors in parentheses.
[a] Estimates of country intercepts excluded.
[b] GDP growth is average of two most recent years.
[c] Time is scaled to be 0 in 1976 and 1 in 1991.
* $p < .10$; ** $p < .05$; *** $p < .01$.

robust and statistically significant association between changes in economic performance and changes in public opinion. That is, on average, more (less) growth is associated with an increase (decrease) in environmental concern.

Although there are not enough years for a regression analysis, the results for the 1990s also generally support the importance of short-term economic factors on aggregate environmental opinion. Economic downturns in Europe, as well as in the United States, are matched by dips in support – in some cases dramatic – for environmental protection. In Europe the only country to prosper throughout the slowdown in the early 1990s, Ireland, was also the only country in which support for environmental protection increased between the 1991 and 1995 surveys.[12]

Although fluctuations in public support for environmental protection may follow the business cycle to some degree, it is impossible to deny that there has been an upward underlying trend. Whether one compares the series of questions on the "importance" of environmental protection or its "urgency," the trend in the proportion of the population strongly supporting environmental protection is up in all countries. (This trend is

[12] Based on the available economic data, the one place where we might also expect stagnation in support for environmental protection is Japan, where the economy has performed poorly in the 1990s.

89

captured in Table 4.2 by the significant positive association between time and change in environmental concern.) The growing importance of environmental problems in popular opinion throughout Europe and the United States is indisputable.

Economic Trade-offs and "Willingness to Pay"

General support for environmental protection is one indication of the importance that citizens attach to the environment, but providing answers to such survey questions generally imposes no constraints on respondents – that is, respondents are not forced to choose how much they value environmental protection over other social priorities. "Trade-off" questions thus provide some indication of the *relative intensity* of citizens' environmental demands. Several questions asked in the Eurobarometer and the second WVS confront people with an explicit trade-off between environmental protection and other goals. The EB 10A (1978) asked respondents:

Among the different possible choices for national planning and development policies which are on the list, which is the one that you would give priority to?

1. Slow up the expansion of large towns
2. Encourage the creation of work in the least developed regions
3. Protect the character and uniqueness of each region
4. Reorganize working times, working week, leisure time and holidays
5. Improve and coordinate the public transport system
6. Protect the environment and fight against pollution

The EB 18 (1982) asked two explicit trade-off questions of the then ten EC member countries.

Sometimes measures that are designed to protect the environment cause industries to spend more money and therefore raise their prices. Which do you think is the more important: protecting the environment or keeping prices down?

Here are two statements which people sometimes make when discussing the environment and economic growth.

Statement A: Protection of the environment should be given priority, even at the risk of holding back economic growth.
Statement B: Economic growth should be given priority, even if the environment suffers to some extent.

Which of these statements comes closest to your opinion?

90

Similarly, the EB 43.1 (1995) asked respondents to indicate whether growth should take precedence over environmental protection.

I am going to read you three opinions which you sometimes hear about environmental problems. Which one comes closest to your own?

1. Economic development should get higher priority than concerns about the environment.
2. Economic development must be ensured but the environment protected at the same time.
3. Concerns about the environment should get higher priority than economic development.

Finally, the second World Values Survey (1990), also asked "trade-off" questions about individuals' "willingness to pay" for greater environmental protection.

I am now going to read out some statements about the environment. For each one I read out, can you tell me whether you agree strongly, agree, disagree or strongly disagree?

I would give of my income if I were certain that the money would be used to prevent environmental pollution....
I would agree to an increase in taxes if the extra money is used to prevent environmental pollution....
If we want to combat unemployment in this country, we shall just have to accept environmental problems.

The percentage of respondents in each country strongly preferring more environmental protection to other goals is given in Table 4.3. (Data for the United States come from a different survey with similar questions.)

The responses to the 1978 question (column 1 of Table 4.3) suggest that the environment was not the top priority in any EC member nations in 1978. Only in Denmark was it rated above concern for relieving unemployment. Moreover, the results also suggest limits to the economic determinism suggested in the preceding section. Denmark and Belgium, two countries attaching relatively high priority for the environment in the survey, also underwent significant increases in unemployment after 1975. Countries with weaker environmental support (e.g., France and Italy) not only experienced smaller increases in unemployment, but their absolute unemployment rates at that time were absolutely lower than those in Denmark or Belgium.

Columns 2–4 in Table 4.3 suggest that in 1982, another year of sluggish or negative growth in advanced countries, large numbers of people in

Table 4.3. *Environment and Traditional Economic Goals*

Country	Biggest Planning Priority (1978)	Eurobarometer					World Values Survey	
		% Saying (1982) Environment More Important Than			% Saying Environment Is Priority to Growth		% Strongly Agreeing (1990) to Give for Environment	
		Growth	Inflation	Both	1992	1995	Income	More Taxes
Austria						18.4	15.3	12.1
Belgium	26.2	50.2	50.4	38.6	22.1	12.5	14.6	10.0
Canada							18.9	14.0
Denmark	33.6	74.5	73.9	65.9	34.7	34.2	38.2	26.2
Finland						21.6	19.6	14.0
France	17.5	57.6	63.0	47.0	13.5	11.3	16.5	11.0
W. Germany	26.9	63.7	54.1	49.0	31.5	21.6	9.9	6.9
Greece		55.6	66.7	45.8	20.8	25.4		
Ireland	13.2	29.4	33.5	23.5	18.5	16.5	13.6	7.4
Italy	18.9	67.1	66.0	55.3	17.5	13.7	17.1	11.0
Japan							7.5	4.5
Luxembourg	7.9	64.0	69.3	52.7	30.4	25.9		
Netherlands	29.3	55.7	71.5	47.4	30.7	20.0	29.1	19.1
Norway					32.5		28.7	26.8
Portugal					18.5	11.9	39.7	21.1
Spain					20.0	17.8	22.7	16.1
Sweden						32.6	35.3	37.6
United Kingdom	26.2	50.4	56.6	39.1	24.4	23.0	14.2	10.6
United States		41.0	52.0				18.4	13.3

Sources: Eurobarometer, World Values Survey, Gilroy and Shapiro (1986); see text for details.

EC countries (and the United States) indicated support for environmental protection even if it meant lower economic growth or higher prices. Although fewer individuals in these countries ranked *both* inflation control and economic growth ahead of environmental protection, majorities in Italy (55 percent) and Denmark (66 percent) did favor environmental protection over these traditional economic priorities. Near majorities did the same in Germany (49 percent), the Netherlands (47 percent), and France (47 percent). In Belgium (39 percent), Britain (39 percent), and Ireland (24 percent), however, support for environmental protection relative to economic concerns clearly lacked majority support. The United States would clearly fall into the low support category.[13] No more than 41 percent of U.S. respondents have a "strong preference" for the environment over economic priorities.

Although pro-environmental attitudes appear considerably weaker once people have to make a choice, there is a close association between these questions and those discussed in the preceding section. For instance, the correlation between the level of general environmental concern in the 1983 survey and the willingness to sacrifice growth and inflation for environmental protection in the 1982 survey is .89. (Because trade-off and concern questions are not asked in the same survey, we cannot perform such an analysis at the individual level.)

The opinion data considered to this point provide information only on about half of the countries for which there are also environmental performance data. The trade-off questions in the 1992 and 1995 EB surveys overcome this problem to some extent because there are more member states and, thus, more countries being surveyed. The information from the 1990 WVS is even more enlightening because it provides survey results for all but one (Switzerland) of the seventeen countries analyzed in this book.

Columns 5 and 6 in Table 4.3 give the percentage of respondents who agreed (in 1992 and 1995) that environmental protection should take priority over economic growth. The percentages are much lower in the 1990s because the question incorporated a third option allowing respondents to choose both. It is hardly surprising that when offered two desirable ends, people more often choose both when given the opportunity to do so. Danish respondents attached the highest priority to environmental protection in

[13] The data source used for the United States gives aggregate figures only.

both polls. Roughly one-third of those surveyed said that the environment should have higher priority than economic growth, *even when offered an option "in favor of both."* The Netherlands, Germany, and Norway (not an EU member but included in this survey) were close behind in 1992, but support in all three of these countries was lower in 1995. The environment receives priority by less than one-fifth of people in France, Ireland, Italy, and Spain in both years. The United Kingdom is somewhere in the middle. Although we have evidence only for 1995, environmental support appears to be very high in Sweden and moderate in Finland, this in spite of the fact that both countries experienced severe economic disruptions in the early 1990s that would be expected to reduce popular support for environmental protection. Based on the evidence for the EU, it is likely, therefore, that public opinion in these two countries would have been at least as high in the early 1990s as it was in 1995.

As we saw with general concern questions, support for environmental protection declined between 1992 and 1995, particularly in Belgium, the Netherlands, and Germany in line with economic fortunes (recall Table 4.2). Growth rates in the early 1990s were at least 30 percent lower in Belgium, the Netherlands, and Germany than in the late 1980s. Support was more or less unchanged in Denmark, as was its growth rate. (Actually, the Danish growth rate was slightly higher in the early 1990s than in the late 1980s.) However, change between the two periods in the United Kingdom and Ireland is not consistent with economic fluctuations. In the United Kingdom, support for the environment is stable in the two surveys, although growth in the early 1990s was much slower than in the late 1980s. Support in Ireland fell despite blistering economic growth in the early 1990s. These "trends" should be considered with caution, however, as they are based on only two data point years for each country.

Finally, the 1990 WVS provides an even better vantage from which to evaluate citizens' willingness to trade-off presumptively valuable personal and social goals for greater environmental protection. This survey provides information for sixteen of the seventeen industrial countries compared throughout this book. Columns 7 and 8 of Table 4.3 give the percentage of respondents who are strongly supportive of devoting some of their income to environmental protection or paying higher taxes for environmental protection.

Denmark, the Netherlands, Norway, and Sweden all exhibit a high proportion of people "willing to pay" for environmental protection.[14] In these countries almost 30 percent or more of the population are willing to devote some of their income for environmental protection, and 20 percent or more are willing to pay higher taxes for environmental protection. On the other hand, Japan, Germany, Ireland, and the United Kingdom have the lowest "willingness to pay" for environmental protection. In these countries not more than 13 percent (11 percent) are willing to contribute income (pay more taxes) for more environmental protection. The remaining eight countries considered in this book fall somewhere in between. Spain is the only one of these eight that is above the mean on both questions. Finland, the United States, and Canada have the next highest willingness to pay, followed by Italy, France, Austria, and Belgium.

The evidence in this section suggests three interesting facts about aggregate opinion toward environmental protection. First, when confronted with possible trade-offs between environmental protection and other social goals, people's "demand" for environmental protection (shown in Table 4.1) drops considerably. However, there does appear to be a correspondence across countries between the public's general concern and willingness to make trade-offs, despite absolute differences in aggregate support for environmental protection. Second, between the mid-1970s and mid-1990s, the data assessed here look much like the more closely analyzed opinion data for the United States. Support for environmental goals fluctuates with economic cycles, but there is a trend toward greater environmental concern.

There are some important qualifications to attach to these results. The opinion data reviewed contain gaps that make it difficult to evaluate comparative trends in opinion about the environment both across countries and across time. The former is due to a lack of comparable survey instruments; the latter, because, even when cross-national surveys exist, the questions asked vary over time or are administered infrequently. In addition, while attention here has tended to focus on economic fluctuations, other factors might also have played a role in moving opinion.

---

[14] This is not a true measure of willingness to pay because the questions do not ask for a more precise *amount* of income. We can take the data as a rough approximation of willingness to pay, however.

Environmental Organizations and Parties

The attitudes and preferences expressed in national surveys show only individual behavior in relative isolation (i.e., responding to surveys). However, the public-good character of environmental problems requires collective action at varying levels, if only to cajole government into forcing polluters to pay for negative externalities.[15] Thus, opinions and preferences at such a "diffuse" level as survey data may not show up as having systematic effects on cross-national environmental performance. Citizens in a democratic country may, for example, believe that environmental problems are important and be willing to sacrifice other goals to improve environmental protection; yet, if those interests are not organized and articulated to those with power over public policy, results will not reflect opinion. This section looks at indications that environmental protection sentiments are organized and articulated via environmental interest groups and political parties. Membership in or support of environmental interest groups reflects "mobilized" support for environmental protection. Support for environmental organizations indicates not only that environmental issues are popular but also that there is a specific organizational vehicle for channeling concern into more organized political demands.

Although there has not been any cross-national examination of the influence of environmental group strength and support on environmental pollution outcomes, it is generally assumed in environmental policy literature that such strength is an important factor in achieving environmental protection.[16] Much of the interest in "new social movements," for example, is based on these groups' representation of new issues – such as ecology, human rights, peace, and feminism – that were not adequately addressed by conventional political parties or movements.

Eurobarometer surveys in 1982 and 1986, and the 1990 World Values Survey asked respondents if they were either members or potential members of environmental and ecology groups. In addition, the 1981 World Values Survey asked respondents if they were members of an environmental

---

[15] As discussed previously, collective action may work directly on polluters (boycotting polluting firms) or on the behavior of group members (not purchasing environmentally damaging products or products made by environmentally damaging processes) rather than through public policy. Even in these other cases, however, similar collective action problems will have to be overcome, for example, for boycotts to have an effect on the firm.

[16] There have, of course, been cross-national studies of environmental group membership and behavior (see, e.g., Dalton 1994; Dalton and Kuechler 1990; Rohrschneider 1990); however, these do not deal with environmental outcomes.

organization. The strength of "environmentalist" parties comes from national election data and is a good indicator of the electoral strength of environmental interests. The classification of parties as "environmentalist" is based on Kitschelt's (1988) study of "left-libertarian" parties. These data provide a basis for examining the impact of the strength of environmental mobilization on national environmental performance. They also provide a basis on which to evaluate implications of the income thesis in the preceding chapter: do higher incomes explain cross-national differences in support for environmental groups (parties) as economic modernization theories suggest?

EB 18 and 25, and the 1990 WVS ask whether respondents are, might be, or definitely would not be, members of an environmental group. (The 1981 WVS asks respondents only if they were a member of an environmental organization.)

There are a number of groups and movements seeking the support of the public. For each of the following [nature protection association, ecology movement] can you tell me

a) whether you approve [strongly or somewhat] or disapprove [strongly or somewhat]?
b) whether you are a member or might probably join or would certainly not join?

Membership and support for environmental interest groups are interpreted here to be ordinal indicators of national environmental concern. Individual membership in an organization reflects a stronger individual preference for collective environmental protection. The larger the portion of environmental group members in a given country, the more we would expect a substantive impact on environmental performance. Membership in ecology groups could be seen as evidence of a stronger preference for environmental protection than membership in nature protection groups because such groups tend to espouse a more forceful "environmental agenda." This is consistent with the previous literature (Rohrschneider 1990; Dalton 1994).

Potential membership in an environmental group is a weaker form of support.[17] It implies that individuals acknowledge the urgency of

---

[17] Environmental group members are more likely to perceive environmental problems as immediate or urgent compared with potential members or others. Similarly, potential members are more likely than the "definitely not" members to perceive the environment as an immediate problem.

environmental problems, but are not yet committed to collective action (though they might be). As with membership, potential membership in ecology groups indicates a stronger preference for environmental protection than potential membership in a nature protection group.

Finally, the unwillingness to join or support environmental (ecology) groups could be interpreted as evidence of a weak commitment to environmental protection, with refusal to join ecology groups reflecting a more ambivalent (rather than negative) attitude. The reasoning behind this decision follows from the previous discussion.

Support for environmental groups provides the organizations themselves (and perhaps the entire "sector" of environmental organizations) with political power that would be lacking in the absence of that support. The reason is that public support gives these groups the political, economic, and moral power to effect change in the direction of less pollution. Consider how a politician (firm) is likely to respond to a demand by an environmental group. If the public does not support environmental groups, then environmental demands are easier to deflect, even if diffuse support for environmental issues is high. On the other hand, strong public support for environmentalists tends to make politicians more responsive to those group demands.

The precise coding uses the following form, which is similar to that used by Rohrschneider (1990). Individuals are assigned a "total preference score" based on the sum of responses asking about their membership, potential membership, or refusal to join environmental groups. Ecology group members receive a score of 3, nature protection group members a 2, potential ecology group members a 2, and potential nature protection group members a 1. Those who cannot foresee joining an ecology group receive a 1 score and those who would "never" join nature groups receive a score of 0. Again, this coding scheme emphasizes the policy aspects of membership and not the organizational-ideological aspects of being in one group rather than another.

Because the questions in the 1990 WVS do not distinguish between nature protection and ecology groups or ask about potential membership, "member" is coded 4, "strong approval" 3, "approval" 2, "disapproval" 1, and "strong disapproval" 0. For this reason, scores based on responses to the WVS are not directly comparable with those for the EB.

The ordinal coding assumption is supported by the EB data. Most ecology group members in all countries (70–100 percent depending on the country) also belong to nature protection groups, and almost all ecology

Table 4.4. *Public Support for Environmental Organizations*

Country	Eurobarometer 1982	Eurobarometer 1986	World Values Survey 1990
Austria			2.74
Belgium	0.42	0.21	2.56
Canada			2.57
Denmark	0.44	0.58	2.4
Finland			2.22
France	0.42	0.36	2.43
W. Germany	1.33	1.32	2.72
Greece	0.87	0.99	
Ireland	0.72	0.69	2.48
Italy	0.87	0.62	2.51
Japan			2.58
Luxembourg	1.18	1.18	
Netherlands	1.13	1.04	2.82
Norway			2.44
Portugal		0.27	2.75
Spain		0.87	2.63
Sweden			2.46
Switzerland			
United Kingdom	0.64	0.57	2.49
United States			2.51

Source: Own calculations (see text for details).

group members are at least potential members of nature groups. Nature protection group members are more likely to be members or potential members of ecology groups than the rest of the population, but support for and membership in nature protection groups is less likely to imply support for ecology groups. In other words, the individual-level responses are reasonably consistent with the idea that ecology groups represent a "more" extreme commitment to environmentalism than nature protection.

Table 4.4 shows the average score in each survey for each country. If all (no) respondents indicated that they were members (would never be members) of an ecology or nature protection group, the country scored a 4 (0). A higher score thus suggests a higher aggregate degree of support for environmental groups. In most countries, support for environmental groups is weak. In the 1982 survey, only in Germany, Luxembourg, and the Netherlands does potential and actual membership in environmental or ecology groups exceed the portion of the population that says it is unlikely

99

ever to join such movements. Environmental groups appear to be the most "legitimate" and popular in Germany, where less than 20 percent of respondents are unlikely to ever join nature protection or ecology groups. On the other hand, in three countries, France, Belgium, and Denmark, more than 75 percent of respondents say they are unlikely ever to become members of either ecology or environmental groups.

In the 1986 survey, Germany, Luxembourg, and the Netherlands remained the only EU countries in which a majority of respondents were at least potential members of environmental groups. However, in the Netherlands the overall intensity of support had fallen considerably. Disapproval increased significantly from 1982 levels in three countries – Belgium, Italy, and Britain – but it declined significantly in Denmark and Greece. Even in 1986, however, nearly two-thirds of the Danish population, by far the most "pro-environment" country, comprises those who report that they were unlikely to join any type of environmental group.[18]

In the 1990 WVS, Germany and the Netherlands again have the highest level of environmental group support. At this time, however, the latter country appears to be by far the most supportive of environmental groups. Portugal and Austria also exhibit a high degree of support relative to the other countries. The lowest support (perhaps surprisingly) is in the Nordic countries. All demonstrate support for the environmental movement, which is lower than in Ireland or Southern Europe.[19]

If we aggregate individuals in each country between (weak or strong) approval and disapproval based the 1990 WVS, almost no one in any country expresses disapproval of environmental groups. If one assumes instead that the salient dividing line then is whether the respondent indicates enthusiastic (i.e., strong) or lukewarm (i.e., some) approval, only eight countries have a clear majority of either members or strong supporters of environmental groups. These countries are Austria, Canada, Japan, Netherlands, Portugal, Spain, Switzerland, and Germany. Except for the Nordic countries, there is a strong plurality of support in the other countries in the survey.

[18] Two other EB surveys (in 1984 and 1989) asked these questions in France, Germany, Italy, the Netherlands, and the United Kingdom only. The results for these countries closely resemble those reported in Table 4.4.

[19] While at first glance one might attribute this to an economic downturn, these problems occurred after 1990. Moreover, these same countries expressed high levels of support on other indicators of environmental concern.

Table 4.5. *Environmental Group Membership*

Country	WVS 1981	EB 1982	EB 1986	WVS 1990
Austria				2.9
Belgium	2.6	1.7	3.1	7.7
Canada	4.8			7.5
Denmark	4.7	9.2	15.6	15.5
Finland	.4			5.4
France	1.5	1.9	1.5	2.3
W. Germany	3.7	4.6	2.3	4.5
Greece		1.4	.7	
Ireland	2.1	1.3	1.1	2.3
Italy	1.8	1.5	2.3	4.7
Japan	.2			1.1
Luxembourg		8.2	15.4	
Netherlands	10.6	13.7	10.5	24.0
Norway	4.5			4.1
Portugal	1.4			1.4
Spain	1.3		1.1	1.3
Sweden	3.2			10.6
Switzerland				10.5
United Kingdom	2.0[a]	1.3	3.0	5.9
United States	6			8.1

Note: WVS = World Value Surveys; EB = Eurobarometer.
[a] Excludes members of animal welfare groups.

Are general public concern and environmental group support connected? It is tempting to answer yes to this question. We naturally expect individuals who are concerned about a problem to support and join groups who pressure for reform on such issues. On the other hand, the "logic of collective action" suggests that people might not support lobbies that "represent" their interest, because their contribution can be expected to have only a marginal impact on whether the public good will be provided (Olson 1965). In fact, aggregate environmental concern and aggregate support for environmental groups are *not* correlated. The correlation between the environmental group support index in Table 4.2 and responses to the concern and trade-off questions is positive but small. This is true whether one uses the EB or the WVS results.

Table 4.5 shows the percentage of respondents in each country surveyed who report *membership* in an environmental group in four different years: 1981, 1983, 1986, and 1990. The first and last percentages are from the

WVS; the other two are from EB.[20] In Europe, the Dutch and Danes have consistently had the highest levels of environmental group membership. In 1990 almost a quarter of Dutch respondents indicated that they were members of environmental groups, while 15 percent of Danes said the same. Environmental group membership was also quite high in Sweden and Switzerland in 1990 (around 11 percent). Other countries with relatively high levels of reported membership in 1990 are Belgium, Canada, and the United States with membership rates between 7 and 8 percent. The next tier of membership (4–5 percent) includes Finland, Germany, Italy, Norway, and the United Kingdom. Membership is between 1 and 3 percent in the remaining countries.

There is a reasonably close association between environmental group membership in 1981 and 1990, though overall membership is much higher in 1990. Excluding the high membership in the Netherlands as an apparent outlier, the correlation between national membership in 1981 and 1990 is .63 (n = 15).[21] Some countries' environmental groups grew, however, faster than others. In Denmark, Sweden, and Finland, the proportion of the population claiming membership in environmental groups more than tripled, and it almost tripled in Belgium and the United Kingdom. Membership also grew considerably in Italy in the 1980s. On the other hand, reported membership declined slightly in Norway, though this difference is less than the sampling error.

We might perhaps expect that societies that are willing to pay for environmental protection would also have higher environmental group membership. The cross-national correlation between environmental group membership and the income trade-off question in the 1990 WVS is indeed strong, provided the Netherlands is excluded as an outlier (.64, n = 17). Given their public's "willingness to pay" for environmental protection, we might say that Norway and Spain have "underdeveloped" environmental movements, whereas in the United Kingdom, Canada, Belgium, and the United States, they are "overdeveloped."

---

[20] The 1981 WVS explicitly included animal rights groups in the question about environmental groups. In the United Kingdom (only), such groups outnumber environmental group members. This is confirmed by results in two other EB surveys (1983 and 1987), which ask about membership in environmental or animal rights groups. Using these surveys as a base line, I estimated that U.K. environmental group membership in 1981 to be 2 percent.

[21] This understates the correlation because the Netherlands should count as being "high" in both surveys. If the 1990 figure for the Netherlands is constrained to be 15 percent (equal to Denmark), then the correlation is .76.

The correlation between environmental group membership and public willingness-to-pay contrasts with the lack of correlation between willingness-to-pay and the more general measure of environmental group support. In fact, if the Netherlands is again excluded, there is a moderate negative correlation between environmental group support and actual membership. This is somewhat puzzling because environmental groups constitute a relatively small portion of the population in all but two or three countries. This may be due to error in the measurement of environmental group support. However, one cannot dismiss the explanation that environmental group membership is higher where there is not a broader consensus in the larger society for environmental protection.

The final facet of public support for environmental organizations that is likely to have an effect on environmental outcomes is electoral support for Green parties. Although more than single-issue parties, much of their political appeal revolves around environmental policies. Green parties function much like environmental interest organizations insofar as they aggregate diffuse environmental demands. They also act as a continual point of political access for such interests and, by virtue of having parliamentary representation, have access to powerful policy-making networks.

Whereas some authors insist on distinguishing nominally Green parties from other "New Left" parties (e.g., Richardson and Rootes 1995), Kitschelt (1988) makes a persuasive argument for looking beyond party labels. He notes, for example, that the weakness of nominally Green parties in countries like Denmark and the Netherlands is due to preexisting parties (Left Socialists and Green Left, respectively) having adopted the policy profile of "green" parties without changing their names. Moreover, as Kitschelt and others stress, like these "non-Green" left-libertarian parties, nominally Green parties embrace a wider platform of New Left issue positions in areas such as defense, immigration, and welfare. Thus, I consider votes for left-libertarian parties, rather than support for nominally Green parties, as the critical indicator of environmental party support.

A good measure of left-libertarian party power is the long-term electoral impact of these parties.[22] Such support is not only likely to impact their

---

[22] Although recently there have been a number of Green parties either in cabinets (Italy, Germany, France, Finland) or supporting minority governments (Sweden), they occur after the period analyzed here and thus cannot plausibly be considered to impact the performance measure.

Table 4.6. *Environmental (Left-Libertarian) Party Vote*

Country	Average Vote Share, 1975–95	Left-Libertarian Parties
Austria	3.2	Green Party
Belgium	5.2	Agalev, Ecolo
Canada	.2	Green Party
Denmark	9.1	Socialist Peoples Party, Left-Socialists
Finland	2.7	Green Party
France	1.9	Ecologist, Les Verts
W. Germany	4.2	Green Party
Ireland	.3	Green Party
Italy	3.0	Green Party
Japan	0	Green Party
Netherlands	5.3	Progressive Green Accord
Norway	7.1	Socialist Peoples Party
Spain	.8	Green Party
Sweden	20.8	Left communists, Greens, Center
Switzerland	4.9	Green Party, Progressive Organizations
United Kingdom	.2	Ecology/Green Party
United States	0	Citizens Party, Green Party

Sources: Parties and Elections in Europe (2001); Kitschelt (1988).

credibility as government partners, but it is almost certain to have a long-term impact on policy making because left-libertarian parties are often closely allied with national environmental movements. Table 4.6 shows the average vote share received by left-libertarian parties in eighteen countries between 1975 and 1995. The names of the parties considered left-libertarian in each country are also included.

The table suggests a wide range of support for environmental parties, led primarily by three Scandinavian countries (Sweden, Denmark, and Norway). In all three countries, average support has been between 7 and 21 percent.[23] These countries have had strong New Left parties from the 1960s as well as dominance by Social Democratic parties in the last half of the twentieth century. On the other hand, several countries have had almost no support for environmental parties: the United Kingdom,

---

[23] Kitschelt also counts the Center Party in Sweden as left-libertarian, due to its strong environmental profile and opposition to nuclear power in the 1970s. However, the Center Party is also the traditional agrarian party of Sweden, and it is very likely that the high left-libertarian vote share he reported for Sweden exaggerates environmentalist electoral support.

United States, Japan, France, and Canada. The explanation in the United Kingdom, United States, and Canada is undoubtedly their electoral systems, which strongly discourage the development of "new" parties. (This is discussed further in Chapter 6.)

Postmaterialism

As previously noted, postmaterialism is one of the most widely discussed explanations for interest in environmental problems. As individuals become more educated and economically secure, they become more concerned with "postmaterial" issues, which include the environment. Although the exact association between postmaterialism and environmentalism is not well developed theoretically and problems exist with the linkage between postmaterialism and environmentalism (as mentioned in Chapter 3), a sizable literature suggests that widespread postmaterial values are an important condition enabling society to address environmental problems (Hofrichter and Reif 1990; Dalton and Hildebrant 1977).

There are two ways by which postmaterialist values are argued to enhance national environmental performance. First, postmaterialism translates directly into greater concern for environmental protection at the individual level, and thus democratic societies with more postmaterialists will be willing to devote more resources to environmental protection. Second, postmaterialism reduces support for traditional, "materialist" causes associated with environmental pollution (e.g., increased consumption of goods, economic growth). This shift may indirectly enhance environmental performance by reducing social support for "high-pollution" causes.

Measures of postmaterialism rely on a battery of questions that have been asked of citizens of all the countries in my group. The 1981 and 1990 WVS contain the four-question battery used to indicate whether individuals tend toward more materialist or postmaterialist values and ask it in fifteen and all seventeen (respectively) of the countries in my sample. Table 4.7 shows for 1981 and 1990 the standard measure of postmaterialist societies: the difference in the percentage of postmaterialists and materialists. (Negative values imply there are more materialists than postmaterialists.)

Finland had the highest degree of postmaterialism in both 1981 and 1990. Indeed, it was the only country where postmaterialists outnumbered materialists in 1981. The Netherlands and Canada also had relatively high degrees of postmaterialism in 1981. Countries clearly dominated by

105

Table 4.7. *Postmaterialism Index*

Country	1981	1990	Change
Austria		11	
Belgium	−16	2	18
Canada	−6	14	20
Denmark	−12	13	25
Finland	21	23	2
France	−14	4	18
W. Germany	−11	14	25
Ireland	−20	−4	16
Italy	−39	7	46
Japan	−32	−19	13
Netherlands	−2	26	28
Norway	−21	−19	2
Portugal		−21	
Spain	−41	−6	35
Sweden	−10	9	19
Switzerland		10	
United Kingdom	−13	0	13
United States	−24	6	30

Note: The index is the percentage of postmaterialists less percentage of materialists.
Source: Abramson and Inglehart (1994).

materialists are Spain, Italy, and Japan. There is an obvious move in almost all countries toward higher levels of postmaterialism by the 1990s. (Annual time-series of postmaterialism in this period confirm this trend.) By 1990 all but four countries had a higher percentage of postmaterialists than materialists, and the mean index of postmaterialism changed from −16 to 4. Nevertheless, there remains a wide range in the levels of postmaterialism in these countries.

The level of postmaterial values in a society may work either through changes in the constellation of national attitudes and behaviors or directly on societal behavior. The former path – that higher levels of postmaterialism lead to higher levels of environmental concern, which then produce better national performance – seems more plausible. Nonetheless, we will also consider the direct effect of basic values on performance, because the linkage between "basic values" (e.g., postmaterialism) and "attitudes" (e.g., thinking the environment is an immediate and urgent problem) is complex and our understanding of such linkages is imperfect.

Does Income Promote Environmental Mobilization?

In Chapter 3, I noted that the mechanism by which differences in wealth facilitated environmental improvement were via structural economic change or change in the public's demand for environmental protection. The evidence supporting the structural change argument was, at best, weak. In this section, I answer that question, using evidence of environmental mobilization as the indicator of demand.

With respect to *general concern* about environmental problems, opinion data are consistent with the idea that income increases the demand for environmental protection in the society as a whole. The correlation between per capita income and the proportion of the country that thinks protecting the environment is a "very important" problem is at least .40 in four of the five EB surveys that asked this question. The one exception is 1983. As noted, the preceding years were periods of major economic turmoil in many European countries. Combined with the small sample, this may account for the weaker result in that year.

Regarding the second measure of environmental concern – the extent to which people feel that the environment is an immediate and urgent threat – the results are *not* consistent with the income thesis. Exceptional countries, rather than a poor theory, however, account for the poor statistical result. In Greece the urgency of environmental problems is ranked much higher than one would expect from its per capita income. This is undoubtedly due in part to a particularly acute problem – high levels of air pollution in Athens that are eroding some of the city's major tourist attractions. In France, on the other hand, citizens attached much less immediacy to pollution problems (given their income level) throughout the 1980s. This low level of concern is somewhat more puzzling because concern was quite high in France in the early 1970s. Although it is often explained by the persistently high rate of unemployment in France since the 1980s, other countries – Belgium, Denmark in the 1980s, and Sweden and Finland in the 1990s – also experienced high unemployment without the same degree of flagging environmental concern. Moreover, French economic growth in the late 1970s and through the 1980s was relatively good.

Willingness to trade-off traditional social (particularly economic) goals for environmental protection is typically what social scientists have in mind when they suggest that income is linked to greater efforts at environmental protection. Indeed, this is one of the most consistent findings in the literature. Here, the evidence linking income and willingness to pay for environmental protection is less clear. Within the EU the cross-country correlation between per capita income and the proportion of citizens willing to accept lower growth for increased environmental protection is relatively high: .53 (n = 10) in 1982, .58 (n = 13) in 1992, and .53 (n = 14) in 1995.[24] However, in the World Values Surveys, which exclude several EU countries (e.g., Greece and Luxembourg) but include Austria, Japan, the United States, and Canada, the expected correlation does not hold; it is −.22 (opposite of the predicted) and .05, respectively.

What about support for environmental organizations? The more comprehensive four-point scale measure of support for environmental movements from the 1982 and 1986 EB and 1990 WVS is not correlated with national income. In the 1990 WVS (column 3 of Table 4.4), the correlation between income and support is consistently negative but very weak. There is, however, a positive correlation between income and environmental group membership in the 1981 WVS, if we again make an exception for the extraordinarily high level of environmental group membership in the Netherlands. The correlation between income and the percentage of the population in environmental groups is .59. The results for 1990 WVS are very similar (.51).[25] Thus, this evidence suggests reasonably strong support for the argument that higher incomes are associated with a greater social *demand* for environmental protection, or at least the ability to mobilize that demand.

Next I examine the relationship between environmental party support and income. The basic logic is similar to that for environmental organizations: if more income implies more and deeper concern for environmental policy, countries with higher incomes will tend to have more people willing to vote for parties promoting environmental causes. Considering all of the countries in Table 4.6 (i.e., the countries for which we have environmental performance data), income is not correlated with support for such parties. However, if we exclude countries with plurality electoral systems – on the basis that such systems place severe constraints on the emergence of new political parties as such – the correlation between income and party support is reasonably strong: .56 (n = 13). Furthermore, if we exclude the vote of Center Party in Sweden's total left-libertarian support, the correlation is even stronger, .70.

[24] For reasons mentioned earlier, Greece was excluded from the calculation in 1995.
[25] The correlation is .39 and .32, respectively, with the Netherlands included.

108

Distilling these results suggests the following conclusions.

- Among EU countries there is consistent evidence that the expressed importance of environmental problems varies with the level of economic development.
- There is little association between the perceived urgency of environmental problems and income.
- There is little systematic evidence that higher national income is associated with a greater willingness of people to trade traditional social goals (e.g., growth and low inflation) for less pollution.
- There is reasonably consistent evidence that wealthier countries have higher environmental group membership.
- There is little evidence that richer countries have higher levels of public approval of environmental groups.
- Where electoral laws do not severely discriminate against new parties, more affluent countries have larger "environmental" parties.

A simple tally of the evidence suggests a mixed picture – three "positive" findings and three "null" findings. However, several factors ultimately suggest overall support for the thesis that income matters for environmental mobilization. First, in terms of mobilizing concern into organization and action (what we might call the aggregation and articulation of environmental interests), the evidence favors the income thesis. (Of course, the fact that environmental group membership is more closely associated with income than any of the other indicators of public mobilization is not terribly surprising.) Organizational membership in environmental groups implies resource commitments in support of a public good. Because environmental group membership, unlike diffuse opinion, is "manifest collective action," the strength of such groups is more likely to indicate a more solid commitment in society to dealing with environmental problems. Second, there is no indication of a consistent *negative* correlation between income and any aspect of mobilization. Thus, there is no reason to think income has an *adverse* impact on public opinion regarding environmental protection. Third, measurement error is probably most likely to occur in the case of more vague concepts where we find no statistical association, rather than those for which there was stronger support. For example, whether a person is a member of an environmental group is less open to interpretation than whether one "strongly supports" or only "somewhat supports" such a group, or "might" or "probably would never" join one.

Table 4.8. *Regression Results: Effects of Income and Values on Environmental Mobilization*

	Growth & Inflation	Growth	Environmental Group Membership[a]	
Independent Variables	1982	1992	1981	1990
Income	.066**	.20	.059**	.063
	(.24)	(.13)	.020	(.039)
Postmaterialism	−.34	.07	−.25	.13
	(.35)	(.20)	(.027)	(.08)
Constant	−29.3	−1.2	−4.3	−3.5
	(27.5)	(16.5)	(2.4)	(5.4)
Observations	8	10	14	16
Adjusted R^2	.45	.09	.35	.27

Note: Standard errors in parentheses.
[a] Estimated excluding the Netherlands.
* $p < .10$; ** $p < .05$; *** $p < .01$.

Finally, the income thesis fares well against postmaterialist value change as an explanation of environmental mobilization. If postmaterial values matter more than income for environmental mobilization, the impact of the former should be felt once present income is introduced as a control. In essence, this approach tests for cultural effects by controlling for the impact of proximate economic conditions. According to the theory, values matter independently of *current* income, though they are correlated with historic income (Abrahamson and Inglehart 1994).[26] The result of regression estimates using the various indicators of environmental mobilization discussed earlier as a dependent variable suggests that postmaterialism *does not* contribute significantly to explaining differences in mobilization across countries. The results are shown in Table 4.8. Because the high levels of reported environmental group membership make the Netherlands a significant outlier, those models are estimated without that case.[27]

[26] Empirically, this seems to be true for these countries. The correlation between 1960 per capita income and postmaterialism among the countries included in Table 4.7 is .55 but falls to .40 if we use 1990 income. The difference is even more pronounced if Finland, which is something of an outlier, is excluded. The respective statistics are then .61 for 1960 income and .41 for 1990 income.

[27] The Netherlands is such an outlier that the option to retain the observation while downweighting its influence on the coefficient estimates failed (see Granato, Inglehart, and Leblang 1996). The robust regression "canned" weighting procedure in Stata 6.0 weights the case 0 (i.e., drops it from the calculation).

In all of the models, current income per capita is at least a marginally significant predictor of the level of public support or mobilization (i.e., estimates are 1.5 times the standard error). This is true of the postmaterialism estimates in only one of the four models. Moreover, in the estimates for the early 1980s, postmaterialism is *negatively* associated with environmental interest or mobilization, once income is partialed out. Although these results cannot rule out an effect of postmaterialism, the evidence should call into question the widespread assertions that rising interest in environmental issues are explained by long-term value change. The results provide somewhat stronger support for the effects of more proximate income effects in the mobilization process.

Combining Indicators of Environmental Mobilization

Before turning to the empirical investigation of the impact of environmental mobilization on cross-national environmental performance, it is worth considering public mobilization using a combination of different items that have been considered individually up to this point. Doing so provides a more comprehensive indicator than any individual measure would. This will be useful later when we assess the impact of public support for environmental protection on environmental outcomes.[28] I rely on the WVS and electoral data to construct the combined measures, because these two sources cover sixteen of the seventeen cases for which we have performance data. Using the EB results would limit the cases that could be considered to eight or nine.

The first combined measure ("Combined 1990") is presented in column 1 of Table 4.9. It consists of the sum of standardized scores for:

1. The average of the two "trade-off" questions asked in 1990 (from Table 4.3).
2. Environmental group membership in 1990 (from Table 4.5).
3. The vote for environmentalist parties (from Table 4.6).[29]
4. "General support" for environmental groups in 1990 (from Table 4.4).

---

[28] This also allows us to collapse a number of variables measuring a similar concept (mobilization) into a smaller number of variables, thus preserving precious degrees of freedom (Lijpahrt 1971).

[29] The Swedish Center Party was not counted toward Sweden's total for reasons previously discussed.

Table 4.9. *Combined Scores of Environmental Mobilization*

Country	1990	1981
Austria	0.24	
Belgium	0.21	−0.24
Canada	−0.67	−0.39
Denmark	3.84	2.54
Finland	−2.68	−1.90
France	−2.34	−1.22
W. Germany	0.03	−0.09
Ireland	−2.83	−1.41
Italy	−1.04	−0.69
Japan	−2.95	−2.12
Netherlands	6.18	4.24
Norway	1.13	1.68
Spain	−0.78	−1.71
Sweden	4.75	1.15
Switzerland		
United Kingdom	−1.96	−0.24
United States	−1.13	0.06

Source: Calculations based on data in previous tables (see text).

The standardized scores exclude Greece, Luxembourg, Portugal, and Switzerland in the calculation, because there are either no environmental scores for them (as for the first three) or the trade-off questions were not asked (Switzerland).

Several results may seem surprising. Contrary to conventional wisdom, environmental mobilization in western Germany is only about average for the advanced democracies.[30] Only the "approval" of environmental organizations is more than a standard deviation above the mean. Although the German Green Party has probably generated more academic ink than all other European environmental organizations combined, it has nevertheless received fewer votes between 1975 and 1995 than the "Green"/left-libertarian parties of six other European countries. German environmental group membership is also about average through the 1980s and 1990s.

[30] If the comparison is limited to large "Western" countries (e.g., Britain, France, Italy, Japan, and the United States), Germany's environmental mobilization profile in 1990 is much higher. The tendency to focus attention on the big countries may partly explain why the conventional wisdom and the results here diverge.

Even on "general importance" questions asked on several occasions in the EB since 1976, Germany has scored only slightly above average.[31]

The level of mobilization may also seem surprisingly low in the United States and Japan. One reason for this is that both countries lack a strong environmental party, partly due to their electoral rules. But even making an exception for this factor, citizens in the United States are below the average for willingness to pay for environmental protection and in general support of the environmental movement.[32] It is only slightly above average in environmental group membership. Japan scores poorly on the first three criteria but has a much higher level of general approval of environmental groups. For other countries, results probably confirm conventional wisdom. For instance, the Scandinavian countries and the Netherlands do well; Ireland, France, and the United Kingdom do poorly.

If we reevaluate the relationship between mobilization, national income, and postmaterialism using this multidimensional measure of mobilization, there is little support for either the income or value change explanations of environmental mobilization. Regression analysis suggests that, while the estimated impact of both variables is in the expected direction (i.e., more income and higher levels of postmaterialism imply higher environmental mobilization), neither coefficient is statistically significant.

Public Mobilization and Environmental Performance

The final goal of this chapter is to evaluate the effect of mobilization on comparative environmental performance. I first discuss bivariate and multivariate results for the different types of mobilization and opinion measures entered separately and then discuss combined measures. The results suggest that environmental mobilization adds little to our ability to account for variations in environmental performance. Where there is a bivariate relationship between one of the combined measures presented in Table 4.9 and environmental performance, the estimated effect disappears when controls for income and geographic advantage are considered.

For general opinion questions – importance and urgency of environmental problems – there is no statistically significant positive relationship between concern and performance. When a large bivariate correlation is

[31] After unification, the EB survey uses separate East and West German samples. I have used only the West German ones here.

[32] Excluding environmental party support from the combined indicator does little to alter a country's position. The correlation with the measure in column one of Table 4.9 is .96.

indicated (i.e., above .40), the statistic is due to a single influential case, differences are better explained by income, or both. For instance, the correlation between the percentage of people saying that the environment was a "very important" issue in 1976 and the environmental performance score is .56 (n = 8). If poor-performing Ireland is excluded, however, the correlation is reduced by half (.22). More tellingly, the estimated effect of concern on environmental performance, once income is controlled, is not close to statistical significance (although the impact is typically in the expected positive direction) whereas the income effect is positive. Comparing the coefficients for models with and without controlling for income (using the 1976 EB data), the predicted effect on environmental performance of a 1 percent increase in the percentage of the population saying that fighting pollution is "very important" drops from more than 8 points to about zero.[33] This finding is consistent with the idea that greater concern is the product of higher income and that the latter is a more consistent determinant of results than the former.

For the public's general willingness to pay or "trade-off" traditional economic goals for environmental protection, the results provide more support for the importance of popular opinion on environmental outcomes, but a reasonable evaluation of the evidence would have to reject any systematic effect. On one hand, there is a bivariate correlation between environmental performance and the percentage of the public (in 1978) placing environmental protection as the top planning priority (.78, n = 8); the percentage of adults (in 1982) willing to accept lower growth (.71, n = 10); and the percentage (again in 1982) willing to accept higher prices (.68, n = 10). All of these are statistically significant, and the results are nearly the same whether or not the data for the United States are included. There is also a significant correlation between performance and the proportion of the population attaching low priority to economic growth in the 1992 EB survey (.65, n = 10). For the 1982 survey, the results suggest that willingness to pay matters even when income effects are taken into account.

However, there is no correlation for trade-off questions when the non-EU members (for which we have environmental performance scores) are included. Performance is correlated with neither the trade-off questions in the 1990 WVS (including all seventeen countries in the sample) nor the 1995

---

[33] The opinion estimate in this case is actually *negative* (−.07). However, for several reasons – the estimate is small and statistically insignificant, estimates using other years are positive, and there are generally so few cases – the result is best interpreted as simply no effect.

trade-off question in the EB (which surveyed twelve of the seventeen). For both the planning question (1978) and the 1992 growth-environment trade-off question, controlling for income lowers the estimates for the respective opinion questions considerably and makes them statistically insignificant.

Finally, all of the positive results mentioned are thrown into doubt if the income squared term is included in the model. Given the severe data constraints (working with fewer than ten cases), such estimates must be treated with great caution. Nevertheless, the results tend to support the contention that income drives both opinion and performance. In other words the evidence suggests that opinion is a spurious cause of performance. Once we take into consideration differences in national wealth, differences in the levels of concern appear to be less important or at least much harder to discern statistically.

Popular approval of environmental groups is also not closely associated with environmental performance whether one considers environmental group membership or public support for environmental organizations (see Tables 4.5 and 4.4, respectively). For 1981 environmental membership data, the correlation between performance and environmental group membership is only .28. Even this very weak positive association is due to the extremely high level of membership in the Netherlands (11 percent). If the Netherlands is excluded, the coefficient falls to near zero (.11, n = 14).

Using the 1990 WVS data improves the results somewhat, as environmental group membership in one high performer (Denmark) increased considerably between 1981 and 1990. The correlation is .43, which is almost statistically significant at the 5 percent level. The Netherlands, however, remains an influential case. Moreover, once structural factors – income, its square, and geographic advantage – are entered as control variables, the estimated impacts are negligible at best. Indeed, the estimated effect of environmental group membership in 1981 (which is as close to the start of the period under consideration as we have), controlling for income and geography is *negative*, though not significant.

Looking at more diffuse measures of public support for environmental organization might provide a better measure of the popular appeal and mobilization potential of such groups; however, the results also suggest a weak correspondence with environmental performance. Whereas some top performers (Austria, Germany, and the Netherlands) enjoyed comparatively high levels of environmental mobilization in 1990, several others (Finland, Denmark, and Sweden) did not. Moreover, at least one poor performer, Spain, has high environmental movement support. Overall, the correlation is low, .09. Finland might be considered an exception here, as it has a low-level environmental mobilization. The low level of support in Finland can probably be explained in part by its economic crisis following the breakup of the Soviet Union.[34] However, excluding it from the calculations does not raise the correlation significantly.

Perhaps the strongest evidence that differences in environmental mobilization positively affect environmental performance comes from the support for environmental parties. Average support between 1975 and 1995 is reasonably well correlated with performance. The bivariate correlation is .56 (n = 17). As earlier, this effect is reduced considerably when geography and income are accounted for.[35] Moreover, as suggested previously, differences in support for environmental parties may reflect difference in political institutions (e.g., a proportional-representation electoral system) more than "inherent" differences in public support for such parties. This issue is discussed more thoroughly in Chapter 6.

An earlier result in this chapter suggested that the difference in the level of postmaterialism among countries was not a good predictor of environmental mobilization. Despite the common supposition that postmaterialist values would lead to pro-environmental attitudes at a societal level, there was not strong evidence to support the claim.[36] Nevertheless, might societies with more postmaterialists still have better environmental outcomes? Might, for example, postmaterial values promote environmental improvement if we control for more explicit evidence of mobilization via environmental groups or parties?

Although evidence for a positive effect of postmaterialism on environmental outcomes is a bit stronger than for mobilization, it is impossible to conclude that differences in postmaterialism are particularly critical; in our sample, too much depends on a single case. The correlation between postmaterialism (the 1981 WVS) and environmental performance is, as predicted, positive and significant (.53, n = 15). Introducing controls for income and geographical differences lowers the size of the estimate (and

---

[34] If true, this argument simply underscores the importance of short-term economic conditions on public support for environmental protection.

[35] Controlling for Sweden's high level of environmental party support due to the "quasi-green" Center Party does not change the significance of the result; nor does using various other indicators of mobilization as controls (such as environmental group membership or the level of postmaterialism). Nor is the result restricted to a subset of countries.

[36] Individuals with postmaterial values are more likely to have pro-environmental attitudes, but the inverse is not true.

its precision) by about half. However, the result hinges entirely on the extremely high value of postmaterialism in Finland, which also has an above average environmental performance score. If Finland is removed (or downweighted in computing the results), the predicted effect of postmaterialism drops by another 40 percent, and the error increases by more than 60 percent. In other words, postmaterial values do not do much to explain differences in environmental protection outcomes once other factors are taken into account. Although it may be true that higher postmaterialism does help to account for the fact that Finland performs better than otherwise predicted, this is an insufficient basis to claim that postmaterial values matter more generally.

As we did for evaluating the role of income on environmental mobilization, measuring environmental mobilization is fraught with uncertainty. Combining partial measures to get at the more abstract concept of mobilization might produce a more accurate measure. To do this, however, the combined mobilization score developed in the preceding section may not be appropriate because it measures mobilization at a time (ca. 1990) that postdates most of the period covered by the environmental performance measure. A correlation between mobilization in 1990 and improvements in environmental conditions between 1975 and 1995 would be better interpreted as a test that performance causes mobilization, rather than the other way around. We want to test the opposite.

This criticism of the measure developed is technically true; however, if the 1990 data are taken as reasonable proxies for environmental mobilization earlier in time, we might infer a correlation between performance in 1975–95 and mobilization in 1990 as a test of mobilization as a cause of performance. (In discussing a more acceptable measure later, I make the case why this may be reasonable to do in this case.)

Because the environmental performance score covers a long period, it seems reasonable to take the average level of mobilization in some part of that period to capture the extent of the explanatory forces at work.[37] We have data on environmental group membership for 1981 and 1990. I use the average of these two measures. In order to include all seventeen countries, I imputed a value for Switzerland and Austria for 1981. We also have data for environmental party support. For this I also use average support – between 1975 and 1995.

---

[37] Ideally, we would have annual data on both variables and fully specify a complex pooled model. However, the available data do not allow that.

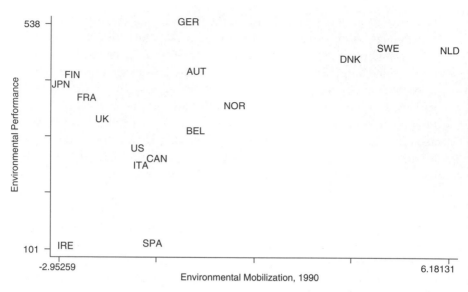

Figure 4.2 Environmental Mobilization and Environmental Performance

For the two (technically three) remaining components of the combined mobilization measure – willingness to pay and general support for environmental groups – there is some evidence that the 1990 results *are* decent proxies for the 1980s. For general support there is a close correlation between the index of environmental group support for the EC countries in 1990 and 1982 (.82, n = 8) and 1986 (.73, n = 9) (see Table 4.4). The percentage of the population's willingness to pay for environmental protection in 1990 is also closely correlated with the inflation trade-off response in the 1982 EB (plus the U.S.) subsample (.71, n = 9) and with the planning trade-off scores in the 1978 EB subsample (.61, n = 8) (see Table 4.3). Thus, there is at least some basis for thinking that the cross-national distribution of public support and willingness to pay in 1990 resembles that in the earlier periods, if imperfectly. This revised mobilization score is almost perfectly correlated with the original (.998).

An alternative indicator of environmental mobilization would be to rely *solely* on data from as early as possible. This would control for the potential endogeneity of mobilization – that poor performance promotes mobilization. This is compelling methodologically, as it seems reasonable to assume that mobilization is somewhat endogenous to performance over long periods of time. Given the data, this restricts the measures of mobilization to those available in the 1981 WVS and electoral data around that time.

Table 4.10. *Regression Results: Environmental Mobilization and Performance*

Environmental mobilization	22.8*	4.7	4.9
	(10.9)	(11.6)	(9.6)
Income		4.47**	28.3**
		(1.8)	(9.4)
Income squared			.0013**
			(.00049)
Geographical advantage		41.5	17.9
		(19.0)	(18.2)
Constant	357.4***	−74.6	−1153.6**
	(29.0)	(177.1)	(443.4)
Observations	16	16	16
Adjusted R^2	.18	.39	.59

Note: Standard errors in parentheses.
* p < .10; ** p < .05; *** p < .01.

Column 2 of Table 4.8 presents the sum of standardized scores for the percentage of people in environmental groups in the 1981 and average electoral support for environmental parties between 1975 and 1985.

The two methods of combining variables produce almost identical indices. (The scores are almost perfectly correlated: r = .91.) Figure 4.2 shows a scatterplot of environmental performance and the 1990 mobilization index. I used the column 1 scores because they include Austria. All countries with high or moderate levels of mobilization – the Netherlands, Sweden, Denmark – have good environmental performance. Results are more varied for countries with lower mobilization. Finland, Japan, and France do very well; but Canada, Ireland, Italy, Spain, and the United States do relatively poorly.

The bivariate correlation between mobilization and performance is moderate (.49). Multivariate analysis (controlling for income and geography) suggests a weaker result, as the estimates in Table 4.10 show.[38] The introduction of controls for income and geography lowers the estimate for mobilization enormously. In other words, excluding structural factors results in a large upward bias in the estimates. Uncorrected, this leads to the mistaken conclusion that environmental mobilization is very important

---

[38] Results do not change significantly if Austria and Switzerland are estimated and included in the calculations.

for environmental performance.[39] Although these results do not prove that mobilization does not matter at all, they do suggest that its effect is relatively small.

Conclusion

What conclusions can we draw from this chapter? Perhaps the main positive, although weak, finding is that higher levels of environmental mobilization – particularly with respect to tangible actions (the proportion of the population in environmental groups or voting for environmental parties) or hypothetical trade-offs (preferring more environmental protection over more economic growth) – are found in wealthier nations. Beyond that, it seems fair to say that the chapter constitutes a series of "nonresults." However, sometimes negative results can challenge the basis for some of our theories. This chapter shows that many conventional assumptions about the role of cultural or attitudinal differences in explaining environmental performance do not systematically account for the good results we see. Indeed, the results suggest that factors such as larger environmental movements, public support for the environment, and beliefs that the environment is an important issue may be epiphenomenal products of higher income (and residing in smaller, more densely populated countries). There is not much evidence that cross-national differences in levels of environmental mobilization affect actual environmental outcomes among the advanced democracies, *once one takes into account that at least some of the increase in environmental mobilization is "produced" by higher levels of national wealth.*

The best evidence that mobilization has had an independent effect on performance lies in differences in the strength of "environmental" or left-libertarian parties. Where such parties have enjoyed greater electoral strength, performance has consistently been somewhat better. However, not only is the evidence for this claim not particularly robust, but, as is discussed at greater length in Chapter 6, what evidence does exist may be attributed more to political institutions than to attitudes.

Several caveats are in order about these results. First, they should not be taken to suggest anything about the relevance of democratic government

---

[39] The geographic advantage estimates are similar to those in the preceding chapter (see Table 3.5). As before, the size of the standard error is due to the fact that Belgium is something of an outlier. The geographic advantage estimate improves considerably if Belgium is removed. The mobilization estimate is not due to any outlying case(s).

for solving environmental problems. Because all the countries considered here are democratic, it is impossible to make inferences about the effects of democratic versus nondemocratic institutions. That more pro-environment opinion is not associated with better performance does not imply that we should all drop our environmental group memberships. Indeed, the fact that outcomes are reflective of opinion (even if spuriously so) suggests that democracy is probably not undermining the positive effects of income on environmental performance. Even economists, who tend to place much stock in wealth as a determinant of environmental quality, emphasize that democracy is important in assuring that increased environmental concerns have some way of becoming reflected in public policies and social institutions.

Second, the results should not be taken to suggest that public support is totally irrelevant to environmental outcomes at all ranges of income and opinion. Expressed support for environmental protection is relatively high (compared with the theoretical minimum) in all countries considered here, as is support for environmental protection if we included poorer countries (cf. Dunlap and Mertig 1995). We might see much lower levels of public support (and thus a larger range of support) if a more diverse group of countries were considered.[40]

Finally, this analysis does not permit a detailed examination of contextual factors that might also intervene in the translation of environmental public opinion into good (or poor) environmental performance. The next two chapters examine two important "contextual" conditions that could affect the relationships found here – economic and political institutions.

---

[40] Dunlap and Mertig found that pro-environment attitudes were *not* more prevalent in rich countries, except for willingness to pay. This implies that the range of opinion here is not truncated. Their results can, furthermore, be taken to imply that wealth effects are more closely linked to stronger commitments (i.e., willingness to commit resources) across a larger range of countries.

5

Pluralism, Corporatism, and Environmental Performance

The two preceding chapters have shown that attitudes, economic structure, and wealth are insufficient, if not problematic, explanations of variations in environmental performance among advanced industrial democracies. This chapter and the next one discuss a crucial factor that mediates between structural or cultural characteristics of countries and national environmental performance: the institutional context. This chapter investigates the influence of institutions linking economic and policy actors and their impact on environmental policy. The subsequent chapter investigates the influence of more traditional political institutions on the ability of countries to provide environmental protection. As with other explanations of environmental politics, studies examining whether institutions matter do not deal with environmental outcomes in a direct manner. Doing so allows us to evaluate competing explanations more systematically.

Garrett and Lange (1996) provide an extensive theoretical treatment of the role that domestic institutions play in mediating exogenous changes in actors' preferences over economic policy. In seeking to explain the specific ways that "institutions matter," they suggest that both the organization of socioeconomic interests (e.g., structure of trade unions and employer groups) and the formal political institutions of a country (e.g., electoral laws, separation of political powers) can strongly influence how nations adjust to a changing configuration of economic preferences.

Although their argument is developed around exogenous changes in the economy brought on by globalization, the model is general enough to be a useful way to conceptualize understanding how countries adjust to influences like the growth of environmental concern since the late 1960s. The recent increase in concern about environmental pollution can be viewed in some respects as a similar exogenous change. As discussed in the preceding chapter, environmental issues have emerged in almost all countries since the 1970s due to a combination of causes: increased pollution, increased knowledge about the deleterious effects of pollution, an increase in the relative importance of environmental "amenities" relative to material consumption. These changes have, like the international economic changes discussed by Garrett and Lange, led to changes in the constellation of actors' choices (and perhaps their preferences) domestically. There is every reason, therefore, to expect that institutions have effects with respect to changes in demand for environmental protection that are not unlike those conditioning national responses to economic globalization.

One might question why I focus on a broadly similar set of institutional factors as Garrett and Lange do – the organization of economic interests and formal political institutions – in trying to explain environmental pollution, not economic policy. This question is answered throughout each of the next two chapters. To preface and summarize that answer, economic actors are an essential part of the environmental problem and its solution, rendering institutional arrangements among such actors important for understanding change. Moreover, economic and political institutions have implications for the provision of collective goods (not just economic ones), including environmental quality. Both socioeconomic and political institutions are thus logical starting points for an investigation of the correlates of national environmental performance.

In this chapter I discuss the general importance of social institutions in affecting social outcomes and provide a brief overview of the literature on social and regulatory institutions and environmental policy; discuss why institutions lead environmental policy making to mirror policy making in other, more traditional, policy areas; introduce key institutional factors expected to explain the differences in environmental performance among nations and discuss the reasons we would expect them to be important; and test empirically the hypotheses generated in the chapter. The theoretical and empirical findings of this chapter strongly suggest that countries characterized by strong, centralized economic interest groups and a more "consensual" approach to policy making (what are often referred to "neocorporatist" institutions) have enjoyed better environmental performance than countries where economic groups are less comprehensively organized and policy making is less consensual. I demonstrate these results in multivariate regression analysis, with different operationalizations of corporatism as well as factors found to be important in previous chapters (i.e., income, geography, and environmental mobilization). The results provide a clear example of the unintended effects of institutions on social outcomes. Furthermore, the results also call into question the claim that neocorporatist institutions necessarily undermine better environmental policies and performance.

Institutions in the Comparative Environmental Policy Literature

Exactly what constitutes an institution seems to depend on the particular whims of individual authors. Peter Hall's definition, however, is concise and captures the essential meaning of the term as used here: institutions are "rules, compliance procedures and standard operating practices that structure the relationship between individuals in various units of the polity and economy" (1986: 19). Institutions can thus be seen as constraints on individual actions.

A number of studies have demonstrated that such constraints have important, arguably essential, functions in creating and maintaining regularity and predictability in human interaction (Knight 1992; Thelen and Steinmo 1992). Although actors may be assumed to behave in a "self-interested manner," the institutional context in which they find themselves restricts the feasible choices in pursuit of their preferences and may even alter them. Here I will be less concerned with answering the question of whether institutions have changed preferences. Such an assessment is difficult if for no other reason than the problems inherent in empirically differentiating preferences from strategies. Instead, I focus on whether differences in economic institutions extend to environmental policy, how these institutions can be expected to alter substantive environmental outcomes, and whether institutional differences across countries can explain differences in observed outcomes.

The importance of institutions in explaining cross-national environmental policy has charted a varied course since the late 1960s. A few early studies suggested that some institutional differences had an important influence on the content of environmental policy. However, later work found that the content of national environmental policies was becoming more similar (Knoepfel et al. 1987). Convergence in policy content led to the (often unquestioned) conclusion that environmental outcomes would also converge. Simultaneous to these studies were others examining ways that environmental policy is implemented. Their results implied that any observed divergence in environmental outcomes might be explained by implementation failure. Most focused on compliance with specific aspects of the law, rather than a broader assessment of pollution problems. The true objective of environmental policy – a less polluted environment – was largely overlooked, save for one largely inconclusive study by Lundqvist (1980).[1]

The first generation of environmental policy studies highlighted broad institutional differences to explain responses to public concern about the environment. The major focus was the *content* of environmental policy (Enloe 1975; O'Riordan 1979; Sabatier and Mazmanian 1981; Solesbury 1976; Wall 1976). These studies suggested that political structures had, in Lundqvist's (1974: 139) words, "considerably more impact on the choice of alternatives than one would have expected." Factors such as democratic institutions, the division of governmental powers, and the strength of political parties were highlighted as potential explanations for how nations would respond to environmental problems. The imperfect state of knowledge about national environmental regulatory systems limited the power of this work and made the results largely speculative. Because these studies were conducted before there were widely available measures of environmental quality trends, little attention was given to the role of social institutions in accounting for altering the actual quality of the environment.

A second wave of environmental studies overcame a number of shortcomings in the first, giving greater attention to in-depth comparative case studies and to the process of environmental policy implementation (Badaracco 1985; Kelman 1981; Lundqvist 1980; Reece 1983; Vogel 1986). Some involved cross-national teams of researchers in collaborative efforts under a common research agenda (e.g., Brickman, Jasanoff, and Ilgen 1985; Kneopfel and Weidner 1986, 1983; Downing and Hanf 1983), whereas others were accounts of existing national policies (Reece 1983). For the most part, these studies cast the U.S. approach to policy making against policy making in other, primarily European, democracies. The adversarial style in the United States – formal procedures for setting rules, intensive politicization of issues, court battles between economic and environmental interests – was contrasted with the more "cooperative" policy-making style of consensus seeking between industry and government, limited politicization of issues, and "voluntary" methods of implementation. On the whole, the results of the second wave of studies suggested few cross-national differences in policy-making approaches apart from those between the United States and everyone else, although the diversity of those differences (at least excluding the United States) was considered quite small.

---

[1] Up until the mid-1980s this review draws heavily on two comparative environmental policy reviews, one by Vogel and Kun (1987), the other by Hoberg (1986).

In contrast to the first wave of research, the studies in the second wave did show that policy *outputs* – policy tools, specific standards, and so forth – were similar across countries. First, "command and control" regulations that compel polluting industries to install particular types of equipment to abate pollution were the dominate instrument in virtually all countries. (The reliance on command and control persists today, even amid a growing use of alternative tools: voluntary agreements, environmental taxes, or tradable emission permits.) Despite the widespread use of command-and-control regulation, some studies did note differences in the emphasis on "control." There was substantial variation in the degree to which "control" was carried out via more legalistic and formal procedures (e.g., the United States) as opposed to more "cooperative" ones (e.g., Sweden) (Lundqvist 1980).

Moreover, relatively recent attention to "economic incentive" approaches to pollution regulation revealed a greater diversity of regulatory tools employed historically, at least in particular sectors of environmental regulation. France and the Netherlands, for example, have relied on wastewater charges since the 1970s to help pay for treatment; and Germany and Denmark began using charges in the 1980s (Andersen 1994, 1999a; Reece 1983). Also, to varying degrees, countries had recycling programs to reduce waste disposal costs and raw material use. Further, although many economic incentives (e.g., gasoline or energy taxes) were not motivated by environmental protection concerns, their existence revealed how economic policy more generally can affect environmental performance.

A second conclusion from this second wave of studies of environmental policy was that countries tended to set similar emission and exposure-level guidelines in their environmental standards. Similar cross-national policies combined with different procedures for making and implementing policy thus showed how "different styles" produced "similar content" (Knoepfel et al. 1987; Kopp et al. 1990). The similar policy content was attributed to the unique nature of environmental policy, to countries being faced with similar problems, to growing economic integration (particularly in Europe), and to ensuing demands for regulatory harmonization.

The implication drawn from the presence of similar policy content was convergent outcomes, although this was not systematically examined. Most studies simply leapt from convergence in the content of policy to convergent outcomes. Thus, the thrust of this second wave of studies was that different styles of policy making were simply not that important in understanding new issues like environmental policy.

Those who did make more systematic arguments for the connection between content and outcomes generally failed to do so convincingly.[2] In their study of chemical regulation, Brickman et al. point to higher administrative costs in the United States than in Europe; however, they make no assessment of whether actual protection levels differ. When Harrison (1995) compared compliance with water pollution laws in the paper industry in the "coercive" United States and the "cooperative" Canada, she found that U.S. standards and compliance rates were higher, suggesting that coercion was "better" than cooperation when it came to actually reducing pollution. Lundqvist's (1980) study of air pollution regulation in the United States and Sweden also provided comparative evidence of outcomes. He found changes in sulfur dioxide concentrations in a six-year period early in the history of both countries' air pollution programs were similar. On that limited evidence he concluded that the differing styles of policy making between the two countries had only limited impacts on pollution outcomes. Just a few years later, however, an empirical assessment of air pollution regulation suggested a different story (Wetstone and Rosencranz 1983: chaps. 6 and 12). The United States was moving away from stringent air pollution regulations, while regulations were tightening in Sweden. Vogel's (1986) case studies of British and American environmental policy-making styles devoted a chapter to why environmental quality was difficult to compare across countries. Yet the critical premise of his argument, that outcomes in the United States and United Kingdom were similar despite their very different styles, was based on a few anecdotal reports of successful policies in both countries. In the 1980s only Badaracco's (1985) study of workplace chemical regulation in France, the United States, Japan, Germany, and Great Britain presents convincing evidence of convergent outcomes; but his study dealt only with the regulation of a single chemical substance (polyvinyl chloride).

In contrast to these sanguine conclusions that environmental outcomes were more or less convergent, the empirical data presented in Chapter 2 clearly suggest a great deal of divergence in performance across countries in core areas of environmental policy. Even if one confines the group of countries to those that were the primary focus of prior studies (i.e., Japan, Germany, the United States, Sweden, and the United Kingdom), comparative environmental outcomes vary considerably. For instance, while performance in Sweden and Germany is high, Japan's is somewhat above the

---

[2] In his review of several such studies, Hoberg (1986) also concludes that the empirical evidence to support converging environmental performance is quite weak.

average, the United Kingdom's is just below average, and U.S. performance is comparatively weak. Although it is true that almost all of these countries made tangible progress in dealing with environmental problems, universal improvement implies neither the end of environmental problems in these countries nor convergence among them.

If similar policy content does not, in fact, produce converging environmental results, what does? One possible answer (in addition to those addressed in the two preceding chapters) is differences in how regulations are implemented. Throughout the 1970s, various governmental bodies and commentators noted that environmental laws were not always implemented to the letter (Aspen Berlin Conference 1979). The "implementation gap," that is, the difference between the nominal standards and the standards imposed, became the focus of serious scholarly attention within the second generation of environmental policy scholarship. If implementation was lax in one country, one might expect that its environmental performance could also be lower, given broadly similar environmental standards.

As with studies of the environmental policy formation process, the implementation literature tended to contrast the American style of enforcement with the more flexible, "good faith" approach to implementation that is often considered to characterize European countries. As a great deal of early environmental regulatory policy was borrowed from American experience and scientific studies, so too was the inference that the "flexibility" of implementation in many European countries (and in the United States itself) was evidence of weak policy. Strict implementation, on the other hand, suggested "good" environmental outcomes.

A major reason for this inference was the presumption that flexibility in implementation resulted in environmental agency "capture" by those they were to be regulating. Capture implied that regulatory agencies subverted public goals (in this case of environmental quality). This criticism came especially from many environmentalists who were concerned that environmental interests would be "papered over" by industry and government in back-room meetings. While sometimes justified, the truth of this claim depends greatly on how national institutions tend to operate.

Unlike other studies in the second wave of comparative environmental policy that were more sanguine about cooperative and flexible styles of regulation, studies focusing on the implementation gap were more likely to suggest that cooperative, consensual policy making produced poor environmental performance. Writing about Swedish policy, Westerlund notes: "All of these ill-defined factors – vague standards, limited resources, politically ruled supervisory boards, and almost complete lack of public participation in planning and implementation – indicate a poor state of air quality control in Sweden" (1980: 36). Similar perspectives could be found among environmentalists in countries with more cooperative systems.

Once again, however, these studies tended *not* to assess environmental outcomes. In one study that did look at comparative outcomes in Europe, Knoepfel and Weidner (1983) confounded the premises on which much work in the field rested. Their findings indicated that detailed policy implementation had a limited impact on observed reductions in pollution. They found little evidence of links between political-institutional factors and policy implementation. For example, they found no difference in implementation based on the openness of the implementation process to appeal by the general public (a key demand of many environmental groups). Most fundamentally, they suggested that the negative interpretation of the "lack of rigorous enforcement" in the area of environmental policy is not necessarily indicative of failed policy or of poor outcomes:

Insofar as institutional patterns of privilege and discrimination are already incorporated in the [environmental] program itself, the notion of an implementation deficit as a shortfall caused by inadequacies of the implementation phase becomes quite relative. Viewed in the context of decisions on program structure and the patterns of interests reflected therein, these deficits represent little more than the effects of the consciously or unconsciously built in biases of the program core which, in turn, is often falsely taken as the only (or most important) point of reference for evaluating implementation performance. . . . implementation research will have to be extended to an integrated analysis of policy that joins both the implementation and program formulation phase. (1983: 201)

Their conclusion sets out the importance of going beyond the means (policy outputs) to study ends (outcomes) and the broader context within which environmental policy takes place when evaluating success and failure.

A final problem confronting the comparative environmental policy literature more generally has been the paucity of broad and rigorous comparative studies, wherein it might be possible to control for competing explanations. Most studies continue to be confined to an examination of one or two countries and one or two areas of pollution. The few studies that do take a broader multicountry approach have important limitations. Jänicke and his collaborators compared some trends in pollution and resource use for both Eastern and Western European countries between 1970 and 1985 (e.g., Jänicke, Mönch, and Binder 1993; Jänicke et al. 1989; Jänicke and

Weidner 1997). Their model emphasized "capacities for modernization": sociocultural, economic, and institutional. They found some correlation between some of these capacities and aspects of environmental performance.

Much of this work takes what might be called a "modernization" approach to the problem of developing environmental sustainability (Andersen 1999). This approach bears a striking resemblance to income growth and value-change explanations discussed in previous chapters. (Indeed, Jänicke also found that income growth was linked to environmental quality.) Two problems make this approach ultimately unsatisfying, both theoretically and empirically. First, there is an absence of "microfoundations" linking causes and effects. For example, it is not clear why the "capacity for consensus" is conducive to solving environmental problems rather than the opposite, or even exactly what such a "capacity" consists of. Second, there is no attempt in this analysis to assess the impact of the different "capacities" that are supposed to be important or to control for competing explanations of environmental performance. For instance, any large-scale comparisons were limited to bivariate associations. This makes it impossible to discern whether the various capacities referred to actually matter for outcomes in a multivariate analysis.

Three other studies in the 1990s also examined the relationship between institutions and environmental performance in a more cross-national approach. Crepaz (1995) assesses the explanatory power of neocorporatist institutions on air pollution levels during the 1980s, concluding that they are correlated with reductions in air pollution. This study also has several important limitations. First, why "consensual capacity" via neocorporatist institutions matters is only slightly more developed theoretically than in Janicke's work. Second, the study considers only one dimension of environmental protection (air pollution), which makes it vulnerable to the claim that air pollution is somehow idiosyncratic. Air pollution is certainly an important component of environmental protection, but it is difficult to conclude that corporatism is generally conducive to environmental protection on that basis alone. Finally, and related to the first two points, the empirical analysis used in that study fails to account for important alternative explanations such as geography, environmental mobilization, or political institutions.

The second broadly comparative study is an unpublished paper by Strom and Swindell (1993). What is innovative about their study is that it argues for a more systematic understanding of environmental politics that is both cross-national, theoretically based, and systematic in its attempt to explain environmental policy and outcomes. However, the theoretical and empirical basis of their results is preliminary (which the authors acknowledge), and they devote their attention to some political institutions (like electoral laws) rather than the socioeconomic institutions considered in this chapter.

Finally, of all the studies to date, Jahn (1998, 1999) has examined comparative environmental performance in a way most closely in the spirit of the current book. His comparison covers multiple pollutants and examines structural, "mobilizational," and political-institutional explanations for differences in national performance. Like Strom and Swindell's analysis, however, his empirical and theoretical analysis is preliminary, and he does not do much by way of explaining the causal linkages underlying major hypotheses.[3] Moreover, he examines only the period from 1980 to 1990, and thus excludes potentially important gains in the 1970s (particularly for "early movers" on air pollution), as well as improvements through the mid-1990s. This shorter time frame increases the possibility that the changes he observes are related to short-term factors (such as differences in the economic cycle) rather than long-term institutional performance.

The Emergence of Institutions for Environmental Policy

This section explains the emergence of national environmental policy institutions and why, despite confronting similar problems, institutions for dealing with environmental problems differ cross-nationally. The results demonstrate the viability of the concept of a general "national policy style" that is rooted in national institutions and show distinct differences in the system of environmental policy making among advanced democracies that may affect environmental performance.[4]

Cooperation and conflict emerge initially in the area of environmental policy due to a combination of factors: preexisting conventions of cooperation and the collective benefits of environmental policy. Although the emergence of a new issue is in some respects inherently conflictual, preexisting patterns of interaction are likely to be emulated in the creation

---

[3] For example, Jahn's empirical analysis relies on a variant of a stepwise regression (backward selection) analysis that is subject to a number of methodological complications.

[4] Richardson's (1982) or Vogel's (1986) books on policy styles are representative. Kelman (1981, 1992) presents a thorough approach to how these institutions emerge and are sustained.

of environmental policy for several reasons. First, incrementalism tends to dominate change in established bureaucratic systems, like those in the economically advanced democracies (Lindblom 1977). Incrementalism is especially likely when relevant actors interacting in a new domain (e.g., environmental policy) have preexisting relationships and organizational patterns in related policy domains. For environmental policy, the relationship between government and industry and existing interactions of governmental and industry groups are likely to influence outcomes heavily because so many environmental problems (even those manifested in individual consumption like the generation of waste) impinge on industry behavior.

In addition to the "inertia" of preexisting relationships, the past policy success of particular approaches to policy making may promote its emulation in new areas. For example, to the extent that corporatist arrangements successfully promoted compromise and stability between interest groups and governments in economic policy and areas of social policy, it becomes a natural model for organizing new environmental policy "sectors." In discussing the concept of policy concertation between the state, labor unions, and employers, Lehmbruch noted the strong tendency for concertation in core economic areas to spread: "The extension of concertation across policy fields . . . appears to derive from the immanent logic of concerted policymaking. . . . A genetic theory of corporatist concertation can be based upon 'rational actor' assumptions. The leaders of interest organizations opt for a corporatist strategy on the basis of an exchange calculus" (1984: 67). As concertation becomes a more extensively employed strategy of mediating socioeconomic conflict, it becomes more and more likely to be adopted (at least initially) in new domains like environmental policy.

In discussing the means by which conventions of behavior are applied in this way, Hardin (1982) also notes more generally that conventions cross over into other domains because preexisting institutional arrangements help to alter the confines of what is "rational" behavior.

Many clubs of backpackers with separate conventions of not littering the wilderness might have a grand meeting on a beach, and they might there readily follow their conventions [even if typical beachgoers litter the beach]. In part this would no doubt be because ongoing relationships among subgroups would make this large crowd less anomic than the usual beach crowd, but it would also be because this crowd [of backpackers] would have a convention already available to it. . . . Is the behavior of the backpackers on the beach somehow necessarily moral, while behavior on the trail was perhaps rational? No. . . . Because we have a convention, we have expectations about each other's behavior; and because we have expectations, we suffer costs if we do not live up to them. (1982: 175)

It is important to note that, based on this logic, deviating from the broader convention within the new policy realm has implications beyond that realm of interaction (i.e., the beach or, in our case, environmental policy making) and may unsettle the prevailing pattern of behavior in other areas (e.g., economic policy).[5] Approaches to environmental policy are the products of, but once established may reinforce, prevailing conventions of policy making. We would expect, therefore, that environmental policy making would look a lot like the prevailing style of policy making (i.e., that corporatist countries would have more corporatist environmental policy, and pluralist countries would tend to have more pluralist environmental policy).

Comparing corporatist concertation in traditional economic policy areas with the extent of "environmental concertation" in individual countries, we can see that this is so. To measure corporatism in traditional areas, I use Lehmbruch's (1984) measure of corporatist concertation in OECD countries. Lehmbruch classifies countries in five categories on the basis of the level of institutionalized negotiation between the state, producer, and labor groups in the conduct of economic policy.[6]

In the category of high corporatist concertation, Lehmbruch places Austria, the Netherlands, Norway, and Sweden. In the moderately concerted category, he places the remaining Nordic countries, Finland and Denmark, as well as Germany and Belgium, and, as a "borderline" case, Switzerland. The "weak concertation" cases are Britain, Ireland, and Italy. The countries with the least concerted policy systems (Lehmbruch calls them pluralist) are the United States and Canada. Spain is not classified. Similar studies of union participation and organization (e.g., Cameron 1984), as well as more detailed assessments of interest intermediation by Aguilar (1993; Aguilar Fernandez 1994), suggest that Spain should be classified as at least weakly corporatist in the time period examined. Two countries, France and Japan, are examples of "concertation without labor." Based on this ranking and the results of my own analysis of environmental

---

[5] This is distinct from the concept of linkage or logrolling in bargaining situations because no one in the convention uses a change in economic policy-making rewards as a carrot for environmental policy. Such logrolling may occur independently of the existence of a convention of behavior.

[6] The rationale behind these categories is the desire of the government to exert either direct or indirect control over the economy. Based on the standard, one would also have to judge concertation as successful (see Katzenstein 1985).

Table 5.1. *Environmental and General Policy Styles*

	Environmental Policy-Making Style	
General Policy-Making Style	More Corporatist	More Pluralist
Strong corporatism	Austria Netherlands Norway Sweden	
Moderate corporatism	Denmark Finland Germany	
Weak corporatism		United Kingdom Italy Spain
Pluralism		Canada United States
Corporatism without labor	Japan	France

Source: Lehmbruch (1984) and Appendix II.

policy making in fourteen countries, Table 5.1 shows the intersection between general and environmental corporatist characteristics.[7] A brief justification for the placement of each of the countries in Table 5.1 is included in Appendix II.

"Environmental corporatism" is most pervasive in countries with similar types of economic institutions. The traditional policy styles of advanced nations appear to have strongly influenced the nature of national environmental policy at least since the late 1960s. These results are consistent with both the "spillover" and emulation effects of institutional arrangements and confirm what comparative environmental policy scholars have noted as different styles.

Critiques of Neocorporatism

Although environmental policy styles bear a striking resemblance to policy making in other areas, a more fundamental question with which we

---

[7] A report on industrial relations and environmental protection among the (then) EC members also found that countries with higher levels of "social partner" consensus in industrial relations (Denmark, Germany, the Netherlands) had relatively more advanced involvement in environmental policy than did more conflict-oriented countries (United Kingdom, France, Italy) (Hildebrandt 1994).

are concerned is how such institutions within nations affect environmental performance. Whereas some have suggested that more consensual-"neocorporatist" arrangements might be conducive to good environmental outcomes, many have argued the opposite: that corporatist institutions systematically impede good environmental performance. This section lays out the major criticisms. I then discuss why many of these objections may be more apparent than real.

To many, the open policy style in the United States is seen as a preferable model to the neocorporatist approach. Environmentalists often suggest that more pluralist institutional arrangements are desirable. We can distinguish two elements of such arguments: those based on the perceived benefits of pluralist systems and those based on criticisms of corporatism. The perceived benefits of pluralism in the American context cannot be dismissed out of hand. Environmental groups in the United States wield some veto power, both electorally and in public policy. Their access to the legal system, a powerful national legislature, and independent state and local government provides numerous points of access to affect policies (Kitschelt 1986). Environmental reformers often support a shift toward more legislative (or parliamentary) control over policy making based on the belief that a strong legislature will produce more effective environmental policies than a corporatist bureaucracy.

Because many environmental groups (and ordinary citizens) in Europe are more often excluded from important policy-making and implementation decisions than in the United States, it is perhaps understandable that a model for environmental reform would be a system that appears to offer environmentalists much more power (Rose-Ackerman 1995). As some of the evidence from Chapter 4 suggests, environmentalist political success has come in arenas – new organizations, parliamentary parties, the "court of public opinion" – whose powers environmentalists wish to see expanded.

Virtually all substantive findings in the comparative policy literature claim that the institutional variation has little impact on outcomes. More pluralist systems are seen to be simply more rancorous, expensive, or unduly confrontational. For example, Lundqvist (1980) concluded that U.S. air pollution legislation, born of political "one-upsmanship" by the Congress, had produced about the same performance as Sweden's more consensual approach. Vogel (1986) suggested that British environmental policy was less expensive and rancorous than the U.S. policy but produced effectively the same (limited) outcomes.

Other arguments favoring more pluralist arrangements stem from a more principled rejection of corporatist arrangements. The major objections surround the interests of the traditionally dominant corporatist interest groups in society: labor unions, producers, and farmers. These "productionist" interests are considered inherently hostile to effective environmental policies and thus, irrespective of the institutional arrangements as such, undermine popular demands in society for greater environmental sustainability. According to the stronger version of the argument, strong concertation between major interest groups and government is a major cause of environmental problems. Referring to the opinions of many supporters of environmental politics, Markus Crepaz characterizes the divide in stark terms:

Corporatism follows an inherently materialist logic of economic growth that represents the smallest common denominator between the antagonistic interests of labour and business. The rise of post-materialist parties throughout Europe, however, questions the philosophy of economic growth because for these parties economic growth is precisely the reason for the environmental crisis our world faces today. There is a fundamental incompatibility between corporatism that follows a materialist logic of economic growth and postmaterialism that favors ecological concerns over economics concerns. (1995: 413, n. 3)

According to this view, the tension between economic and environmental goals is more or less zero-sum. Economic growth and environmental protection are incompatible goals, and the maintenance of policy institutions where economic interests have considerable power necessarily implies poor environmental performance.

Even when not considered inherently hostile, corporatist institutions are considered by many to be structurally incapable of accommodating new ecological issues into a modern environmental policy. According to this second criticism, the "logic" of neocorporatist institutions undermines the development of sustainable environmental policies. Hukkinen states this clearly:

There is nothing inherently incompatible between labour, capital and nature that could not be resolved through negotiations. In practice, however, this is impossible due to the very logic of corporatism. Even the most inclusive corporatist societies... effectively prevent ecological sustenance from ever entering as a party in corporatist negotiations because decision makers themselves conceptualize environmental issues in terms of non-problematic operating assumptions. (1995: 69)

Here, the conflict with traditional economic interest groups is not necessarily zero-sum but effectively so. Corporatist arrangements, originally

136

created in the absence of environmental demands, prevent the incorporation of such demands and preclude progressive environmental policies and improvements in environmental quality.

Both varieties of the objection that corporatism and strong environmental protection are incompatible rely on three problematic assumptions. First, they assume the existence of a deep-seated incompatibility between economic and environmental goals that is demonstrably false. Second, they assume that economic interest groups in corporatist societies have an overly narrow view of their interests. Finally, they assume that corporatist policy arrangements must exclude environmental interest groups as social partners.

False Economic Trade-offs

The argument that producer interests are inherently opposed to environmental protection for material reasons is premised on what are often false trade-offs between economic and environmental outcomes. A popular one is the negative association between employment and environmental protection: that environmental protection means job losses. This impression has been disputed in econometric studies (and often today by environmentalists themselves), which tend to find that environmental regulations, if anything, generate net employment for the economy as a whole (Goodstein 1994; Kopp et al. 1990; OECD 1978). Morgenstern, Pizer, and Shih (2000) even find that environmental regulation has been, if anything, a net creator of jobs in several pollution-intensive industries (petroleum, plastic, steel, and paper-pulp). Moreover, the aggregate employment effects of environmental policies (generally found to be small under standard macroeconomic assumptions) are – as the politics of full employment has perhaps always been – a matter of distributional politics. There is simply little evidence that the full employment consensus in neocorporatist countries was threatened or undermined by environmental policies, or even perceived to be. Indeed, trade-union movements in Europe increasingly took up the idea of environmental protection as a way to *create* jobs in the early 1980s (Hildebrandt 1994: 135).

A second false trade-off is between productivity and environmental protection. Investment in pollution abatement equipment is sometimes seen as taking away from more productive forms of investment and ultimately leading to lower investment and employment. This argument is also largely untrue according to most economic studies (Jaffe et al. 1995). The costs of environmental protection have been small at the macroeconomic level

137

(though they have been quite high in specific sectors). Moreover, environmental protection can enhance economic productivity, via its effects on worker health, the costs of industrial inputs, and productivity enhancing technological innovations (Jaffe and Palmer 1996; Porter 1990). A consensus of economists and ecologists suggest that it is not growth, per se, that is the problem, but the type (or structure) of growth (Arrow et al. 1995).

In summary, the objection that the political consensus for economic growth in corporatist countries is necessarily incompatible with environmental protection is not valid. Environmental considerations may place a constraint on some avenues available for achieving economic growth, but there have always been constraints (many of them "external") in that pursuit. Evidence for this was presented in Chapter 3: economic growth is not systematically correlated with environmental performance.

The Pursuit of "Postmaterialist" Goals

Another argument made by many critics of corporatism is that cooperation between unions and employers requires the pursuit of strictly economic benefits. Some suggest that unions and employers simply ignore issues like the environment on which there is not clear policy consensus (Jahn 1993; Kitschelt 1988; Micheletti 1990). The implication of this argument is that the historical "class compromise" between capital and labor makes the integration of environmental protection into economic and social policies all but impossible.

This view is subject to three objections. First, environmental degradation often involves class and material issues. Because the impacts of pollution often fall on the poor, good environmental outcomes tend to increase social equality, a general goal of trade unions (especially where unions are highly organized into encompassing groups, as they are in corporatist countries). Insofar as environmental protection is more labor-intensive, it may actually bolster employment, something at least unions are interested in.

Second, producer groups do pursue what are more or less "issues of principle," such as work flexibility or workplace democracy, that are not easily fungible. Unions in some of the more corporatist of European polities – Germany, Sweden, and Denmark, among others – pursued extensive quality-of-life demands, including health, safety and environmental reforms, throughout the 1970s and 1980s. Many of these demands – for example, work time reductions in Germany – were defended explicitly as means of increasing workers' leisure (Markovits 1986). Even the intra-union conflicts over the proper form of the work time reduction policies (thirty-five-hour workweek vs. early retirement) are framed as efforts to reduce unemployment by providing for greater leisure. Such pursuits are consistent not only with the "new politics" demands emerging in advanced democracies since the 1960s but also with the interests of union leaders themselves. Attitude surveys in the early 1980s have shown, for example, that union leaders are close to environmentalists' positions on many production issues (Milbrath 1984).

Finally, quality-of-life demands are consistent with the equality-solidarity approach that unions are prone to pursue. The provision of basic environmental amenities, which are available to all, can be defended as enhancing the equality of "life-chance" opportunity in ways that are natural extensions of social welfare states.

The willingness of producer organizations in corporatist countries to pursue quality-of-life issues and in particular union interests in distributional questions highlights two important insights about the compatibility of strong, concentrated economic interests and environmental protection. First, producers are also citizens and consumers. As such, their work and "life" interests are not always easily distinguished. This fact can explain why unions and employer's associations pursue policies that maximize more than short-term gains. (Again, this is most likely to be true where the associations encompass the majority of workers or firms in the society.) The other point is that substantive environmental policy issues are subject to negotiated compromises. The idea that ecological issues are nonnegotiable is reminiscent of "fundamentalist" strains of the union movement in the early twentieth century that suggested that participation in bourgeois democracy would further impoverish workers.

The Exclusion of Environmentalists from Policy Making and Implementation

A third argument made by critics of neocorporatist institutions suggests that they exclude environmental interests from meaningful participation in the policy process. Part of this criticism is answered by the prior point: the interests pursued by the main corporatist groups can include environmental issues (or the relevant compromise space could simply be constrained by government), independent of formal representation by environmental groups. But it is also the case that countries that are most consistently considered neocorporatist – Sweden, the Netherlands, Denmark – have had environmentalist participation on environmental policy matters. The inclusion of such groups into the process has, furthermore, often been prompted by unions (Hildebrandt 1994: xvi).

Admittedly, environmental groups do not typically enjoy the access to policy making that producer and worker organizations have; but environmental interests are consulted by environmental ministries and also can be found on official advisory boards (Blom-Hansen 2000; Peters 1984: 174–81; Ruin 1982; Tellegen 1981). Meanwhile, the nature of decision making in corporatist countries, when it incorporates environmental groups, has retained its essential corporatist features: it is consensus-based, only a few officially sanctioned interest associations (including environmental ones) participate extensively in the process, and aspects of policy agreements are implemented by industry associations "on behalf of" their general membership.

Thus, the major objections to corporatist institutions do not necessarily imply poor comparative environmental performance. The threats posed by strong economic interests are often more apparent than real, particularly when those interests are centrally organized. When considering the objections to corporatist institutions, it is also important to bear in mind the performance of the alternative arrangements being advocated (e.g., a more pluralist model). The relative virtues of either system should be evaluated by comparing cases with these different institutional arrangements and examining their environmental performance. This makes the empirical tests provided at the end of this chapter a critical part of evaluating the relative effects of pluralist and corporatist institutions on environmental performance.

Comparative Advantages of Neocorporatism

Refuting the claim that corporatism is "bad" for environmental performance only takes us halfway toward a more fully developed argument that corporatist institutions should generally be associated with good environmental policy performance. This section goes the rest of the way by suggesting some reasons to expect corporatist institutions to provide distinct advantages over pluralist arrangements in achieving good environmental performance. At least three aspects of neocorporatism facilitate better environmental performance: provision of information to regulated and regulating parties, flexibility in the ultimate implementation of policy by regulated actors, and the organizational structure of corporatist interests. All of these factors help to overcome natural collective action problems that plague efforts at environmental protection in all societies and reduce uncertainty among producers about their ability to comply with these regulations.

One of the "inherent" barriers to effective government environmental regulation is the uncertainty surrounding the costs and benefits of regulation. At least some of this uncertainty comes from the regulator's lack of information about the abatement costs in industries to be regulated, but it is also true among industries themselves. This lack of information makes traditional regulatory policy socially suboptimal unless all firms have the same marginal abatement cost (Baumol and Oates 1988). The regulator's imperfect information problem is a major source of the inefficiency of command-and-control regulatory tools in economic theory. (If the government knew all firms' abatement cost curves, they could set each firm's abatement limits to equalize marginal costs and benefits.) It follows that where institutions help to communicate quality information about the abatement costs of firms and are able to act on that information accordingly, there will be greater regulatory efficiency and thus better (or at least cheaper) environmental performance.

A popular claim for the more pluralistic and adversarial approach to making policy is its alleged advantage in providing more information for decision making. By requiring the opposing sides to state their case for or against regulation, the adversarial approach purportedly provides more information with which to make the appropriate decision. However, Kelman (1992) suggests several problems with such pluralist assumptions. First, more adversarial and conflictual processes create incentives for misinformation, as the competing parties attempt to suppress insider data that undermine their own general argument. Second, a more competitive process leads advocates on both sides to indict any information produced by opponents (even if it is true) that may be harmful to their own position. Third, the rancor of confrontation creates "bad will" among the opposing sides and can bolster confrontational stances even in areas of mutual agreement. Fourth, as many have pointed out with respect to the United States, pluralism has led to the juridification of environmental policy, making it less flexible, increasing transactions costs with few if any clear advantages in performance, and often resulting in environmental policy being made by courts with little expertise (or interest) in environmental issues (Wilson 2002; Vogel 1986). Finally, while the adversarial approach may produce information about the problem (e.g., how great is the threat of chlorine in the environment?), this can do little to produce solutions (e.g., how do we best reduce or eliminate chlorine?). All of these reasons suggest that adversarial processes might not be the best way to gather information about environmental policy.

The information-gathering process for environmental regulation is complicated by the fact that firms typically have information that is not available to others – their real cost of abatement under alternative policy schemes. It may be difficult for an adversarial process to produce good estimates of facts that only firms have. The more incentives there are for firms to overstate their costs of compliance, the more likely it will be that regulations are either too lax or too expensive.[8] In the long run, continued public uncertainty and long-term overestimation of costs by firms can result in less than optimal environmental standards for particular pollutants. Thus, even with perfect compliance, environmental standards (at least if they are instituted with a general "social cost–social benefit" calculus) will tend to be inefficient if regulators do not get the abatement costs near right ex ante.[9]

The general features of consensus policy-making institutions – ongoing consultation with a variety of interests having specific knowledge of the technical areas of regulation – avoid some of these problems by producing more quality information about the real impact of regulation on industry. Such knowledge is, of course, not exactly what the firm has at its disposal but reduces the scope of uncertainty as well as the room for negotiation for particular firms that might subsequently attempt to claim that they are unable to comply.

Perhaps a more important benefit of corporatist arrangements is the ongoing nature of regulatory negotiation. It results in more accurate evaluations of firms' own costs by the firms themselves. There is a natural incentive for firms to exaggerate their compliance costs with any regulation in order to soften the demands placed on them. Part of this may be "honest" insofar as firms are uncertain about their liability under an uncertain level of environmental controls. Can costs be passed through in prices? Will shareholders bear costs or can firms offset them via transitional subsidies?

---

[8] Harrington, Morgenstern, and Nelson (1999) find that costs are consistently overestimated by regulators in the United States. They also note that debates about over- or underestimation of costs tend to follow the "bias" of the source – environmentalists tend to claim costs are overestimated and industry the opposite.

[9] Even if standards that are "too tight" and "too stringent" balance out, the social implications are negative. Having too much lead in the air is not balanced by having "too little" sulfur.

142

Will efforts to minimize costs in achieving the standard be thwarted by overly rigid rules for compliance?[10] These problems are all the more severe if firms are imperfectly informed about what their real costs will be after the regulation is in place (DeCanio 1993). Indeed, this may be a (benign) reason why firms consistently overestimate compliance costs in the United States (Morgenstern, Pizer, and Shih 1997).[11]

When environmental consensus seeking occurs early among broad encompassing groups in a regulated industry, it can generate more accurate information about compliance costs. One mechanism by which this can occur is via the institutionalization of environmentalism in the bureaucratic structures of firms. For example, Lundqvist suggests that this is exactly what occurred as a result of Sweden's corporatist approach:

The traditional political style [of neocorporatism] brought polluting industries very early on into the development of emission guidelines for implementing the 1969 Environmental Protection Act. This was in turn probably also instrumental in the emergence of environmental units or divisions within 35 industrial branch organizations in Sweden. The comprehensive business and industrial federations, most individual branch organizations and individual enterprises of some size now have environmental divisions. (1997: 56)

Kelman (1981: 184) makes a similar argument for health and safety regulations in Sweden. A greater attention to the interaction of environmental issues and production that is integrated into branch and company policy helps to reduce intrafirm resistance to new environmental regulation by demonstrating benefits and "institutionalizing" an assessment of benefits (as well as costs) of regulation within industries. This means firms will be more accepting of environmental policy requirements in general.

The quality of information about environmental standards produced by more cooperative forms of policy making may have other benefits. When competing actors seek to achieve a consensus around particular environmental policy goals and standards, they must publicly acknowledge the validity of information or particular goals that deviate from their original positions. This process can dissolve some of the potential "ill will" among contending parties. Institutionalized negotiations also help to

---

[10] A standard implying an abatement method or technology assumes a process of production. If the standard is inflexible (e.g., firms must buy and run this abatement technology), it may "lock in" a production process that pollutes more than an alternative.

[11] This is not to assert, as Porter (1990) does, that regulation lowers costs for firms below preregulation levels; only that costs of compliance may fall once firms "optimize" under the new regulatory constraints.

alter policies to undermine the free-rider problem (Kelman 1992). This can be beneficial in both directions – regulators get better information about firms, and firms get (and are more likely to trust and thus use) information provided by government. Regulatory flexibility in the actual technology standards of abatement (allowing firms to use any technology to achieve emission levels) also brings with it greater possibilities of technological innovation than required standards and gives firms some leeway in complying.[12]

Moreover, the potential costs of a lack of consensus may produce more violent "swings" in policy. For example, what today might seem like outrageous legislative promises in the 1970s – that the United States would achieve zero pollution in a decade or two – were a product of the competitive political process that sparked resentment and backlash a few years later, perhaps undoing progress made to that time (Andrews 1999). Although such swings may equilibrate (and the prospects for this type of action by political parties are not absent in countries with neocorporatist institutions), they may take a long time to do so. And when they do, they may end up looking much less like either (good or bad) extremes.[13]

Of course, good information *need* not be produced by consensual systems. If firms are never pressed to implement strong policies, for example, then better information for the government is not relevant. Indeed, a condition for regulators getting information is the promise not to exploit it fully or reveal secrets.[14] There must be pressure on regulators and industry from "pro-environment" forces, whether from within the policy-making setup or from without. This is one feature of environmental performance in which the importance of a minimal level of environmental mobilization is probably vital. Without some general sentiment in favor of environmental protection,

---

[12] The generalized exchange that characterizes well-developed corporatist arrangements may also facilitate such innovations (Crouch 1993). Firms may get "credit" for innovations.

[13] Andrews also discusses the pendulum swings in American environmental policy since the 1970s, attributing them in part to shifts in the ideology in government. It is instructive to place those in comparative perspective. European nations had similar rightward swings in the partisanship of government (Sweden in 1976; the United Kingdom in 1979; Norway in 1981; and Denmark and Germany in 1982) and cries for environmental regulatory relief in the face of economic recession. A major distinction between Germany and the Scandinavian countries and the United States and United Kingdom is that the former had established consensual-corporatist institutions.

[14] Spence and Gopalakrishnan (2000) argue that this presents barriers to negotiation-based environmental policy in the United States because environmentalists often insist on eliminating any mutual gains from greater regulatory flexibility.

144

governments are unlikely to pursue environmental regulation seriously.[15] Of course, such sentiment is just as necessary in more pluralist systems.

Although an environmental agency may have the incentive to obtain as much information as possible to produce cost-effective regulations, the reasons for industry to cooperate are less clear. Even if regulations provide firms with incentives to "discover" their costs of compliance, firms may have incentives to hide this new information because they are likely to incur some increasing costs as the stringency of an environmental standard increases. Assume a firm faces an agency offer of standard X. A firm finds that compliance with any standard up to X costs it half what the agency assumes. Because the firm still incurs positive costs for any standard, might it be best to express opposition to standard X in hopes of getting a lower standard and lower abatement costs?

Several factors suggest that this is less likely to occur within a more corporatist institutional framework. First, if the firm's lower cost is due to a firm specific innovation, it has a comparative advantage that probably increases as the standard becomes more stringent. It can either sell the innovation or enhance its market position from its lower costs after the new standard is implemented. This makes the firm a potential ally of the agency in support of a stricter standard. (Of couse, this is true in a pluralist or corporatist setting.) Second, if there is an industry (rather than firm) advantage, the consultative regulatory process characteristic of corporatist countries involving specialized expert panels of industry, government, scientific, and "public interest" officials may result in fewer incentives to "hide" industry secrets. Such expert groups may even have a greater tendency to be "pro-protection" compared with the groups' general membership.[16] Specialization, more "pro-environment" attitudes, close face-to-face interaction in advisory and decision-making bodies, and some degree of isolation from particularistic interests undermines the strategic use of individual firm's information in the policy process.

In summary, the procedures for policy making in corporatist countries produce a great deal of valuable and effective information for industry and

---

[15] This point is made by Crepaz (1995).

[16] Kelman (1981) found that industry association experts in worker safety were much more willing to adopt high workplace standards that exceeded those that might have been adopted by ad hoc groups of general managers. He attributed this to common socialization (e.g., education, socioeconomic status), reinforced by close interaction among the expert groups in isolation from the particularistic demands of particular firms or industries.

regulators. Government and industry can get a better idea of the likely costs and benefits of particular policies and may be able to negotiate more efficient regulation in the process. Industry is less likely to be "surprised" by regulatory demands, making it potentially easier to adjust to stringent regulations. Finally, bargaining by encompassing associations rather than more fragmented associations helps to produce a more "pro-protection" consensus, particularly in a context in which business is granted some flexibility in implementing regulations in greater accord with other investments in exchange for stringent standards. Such bargaining increases the likelihood that firm-specific information goes to the government (or other firms). All of these factors make it more likely that corporatist institutions will achieve comparatively better overall environmental outcomes.

A former Swedish environmental official provides an excellent exposition of how the corporatist policy process can be stringent, not simply while accommodating producer interests, but because it does so:

During the permitting process, the dialog normally results in broad consensus regarding a great deal of the terms to be met in the [environmental] license. Emission limit values set are normally very stringent, in an international comparison, but give consideration to possibilities for companies to phase environmental protection measures into their normal investment plans that could often be accepted by the polluter as conditions in their license.

That flexibility has another advantage: it allows for the selection of a more environmentally friendly process to start with, reducing end-of-pipe treatment. This flexibility substantially reduces the costs for environmental protection, and normally results in lower emissions than is the case when square medium-based emissions standards form the basis for environmental measures.

From the environmental point of view the procedure also has the advantage that the terms are not tied by standards, so new innovations in process and environmental technology can progressively be considered in each new license. The [Swedish] EPA also allows for trial periods before limit values or other conditions are fixed [in the license]. That possibility makes the polluter more open to test new innovative designs. (personal communication, December 9, 1999)

In addition to informational advantages of cooperative policy making characteristic of neocorporatist institutions, another factor favoring the effectiveness of regulation by consensus is that regulations will have a higher level of "voluntary" compliance. As the preceding quotation suggests, flexibility in the ultimate implementation procedure can result in dynamically progressive policy outcomes, provided that regulators insist upon (and producers accept) upgrading over time. This is precisely the kind of "generalized exchange" that Crouch and others are referring to when they discuss traditions of state and (economic) interest group inter-action (Crouch 1993). This type of industry "overcompliance" in exchange for more flexible policy is backed, of course, by both the shadow of more invasive government regulation and sanctioning. But it is the coordinating capacity of strong business associations that overcomes an industry coor-dination problem. Firms that run afoul of government and their industry associations may undermine the benefits that can come from a generally more cooperative regulatory environment, where industry has influence and legitimacy in policy making (Soskice 1999). Although this may not elimi-nate temptations to cheat, it provides varied incentives among noncheaters to cooperate both within the industry at large (e.g., through an industry association) and with government, to sanction firms that threaten coop-eration by cheating. In Denmark, for example, firms unable to comply with a particular regulation were granted extra time to comply (subject to the approval of state regulators) only so long as they joined the Associa-tion of Danish Industry, which helps to enforce the agreement (Wallace 1995).

Where we might expect to see *lower* standards as a result of such coopera-tion is where there is very limited access for nonindustry and nonregulatory groups and where interactions in implementation at the associational level are limited. An example of this appears to be air pollution regulation in Britain. There, policy is decided primarily between firms and regulators that are closely tied to one another, but whose dealings are not subject to the checks that formalized consultation among a broader group of inter-ests (i.e., unions, consumer or environmental groups) imposes. Indeed, it is precisely in countries *without* established corporatist institutions that "coop-erative" policy making between firms and government can tend to produce something more akin to "agency capture," something many critics of cor-poratism fear. Some otherwise pluralist countries have such relatively secre-tive implementation procedures (e.g., in addition to the United Kingdom, Canada).[17] This is, of course, an important thing to consider in attempting reforms of more adversarial regulatory systems. Simply moving to "flexible implementation" may not produce large performance improvements in

---

[17] Weale, O'Riordan, and Kamme (1990) suggest that the Confederation of British Industry opposed the movement of the Alkali Inspectorate into a more tripartite administrative structure in part because of its secretive relationship with the inspectorate. This underscores the importance of the extent of *preexisting* corporatist arrangements in helping to determine if cooperation as such is really conducive to good performance.

the absence of changes supporting more broadly consensual policy-making institutions.

Organization of Interests

Thus far, the focus of the beneficial effects of corporatist regulatory processes has centered primarily on the relations between regulated and regulating parties. It is important to emphasize that the internal structure of the corporatist producer groups themselves is also important for understanding how institutions can be expected to enhance environmental performance.

Environmental protection is quintessentially about the provision of a public good and is thus subject to collective action problems. No individual has an incentive to provide a public good as long as she cannot be assured that others will contribute. And although all may desire less pollution, everyone also has incentives to free-ride on the efforts of others.

This environmental free-rider problem is much like the economic free-rider problems that encompassing interest groups supposedly overcome (Lange and Garrett 1985; Olson 1965, 1982). The same logic of collective action in economic policy is transferable to the arena of environmental policy. For example, peak associations in corporatist labor organizations tend to include most workers and, by extension, most households (and, on the industry side, most large firms). This provides two main advantages in overcoming problems of collective action in the area of environmental protection.

First, the authority of national peak associations over local units permits the pursuit of general, rather than particularistic, group interests. This helps to reduce (though certainly not eliminate) policy paralysis led by small groups of intensely interested workers who stand to lose from an environmental regulation. In societies with nonencompassing groups, such small groups would be more likely to pursue their maximum advantage. In Olson's terminology, they will pursue distributional or rent-seeking strategies. Such strategies can have pernicious effects when pursued by economic interests but also by overzealous environmental groups. In the latter case, excessive standards, inflexibility, or misplaced environmental priorities can undermine environmental policy in the long run. The overall effect of policies that are not stringent enough in some areas and overly stringent in others can lead to the worst of both worlds – high costs and limited benefits. Decentralization among economic actors may also result in perverse (i.e., economically inefficient) outcomes when environmental policies are

148

ultimately enacted. This suggests not only less environmental protection in pluralist countries but also less efficient regulatory outcomes.

Second, corporatist arrangements are noted for facilitating compensation for losers in economic adjustment (e.g., via generous retraining or unemployment benefits or subsidies), thereby socializing some of the distributional costs of policies (Katzenstein 1985). Because environmental adjustments following environmental regulations will produce economic "losers" (even if net social benefits are positive), existing avenues for temporary compensation will reduce the likelihood that intense producer interests will undermine the collective environmental interest.

Indeed, environmental policies can be incorporated into the broader arena of distributional politics, making environmental policy serve economic goals in the society. For example, the Swedish government provided subsidies for public and private environmental investments in the early 1970s as a means to stimulate the economy (OECD 1977b). Similar "environmental reflation" projects were undertaken in Belgium, Denmark, and Austria (all corporatist countries) in the late 1970s (OECD 1978). The labor-intensive nature of many environmental policies has also been recognized and promoted by unions and environmental groups in most countries as ways to reconcile overall environmental and labor demands. Finally, changes in agricultural policy in many of these countries also demonstrate how compensation mechanisms are used to soften the blow of sweeping environmental reforms (Vail et al. 1994). A more recent example is the debate about green taxation as a mechanism for reducing taxes on "goods" (like employment). Although these gains often fall short of the proclaimed "double dividend," they can reduce some undesirable distortions in the tax code.

Third, as Peter Katzenstein argues, the strategies of adjustment found in corporatist countries stem from the need to adapt to change in the international economy. "In linking international liberalization with domestic compensation, the small European states respond to economic change with flexible policies of industrial adjustment. They neither export the costs of change through protection nor preempt the costs of change through structural transformation. Instead, they deal with the problems of change rather than wishing them away" (1985: 8). Because structural adjustments are constant features in corporatist countries, the ability of corporatist countries to adjust to environmentalism may stem from their ability to adjust quickly to an international shift in the types of products and services demanded, especially among the large states. It is no accident that Germany, Denmark, and Sweden are on the cutting edge of "ecotechnology" compared with other large countries, including the United States (Moore and Miller 1994).

Finally, corporatist peak associations help to overcome temptations among members to "defect" from a policy in pursuit of greater social environmental benefits. This can perhaps best be explained by an example. Although economic and environmental goals do not necessarily conflict, if workers or employers believe there are economic trade-offs or that they will face undue economic risks if they accept environmental measures, they may (mistakenly) oppose environmental regulations. In particular, a worker or individual union may be vulnerable to "job blackmail" – false information about the impact of an environmental policy on an employer – because she has little information about a firm's intentions or the cost of the regulation.

Even without explicit blackmail, individual firms and workers in a pluralist society have few reasons *not* to resist specific regulations that may disadvantage them, *even if they all individually prefer less pollution*. Based on their incentives and institutional arrangement, they may fight to make others bear the costs of regulation. On the other hand, the potential economic beneficiaries of environmental policy more generally represent a latent group that is more likely to be overlooked than would be the case in a more organized corporatist arrangement. The alleged "relative power" of environmentalists in pluralist systems (vis-à-vis industry) may increase the prospects of stringent policies; however, the price paid is often, as Scholz (1991) points out, a policy regime that is overly rigid.

The peak associations that characterize neocorporatist institutions also have incentives to identify false trade-offs (e.g., to inform their members that the overall employment effects of environmental regulation are small). Although this is true for any peak association, even where their power is circumscribed (e.g., the Trade Union Congress in Great Britain or the AFL-CIO in the United States), peak organizations in corporatist countries tend to have more influence over member groups to build consensus. They may be able to induce collective support for policies in spite of negative impacts on small groups. Finally, their location at the center of social policy making also makes it easier to coordinate environmental policy to ease social disruption just as they facilitate other economic adjustments. The net result of hierarchical producer and consumer institutions is that false trade-offs can be exposed, thus enhancing the general support for regulations.

Empirical evidence from the environmental policy process in corporatist and noncorporatist countries supports the vulnerability of environmental policy in more pluralist systems to the aggregation problem. For example, in the United States and United Kingdom, both pluralist systems, the jobs-environment trade-off is constantly invoked as a reason to be concerned with environmental policies. For example, even though trade-union leaders acknowledge that there are very few overall employment effects, public statements by the British Trade Union Congress (TUC) even in the 1990s reflect continuing efforts to suggest that environmental regulation does not significantly affect employment (TUC 1996). The process of persuasion is barely underway (and apparently not very successful).

By contrast, officials in corporatist countries like Sweden and Denmark report that the issue of "employment versus environment" seldom comes up in official discussions of environmental policy. Government officials in Denmark suggest that such a conflict has not really been an issue since the early 1970s. (This is in a country with very high unemployment in the late 1970s and early 1980s.) Although such evidence is not conclusive proof that encompassing producer groups affected the outlook of their members, it is consistent with the idea that organized union movements adopt more progressive attitudes toward environmental protection more quickly.

Recent work on differences in the organization of production in advanced economies also points to several microlevel factors that are consistent with my argument. Soskice (1999), for example, argues that the dominant "production regime" in the neocorporatist countries is a coordinated market economy (CME) that provides numerous mechanisms that are conducive to effective environmental regulation. First, coordinated production is national in scope and permits the state to negotiate collectively with companies to determine the framework in which individual companies operate. This helps to ensure that policy comes closer to reflecting collective goals (both the government's and industry's) than a fragmented, "pluralist" approach.

Second, there is close cooperation and information sharing between firms, which helps to diffuse innovations so that firms are not unduly disadvantaged (vis-à-vis other domestic producers) by national regulations. Strong business associations monitor arrangements among firms to ensure that some firms do not simply free-ride on innovations by others. Soskice notes that strong associations "ensur[e] that companies make 'fair' contributions to the flows [of technical exchange] and guarante[e] to the companies that the inside information acquired in the process will not be misused" (1999: 116).

Summary

This section has suggested that corporatist institutions are more beneficial for environmental policy than is often supposed. In summary, three
aspects of neocorporatist societies make a compelling case for a positive
link between corporatism and environmental performance. Neocorporatist
and consensual policy-making institutions, and the countries dominated by
such institutions, have several comparative advantages for attaining good
environmental outcomes.

1. They provide informational and efficiency gains in making policy.
2. They provide a regime where flexible, cost-effective implementation
   of high standards can occur.
3. They provide "built-in" conditions that facilitate internalizing production and consumption externalities.

Critics of corporatist institutions often fail to take into account these *comparative* advantages of corporatism in dealing with environmental issues.
Because many critics of corporatism advocate alternative political institutions that mostly resemble pluralist arrangements, only a comparative approach that evaluates the environmental outcomes of corporatism against
this alternative arrangement can provide an appropriate basis for an evaluation of the consequences of corporatist institutions. It is to this empirical
analysis that we now turn.

Empirical Analysis

The two preceding sections suggest competing hypotheses about the ways
that social institutions affect important environmental outcomes. On the
one hand, the critics of corporatist institutions suggest that such arrangements will have a negative impact on national environmental performance.
On the other hand, I suggest a number of reasons why corporatist institutions are more conducive to good environmental performance than are
pluralist ones. This section tests this hypothesis. First, I discuss the operationalization of corporatism. I then present bivariate and multivariate
evidence showing the association between environmental performance and
corporatism. The multivariate evidence incorporates factors suggested to
be important in previous chapters – income, geographical advantage, and
environmental mobilization.

152

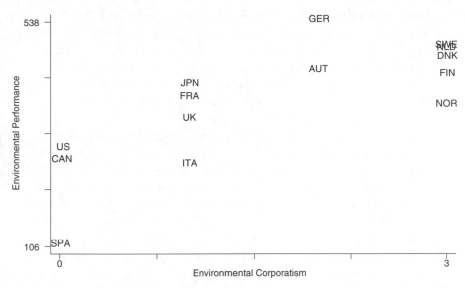

Figure 5.1 Environmental Corporatism and Environmental Performance

The results are dramatic. Countries with corporatist institutions have systematically higher environmental performance than do countries with more pluralist arrangements. Controlling for competing explanations of environmental performance does not seriously affect the positive impact of corporatist institutions. The empirical record thus implies that consensual politics among the state and major social actors combined with the presence of encompassing economic interest groups has produced superior environmental performance during the first two decades of the modern environmental era.

An immediate complication of discussing the "impact" of corporatism is how to operationalize "environmental corporatism." Relying on rankings of the fourteen countries from Table 5.1 is one possibility. The correlation between those rankings and environmental performance is high: .76. Figure 5.1 plots "environmental corporatism" against performance and shows that there is a clear consistent relationship from low to high.

There are several shortcomings of using this evidence, however. First, the rankings exclude some countries for which I have environmental performance data. In an effort to retain as many cases as possible for statistical analysis, alternative measures are more desirable. Second, as suggested earlier (and following the advice from Knoepfel and Weidner's [1983]

153

study), the broader institutional setting in which relevant actors (particularly regulated interests) operate, not simply at the environmental policy arena, is likely to be important in effecting environmental outcomes. Third, given the subjective aspects of creating it, using my own classification of countries as "corporatist" invites the charge that the classification is constructed to confirm the main hypothesis. All of this suggests using a measure of neocorporatist institutions that is more general, covers more countries, is based on more systematic observation, and is derived independently. The measures of corporatism discussed in this section meet these conditions.

There are many categorizations of corporatism in the literature. Not only do different authors often have different goals in mind when classifying countries, but there is also variation in "expert judgment" when the understandings of the concept are shared. I use three different measures – including one that combines a number of categorizations by "experts" into a single standardized measure – rather than relying on one. Assuming that the results are similar across the measures, we can be more confident that the relationship I have suggested is robust.

1. *Lehmbruch's corporatist concertation* (Concertation): Lehmbruch's rankings, discussed earlier in the chapter, are based on the role of peak interests in policy making, particularly the inclusion of labor groups in the making of economic policy. Concertation is distinguished from the more rigid sectoral corporatism and is based on the *relationship* among more or less sectorally corporatized groups and the government.
2. *Lijphart and Crepaz's "expert" corporatism score* (Corporatism): This indicator is constructed based on country rankings from twelve separate classifications by experts. Thus, the measure represents something of an average rating from the literature. I assigned Spain, excluded from Lijphart and Crepaz's (1991) paper, a score of -1 to reflect the general descriptions from other literature that it is less corporatist than Japan (which is scored .05), but not as pluralist as the United States (-1.34).
3. *Siaroff's measure of economic integration* (Integration): Siaroff's (1999) article attempts to rectify several problems that exist in categorizations used in the corporatist literature and provides critical information on the degree of corporatism since the mid 1980s.[18] His classification

---

[18] In particular, Siaroff addresses the problematic categorization of Japan and Switzerland and includes measures of the degree of integration (i.e., corporatism) for the late 1960s,

Table 5.2. *Neocorporatist Institutions*

Country	Lembruch Concertation	Lijphart & Crepaz Corporatism	Siaroff Economic Integration
Austria	3	1.60	4.6
Belgium	2	.26	3.9
Canada	0	−1.34	1.7
Denmark	3	.52	4.2
Finland	2	.43	4.1
France	1[a]	−.73	2.1
W. Germany	2	.48	4.1
Ireland	2	−.53	2.4
Italy	1	−.85	2.5
Japan	2[a]	.05	3.5
Netherlands	3	1.01	4.0
Norway	3	1.53	4.6
Spain	1	−1.00	1.9
Sweden	3	1.40	4.6
Switzerland	2	.51	4.1
United Kingdom	1	−.86	2.0
United States	0	−1.34	1.9

[a] Classified as corporatism without labor.

focuses more on the general functional and behavioral (as opposed to the mere contextual) elements of corporatism and is perhaps more in the spirit of my interpretation of the concept. Moreover, unlike the two other measures, Siaroff takes into account changes in corporatism after the mid-1980s. Countries are scored based on the average score for four periods (the late 1960s, late 1970s, late 1980s, and mid-1990s).

Table 5.2 provides a summary of the country scores on four measures of corporatist institutions, the ranking from my own analysis, and the correlation of each with national environmental performance. The correlation statistics – .55 for Concertation, .67 for Corporatism, and .72 for Integration – suggest that all three measures of neocorporatism are closely correlated with environmental performance, in particular Siaroff's more up-to-date measure.

late 1970s, late 1980s, and the mid-1990s. His results suggest the decline in centralized collective bargaining, which many consider the "end of corporatism," has not reduced corporatist policy making in other areas of government policy.

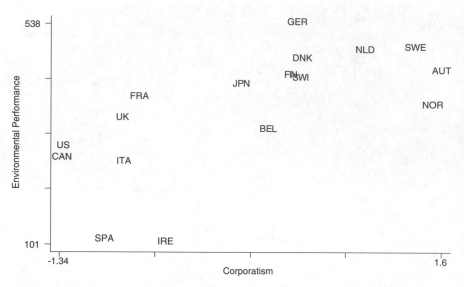

Figure 5.2 Lijphart-Crepaz Corporatism Score and Environmental Performance

As the preceding chapter demonstrated, simple correlation statistics can be deceptive. Figures 5.2–5.4 show scatterplots of environmental performance and Corporatism, Concertation, and Integration, respectively. All three figures show clearly a consistent, positive impact on performance. There are really only two major deviations. First, Germany performs better than its moderate Concertation or Corporatism ranking suggests. However, Germany has consistently been characterized by several scholars as having a high degree of formal environmental corporatism, though of a variety that has, until the 1990s, tended to provide limited access by environmental groups (Lenschow 1997; Pehle 1997; Weidner 1995). Second, Ireland performs somewhat worse than its moderate Corporatist and Concertation scores indicate.

These results are striking. Of course, as we have already discovered, bivariate correlations may disappear once we take other explanations into account. To find out, I controlled for the alternatives discussed in previous chapters – income, geographical advantages, and environmental mobilization – in a multivariate regression. Table 5.3 shows results of several regression models estimated using different measures of corporatism and these other variables. The first result simply serves as a reference and

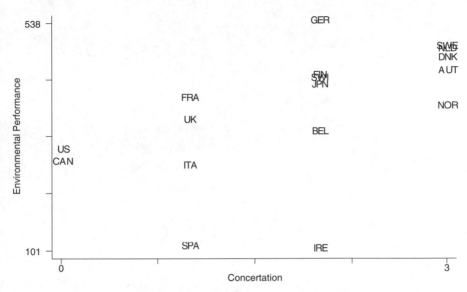

Figure 5.3 Concertation and Environmental Peroformance

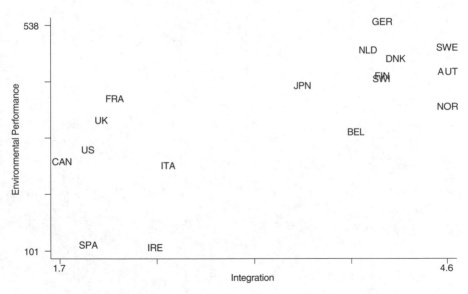

Figure 5.4 Economic Integration and Environmental Performance

157

Table 5.3. *Regression Results: Corporatism and Environmental Performance*

	1	2	3	4	5	6
Corporatism	28.3** (9.4)					
Concertation		69.0** (23)	83.6*** (23.3)			
Integration				59.3** (20.0)	49.6** (16.5)	55.2*** (15.2)
Income (1975)		18.9** (7.8)	22.1*** (6.7)	18.9** (7.8)	21.7*** (6.6)	22.7*** (6.4)
Income squared	−.0013** (.00049)	−.00073 (.00041)	−.00084** (.00036)	−.00076** (.00041)	−.00094** (.00033)	.001*** (.0003)
Geographical advantage	17.9 (18.2)	22.7 (13.9)	13.6 (11.0)	17.3 (13.9)	9.6 (10.8)	
Environmental mobilization	4.9 (9.6)	−10.9 (9.0)	−18.5 (12.2)	−7.1 (8.4)		
Constant	−1153** (443)	−761* (362)	−1174*** (293)	−927** (347)	−987*** (304)	−1037*** (297)
Observations	16	16	16	16	17	17
Adjusted R^2	.59	.76	.80	.76	.77	.77
Turning point	$10,885	$12,945	$13,155	$12,434	$11,543	$11,350

Note: Standard errors in parentheses.
* p < .10; ** p < .05; *** p < .01.

includes income (and its square), geography, and environmental mobilization. The next three columns show the results with the corporatism variables included separately, and the final two columns drop marginally significant variables – geographic advantage and environmental mobilization. The corporatism estimates are all substantively and statistically significant.[19] Holding other variables constant, the approximate change in environmental performance moving from the lowest to highest level of corporatism is 200, 250, and 175 points (respectively for Corporatism, Concertation, and Integration).[20] All of the models explain most of the variation in environmental performance: between 75 and 80 percent.

The results for two of the three other variables are largely consistent with findings and expectations developed earlier. Income remains related to performance in a curvilinear fashion. Up until $12,000 to $13,000 per capita (in 1975), higher income is associated with better performance. After that, more income is associated with worse environmental performance. Geography is also not significant in any of the models estimated but does retain the correct sign in all estimates.[21]

Contrary to expectation, however – but consistent with findings in the preceding chapter – the impact of greater environmental mobilization is negative, but *not* significantly different from zero.[22] One (tempting) explanation is that environmental mobilization is stronger where policy makers have failed to respond successfully to pollution problems and weaker where policy has been more responsive. Examining the cases more carefully, however, casts doubt on the claim. Some of the best performers (Sweden and the Netherlands) are also among the most highly mobilized.

Most important for the claims made in this chapter, regardless of differences in estimates for the other variables, all measures of *corporatist*

---

[19] Using other explanatory variables discussed previously (postmaterialism, growth rates, heavy industry, etc.) does not substantially affect estimates for the corporatism variables.
[20] Estimates using the environmental corporatism ranking for fourteen countries in Appendix II are consistent with these.
[21] If the income-squared term is removed from the models, the magnitude of the other estimates increases, but the signs and significance levels remain about the same. In addition to the combined measure, Geographic Advantage, I estimated models with country areas and population density separately. The resulting estimates are consistent with expectations – Population Density has a positive coefficient, Land Area a negative one – but very imprecise.
[22] The results for environmental mobilization do not change if I use the measure based on the 1981 WVS.

159

institutions are positively and significantly associated with environmental performance.

Conclusion

This chapter has argued that there are several reasons for us to expect that prevailing socioeconomic institutions have an important impact on environmental performance in advanced democracies. As with many forms of complex regulation, controlling pollution inherently involves the knowledge and commitment of polluters and coordination among regulating and regulated actors. By providing means to overcome collective action problems, promote consensus between regulators and polluters, and promote and implement those environmental policies in a manner that is cost-effective, corporatist institutions belie the claims of many of their critics that they are incompatible with strong environmental protection. The evidence presented here strongly supports this argument. Corporatist institutions contribute positively and strongly to environmental policy performance, even when the other explanations for environmental performance are controlled for.

One question that arises from the empirical results is whether corporatist institutions as such are really responsible for environmental performance. In some respects this is a difficult question to answer definitively. I have tried to make a strong case for why they should matter. In so doing, I employed both quantitative and qualitative evidence to demonstrate that corporatist institutions do indeed seem to facilitate better performance. Small states in Europe have certainly adopted corporatist institutions partly out of economic and political necessity (Katzenstein 1985). Yet, as we have seen, corporatist institutions are important *even if one controls for the structural characteristics of small states*. Indeed, even if we ignore the smaller states and focus on France, Germany, Japan, the United Kingdom, and the United States, the more corporatist-consensual the country, the better its environmental performance.

Economic performance is also an important cause of environmental protection. To the extent that good economic performance is a product of corporatist institutions, the economy, rather than the institutional differences stressed here, may be the critical causal variable. There are two problems with this claim, however, that reinforce the importance of institutions. First, the balance of evidence tends to show that pluralist institutions produce economic performance that is as good as that of corporatist countries (Lange and Garrett 1985; Scruggs 2001). Moreover, as suggested in Chapter 3, economic growth rates are not systematically linked with environmental performance.[23] Second, economic growth in corporatist countries has been less spectacular in the past decade or so, yet this seems to have had little negative impact on their environmental performance.

Finally, one might argue that the organization and institutions of policy making among economic actors are really only one important aspect of a much broader system of arrangements called consensual democracy and that the institutions discussed here are secondary to differences in political institutions (Lijphart 1999). The next chapter addresses this claim directly.

---

[23] Although the results reported in this chapter did not include an economic growth variable in the model, including it does not add explanatory power to the model and does not affect the estimates for pluralist-corporatist institutions. Nor does including a more encompassing measure of economic performance – the misery index (unemployment rate plus inflation) – for the period considered.

6

Political Institutions

This chapter examines the relationship between differences in national political institutions and differences in environmental performance. Unlike the preceding chapter, which addressed the implications of patterns of interest group influence on environmental outcomes under an assumption that environmental interests are on the policy agenda, here I deal directly with barriers to the articulation, aggregation, and representation of environmental interests in the political arena.

A major reason for caring about political institutions is their effect on democratic responsiveness. In *Democracies* (1984) and *Patterns of Democracy* (1999), Arend Lijphart suggested that differences in institutional practices used to translate citizen preferences into policy have an important role in explaining differences in national policies. The significance of political institutions in effecting social choices and outcomes has received considerable attention in comparative politics and political economy (e.g., Alt and Chrystal 1983; Huber and Stephens 2001; Knight 1992; Lijphart 1999; Persson and Tabellini 2000; Powell 1982). This includes environmental performance. In particular, political scientists have proposed a number of hypotheses about the relationship between varieties of democratic institutions and the ability of society to respond to "diffuse interests" such as environmental protection effectively (Vogel 1993).

Environmental protection can be generally classified as a diffuse benefit because the benefits to individuals from the provision of environmental protection are relatively small or uncertain. Such benefits tend to be underprovided because of collective action problems. Small benefits for individuals may discourage them from acting to pay the costs of change, particularly when their own contribution is not likely to affect the outcome significantly. Environmental protection is also problematic because the sources of pollution are often few in number and face large costs of change. That is, costs are concentrated. Although groups of polluters also face collective action problems, their smaller numbers and greater cost owing to environmental regulations may provide them with comparative advantages in political struggles over environmental policy. In short, the logic of collective action conspires against environmental protection.

The ability to have diffuse interests articulated and acted upon is a rationale for representative democracy. Indeed, the supply of public goods (such as environmental quality) is a major rationale for government of any kind. This chapter first lays out the main dimensions of difference in democratic political institutions, and the theoretical debates about the role of each type of institution and its ability to represent diffuse interests over concentrated ones. This analysis draws almost exclusively on existing categories of institutional difference widely discussed in the literature. While examining the hypothesized effects of these institutional differences on environmental protection issues, I emphasize national differences along these dimensions. Next, I examine the empirical relationship between political institutions and environmental performance and then conclude by discussing the implications of the empirical results in light of expectations of the effect of political institutions on environmental performance.

Dimensions of Institutional Variation in Democratic Society

In this section, I lay out major categories of institutional variation among major democratic countries and discuss the hypotheses linking these institutions to governmental performance. I focus on four main dimensions of institutional differences:

1. Prevalence of coalition (as opposed to single-party) government.
2. Extent to which political power is unified or separated at the national level (separation of powers).
3. Extent to which political power is dispersed geographically (federalism).
4. Difficulty of entry for new political parties.

Although other institutional differences might be added to this list, these four are often considered important factors affecting public policy in comparative politics and comparative political economy. Because the purpose of this work is to advance the integration of environmental politics, policy, and outcomes into the more general comparative literature, these four dimensions are a natural starting point.

Single-Party versus Coalition Government

An important distinction among democracies is whether they are ruled by a single party or a coalition of parties. Whereas some political systems (such as in the United Kingdom) virtually guarantee majority government, other countries have had no single-party government since World War II.[1]

Scholars have advanced several explanations for the greater effectiveness of coalition government in general and particularly oversized coalitions (where the coalition is greater than that necessary to produce a voting majority in the legislature) for the representation of diffuse interests such as the demand for environmental protection. First, to the extent that government *parties* represent distinctive electoral platforms, there is a greater chance that environmental interests will gain favorable access to legislative power where more parties are needed to form one.

Second, if multiple parties share governmental power, the chance that a coalition will have to confront environmental issues is greater insofar as the environment is an issue separating potential coalition parties. For instance, the necessity of a coalition government in Germany has provided the Green Party with extensive access to and influence over environmental policy among German Länder (where they have sat in government), and influence as a result of competing for votes with the Social Democrats and Free Democrats. Their coalition *potential* – realized in 1998 when they entered into a coalition with the Social Democrats – has fostered environmental reforms in Germany since well before that time.

Critics of the effectiveness of coalition government point to a number of problems with this assessment. First, the presence of environmental factions within large parties may make the existence of an environmental party per se irrelevant. For example, there are strong environmentalist factions in both parties in the United States, particularly in the Democratic Party.

Another criticism focuses less on the question of *representing* environmental interests than on the possible effectiveness of that representation,

---

[1] The United States is often characterized as having *divided* government (legislative and executive branches controlled by different parties). Although this is not typically considered a "coalition" government in the comparative literature, it should be because executive-legislative powers are rather evenly divided in the United States.

or *responsiveness*. Some suggest that coalition governments undermine executive power and democratic accountability, and undermine the provision of collective goods like fiscal responsibility (Grilli, Masciandaro, and Tabellini 1991). This criticism is made particularly of countries with long histories of coalition government (Weaver and Rockman 1993).

For their part, advocates of coalition party government maintain that the discipline of party platforms and governing, even if diluted by power sharing, ensures greater responsiveness to diffuse issues like environmental protection. In *Patterns of Democracy*, Lijphart suggests that democracies dominated by coalition government (along with other factors) perform better on a number of public policy dimensions – macroeconomic outcomes, representation of women and minority groups, political violence – than those dominated by single-party government.

To quantify the idea of "coalition intensity," researchers use a measure that captures not the number of parties in government but the proportion of seats in the legislature held by the government – for example, the proportion of "minimal winning cabinets" (Lane and Ersson 1999). What is crucial in our case is not whether governments have the correct "size" but the proportion of single-party governments. To capture this idea, I use the *frequency of one-party cabinets* (weighted by time served) between 1971 and 1996. This is calculated based on Lijphart's analysis with the following modifications. First, single-party minority governments are counted as single-party governments. Although such governments do require legislative coalitions for passing environmental legislation, there is less of a dispute about political responsibility for how the bureaucracy (an important element is making environmental regulations from much more general laws) operates. This implies, inter alia, that Japan is always coded as a single-party majority when one party controls the cabinet. Second, the United States is considered a single-party government only when the president and the Congress are from the same party. This makes sense in the context of U.S. environmental policy, since Congress historically uses legislation to place severe limits on bureaucratic (and hence presidential) discretion in implementation (Rosenbaum 1998).

The data for this measure are presented in column 1 of Table 6.1. Four countries (Spain, Japan, the United Kingdom, and Canada) are run by a single party for more than 90 percent of the period. Two others (Sweden and Norway) are run by single parties more than two-thirds of the time. On the other hand, seven countries – Belgium, Finland, Germany, Italy, the Netherlands, Switzerland, and the United States – are never, or almost

Table 6.1. *Characteristics of Political Institutions, 1970–1995*

Country	% Single-Party Government[a]	Executive Dominance	Bicameralism	Federalism	Electoral Threshold	Veto Structure	Multipartyism
Austria	52	5.5	2	4.5	2.6	-.91	-.66
Belgium	0	2.0	3	3	4.8	1.18	-1.83
Canada	100	4.2	3	5	35	1.18	3.04
Denmark	42	2.1	1	2	2	-1.50	-.96
Finland	3	1.5	1	2	5.4	-1.14	-1.71
France	58	5.5	3	1.2	35	-2.10	1.95
W. Germany	0	5.5	4	5	5	1.38	-1.81
Ireland	44	2.5	2	1	17.2	-1.42	.24
Italy	18	1.1	3	1.3	2	.60	-1.58
Japan	91	3.0	3	2	16.4	-.08	1.39
Netherlands	0	2.7	3	3	.7	.76	-2.14
Norway	78	2.6	1.5	2	8.9	-1.31	.49
Spain	100	4.4	3	3	10.2	-.26	1.15
Sweden	69	2.7	1	2	4.0	-1.86	-.11
Switzerland	0	1.0	4	5	8.5	4.08	-1.55
United Kingdom	100	5.5	2.5	1	35	-2.72	3.04
United States	23	1.0	4	5	35	4.08	1.05

[a] See text.

Source: Author's calculations based on Lijphart (1999).

never, run by single parties. The presence of the United States in this group reflects the prevalence of divided government. Only in 1977–80 and 1993–94 was there a government with an executive and legislative branch majority of the same party. The remaining four countries (Austria, Denmark, France, and Ireland) have a more balanced division, with single-party governments in place 40 to 60 percent of the time.

Unified versus Separation-of-Powers Systems

In an early assessment of the effects of political institutions on environmental policy making, Lundqvist (1974) suggested that the distinction between the U.S. presidential (separation-of-powers) system and the parliamentary systems of Canada and Sweden might have important implications for environmental policy outputs and outcomes. Twenty years later Strom and Swindell (1993) noted that little subsequent work had investigated the effects of this major institutional difference on environmental policy. This oversight is surprising given the importance attached to these differences in the mainstream political science literature (Shugart and Carey 1992; Lijphart 1992; Weaver and Rockman 1993).

In distinguishing between these types of political institutions, I take a relatively narrow view of the separation of powers and the extent to which the executive and legislative functions of government are separated. There are clearly other forms by which power might be separated – for example, federalism, judicial review – and I address some of these later in the chapter.

Under a presidential system, there is separation of political powers between main branches of government (legislative, executive). This structure provides multiple channels of access for interests wishing to substantially influence policy and complicates policy making.[2]

There are several potential policy benefits of such a system for problems characterized by diffuse benefits and concentrated costs (like environmental quality). First, by allowing multiple avenues for groups to influence policy, separation of powers (SOP) can overcome entrenched opposition from one branch of government. Second, SOP can preserve past victories that are the result of popular will, even after broad support for them wanes. Finally, SOP may create a "virtuous cycle" of reform. Branches of government may outbid each other for progressive reform when issues are popular. Vogel (1993),

[2] Dahl (1956) provides a critical analysis of Madison's theoretical foundations of separation of powers.

167

for example, concludes that U.S. environmental policy fared better in the 1980s when political and popular conditions were more unfavorable than did policy in parliamentary countries like Japan or Britain, because SOP helped to create a "ratcheting up" effect on regulation.

Shortcomings of SOP, however, are similar to a shortcoming of coalition governments mentioned previously: access and influence do not necessarily translate into policy impact. Multiple points of access can undermine accountability. This is especially problematic for environmental policy because collective action problems work against the large, diffuse interests in favor of protection and in favor of small, concentrated interests who oppose it. If the separation of powers produces divided government (which it has tended to do in the United States since 1970), additional veto points may prevent meaningful policy innovation and its uptake. The lack of coherent policy response under more fragmented systems can have lasting implications for the long-term institutionalization of new policy and thus hurt environmental performance.

Finally, some have disputed the ultimate benefits of what Vogel called "bidding up" opportunities under SOP. In his study of air pollution policy making in Sweden and the United States, Lundqvist (1980) suggested that the "bidding up" process in the United States helped to produce unreasonable demands on industry and polarized the environmental policy debate. Whereas supporters of SOP point to the inability of an antienvironmentalist Reagan administration to make as much progress in gutting environmental regulations as it would have liked, critics argue that polarization and environmental backlash were due to the "irrational exuberance" of the bidding up process in the early 1970s.

Supporters of more unified political institutions – where political power tends to be concentrated in the hands of the majority party or coalition – suggest that a concentration of power can produce more responsive environmental policies. The strength and cohesiveness of a parliamentary form of unified government may make it better able to resist the demands of particularistic interests that could effectively oppose policy change if political power was more fragmented. The logic underlying this argument is similar to that of encompassing groups discussed by Mancur Olson and in the previous chapter of this book: parliamentary systems may be more responsive to environmental interests because unified political institutions reduce the risk of political deadlock.

Another reason that a unified parliamentary government may be more effective than SOP is the continuity between policy making and implementation characteristic of a unified government apparatus.[3] The cabinet's control over the entire policy process (from initiation of legislation to political control over ministries) encourages them to reconcile technical-bureaucratic elements of policy with political ones, resulting in more effective and efficient policy. In contrast, effective and efficient policy in SOP systems may be undermined by constant conflicts over control among different branches of government. The close link between the bureaucracy and legislature in parliamentary systems may also eliminate another means of displacing responsibility: by preventing legislatures and executives from blaming each other or other branches of government for failure. In other words, "responsible party government" may ultimately outperform "divided government."[4]

In summary, arguments in favor of both more unified and divided legislative and executive power have been advanced in the literature. Despite these conjectures, however, little systematic evidence has been presented to clearly substantiate one view over the other in the area of environmental policy. Lundqvist's (1974, 1980) initial assessment and his more in-depth comparison of Sweden and the United States were equivocal but favored the advantages of unified government. Vogel's (1993) comparison of Japan, Britain, and the United States reached the opposite conclusion. Strom and Swindell (1993) obtained results that were largely inconclusive.

Among the seventeen advanced democracies considered here, only three have a chief executive who is elected by the public and is not removable by a legislative vote of no confidence: the United States, France, and Finland. All other countries, except Switzerland, have an executive subject to a vote of no confidence.[5] This simple distinction is misleading as an indication of

---

[3] A secular shift in the locus of policy making to the executive and bureaucracy has been noted in many areas of government regulation among all advanced democracies. A major reason for this trend is that the growth of government regulatory responsibilities and their technical demands exceed the relatively nonspecialized abilities of most politicians. This trend is especially important in environmental policy due to the fact that the highly technical nature of environmental problems leaves the executive with a great deal of discretion in translating legislation into substantive achievements.

[4] There are, of course, conflicts within "unified" government. Executive control over the bureaucracy may be limited by differences in the technical specialization and career tracks of bureaucrats and the information and incentives of politically appointed cabinet ministers. The point is that they tend to have comparatively fewer conflicts.

[5] Switzerland has an appointed executive leader who is *not* removable by the Parliament and is considered a presidential system in all but name. Furthermore, among Western democracies the degree of presidentialism in the United States is somewhat exceptional (Lijphart 1999: 117–24).

the true fragmentation of power, however. The dominance of the executive vis-à-vis the legislature varies within and across nominally presidential and parliamentary systems. This de facto separation is critical when evaluating implications for environmental policy. If a parliamentary system has more balanced power between the executive and the legislature, or if a parliamentary executive confronts two legislative bodies with equal power, the prospects for "executive control" are reduced. In contrast, where power rests more firmly in the hands of the executive, appeals to "dissident" forces in the legislature are less likely.

A standard approach to the relative strength of executives (vis-à-vis legislatures) is the durability of the executive. An advantage of this measure is that it is informed by extensive detailed knowledge of the individual cases. In this scheme, parliamentary systems with long-lived executives are considered to be more "executive-dominant." The values are provided in column 2 of Table 6.1. Relative cabinet strengths are constrained, with the British (Swiss) cases defining the extremes of strong (weak) executives. The "presidential" systems – France, the United States, and Switzerland – are evaluated by Lijphart on a qualitative basis of the relative powers of executive and legislature, as they are not subject to votes of no confidence. I rely on his judgments here.

On these criteria, Switzerland, the United States, Italy, Finland, Belgium, and Denmark have weak executives and stronger legislatures (government duration less than 2.5 years), or at least balance between the two bodies. Austria, Canada, France, Germany, Spain, and the United Kingdom all have had relatively powerful executives in the past three decades, with their governments lasting more than 4 years on average. The remaining five countries – Ireland, Japan, Netherlands, Norway, and Sweden – fall somewhere in the middle, with average government longevity of between 2.5 and 3 years.

A second important dimension of national SOP lies in the presence of a strong second chamber of the legislature. Where the power of a second chamber is strong – for example, the second chamber has effective veto power over important legislation and its representation incongruent with the first chamber – power can be considered more dispersed. Where a second chamber is nonexistent, has little veto power over legislation, or is indirectly elected by the executive or lower chamber, there are few formal political checks on government-executive power. In other words, "robust bicameralism" implies less unified government, whereas "weak bicameralism" or unicameralism suggests more unified government.

Following the literature on the structure of legislatures, I assign countries to a four-point scale of unicameralism and bicameralism, based on the distinctions made by Lijphart (1999). The scores are presented in column 3 of Table 6.1. Two countries, the United Kingdom and Norway, merit special attention as they are placed in intermediate categories. Norway is nominally a unicameral legislature, but it splits into two chambers after the elections. However, because the elections of these bodies are congruent and most work in the Norwegian Storting is carried out in joint sessions, Norway cannot be considered a case of strong bicameralism. The United Kingdom has a formally independent second chamber (at least for the period considered here) in the House of Lords that is appointed; but it has limited authority to affect legislation desired by the lower house and government.

Overall, although there are only four systems with nominally separated powers (the United States, Finland, France, and Switzerland), several parliamentary systems have a relative balance between legislative and executive power (Belgium, Denmark, and Italy). Several other countries with relatively strong second chambers belie their unified parliamentary systems (Canada, Germany, Japan, the Netherlands, and Spain). Thus, of the thirteen parliamentary countries considered in this study, nine deviate in at least one important respect from being true unitary political systems. Belgium and Italy both have relatively independent lower houses and additionally have strong second chambers. They should be considered to have strong separation of powers. The Netherlands and Japan have moderate separation of powers along each of these two dimensions. Of our seventeen countries, only Austria, Norway, Sweden, and the United Kingdom fit closely to the model of unified national government. Deviations from conventional ideas about the separation of powers also permeate presidential countries. Both France and Finland more closely resemble a system of unified, rather than separated, powers. In both cases the powers of the president depend primarily on a legislative majority and are otherwise quite weak.

In summary, if one examines the de facto division in national political institutions, the distinction between "divided" presidentialism and "unified" parliamentarism dissolves somewhat. Based on the sum of standardized scores for executive dominance and bicameralism, the most unified systems are Austria, the United Kingdom, Sweden, France, Denmark, Norway, and Finland, whereas the countries with the greatest "separation of powers" are the United States, Switzerland, Italy, and Belgium. Germany scores a rough balance between SOP and unity, although it has both a dominant executive and a powerful second chamber. Independent evidence of the power of the governing parties over the legislature, the impact of the opposition on policy, suggests a lack of institutional autonomy for the legislature (Laver and Hunt 1992).

Federal versus Unitary Political Systems

Another dimension of the separation of power within a country and one that offers potential points of access for actors with interests in the environmental policy arena is that between the national and subnational levels of government: federalism.[6] Much of the debate surrounding the impact of federalism on environmental policy mirrors the debate over the importance of the degree of separation of powers discussed in the previous section. The critical issue is whether it is better to have multiple avenues of possible representation for environmental interests or centralized channels. "Even if the federal structure provides more channels for participation, and is compatible with a flexible approach, it may in fact lead to excess flexibility and time costs. Key interests in the provinces or states may be able to delay action or push through standards more lenient than is scientifically or technologically defensible" (Lundqvist 1974: 140).

Students of the impact of environmental movements make a similar point. For example, Kitschelt (1986) suggests that the ability to intervene at multiple levels of government (national, state, and local) enhanced the ability of protest to block the expansion of nuclear power in Germany and the United States but prevented the development of a more coherent alternative energy policy.

Overlapping authorities in federal systems tend to increase the costs of creating coherent policy (Holland, Morton, and Galligan 1996). This is true not only between the levels of government but also for interest groups that must operate at both the federal and state or provincial levels. The increased cost often works to the disadvantage of the most weakly endowed groups and the ones pursuing the more diffuse benefit because resources for that group will tend to be hardest to organize.

Other arguments suggest that federalism leads to more effective environmental policy. Autonomous, subnational units, acting as "policy laboratories," ultimately produce more policy innovation. This laboratory

---

[6] Federalism could be considered as just another feature of the separation of powers. I distinguish it here because it is not a division within the national government but between the national and regional levels. In the next section it is combined with them.

172

model is based on two central assumptions: that many units addressing a particular problem will raise the probability of innovation and that, when innovation occurs, the most effective policy innovations will be adopted by others or by the federal government itself. These two assumptions are based, in turn, on a model of a well-functioning "market" process for policy innovation.

Unfortunately, such a model tends to be exactly what is lacking in areas of regulation, such as environmental protection. First, whether federal environmental policy forecloses innovation "from below" is not clear. Because environmental pollution is a negative externality of production, federal subunits have few incentives to internalize their own externalities, especially when others do not. Paying for clean-up costs imposes economic costs on businesses or citizens, which they can easily flee by moving to another state. For many areas, then, the choice may be between a strong federal policy or weak state policy as states or provinces become caught in a proverbial race to the bottom. Such competition will not eliminate environmental standards but may undermine their stringency. Indeed, state inaction prompted the federalization of environmental policy beginning in the 1960s in the United States.

A second problem is the type of innovation produced by decentralization. In innovating to solve pollution problems, federal subunits (states, provinces, etc.), like firms, may be indifferent between policies that alleviate pollution and those that simply displace pollution onto others. Thus, *more* innovation by states in a federal system may have little effect on *national* environmental problems. Indeed, Rosenbaum notes that in the United States "state governments have a habit of using their Congressional representatives to influence federal environmental regulation to their own advantage" (1998: 113).

Third, the federalist model of competition among subnational jurisdictions assumes that diffusion occurs on the basis of an evolutionary selection mechanism. Yet federal subunits can probably survive "stupidly" for a long time. In other words, the assumption that decentralization results in competition for the best environmental policy is not particularly credible.

Fourth, it is not clear that the result (to take the U.S. example) of fifty state environmental agencies, even if working effectively on their own, will be a more effective national policy than a single federal agency. There is a great deal of variation among U.S. states – for example, California or New York versus Louisiana or Alabama – in the area of environmental policy. Although there are certainly different problems and capacities for solutions, the wide discrepancy of efforts suggests that policies do not necessarily converge, except when regulations are eventually adopted at the federal level.

Finally, a problematic assumption of the federalism model is the fundamental tension between a specificity argument for decentralization (that different states have different regulatory needs necessitating freedom over goals) and the diffusion argument (that all units, or the federal government, adopt the best policy innovations). This tension seems to be best overcome if the laboratory model is the informal strategy of a strong central government but not a component of the country's constitutional structure. The national authority to impose the best innovations on everyone is as important for good outcomes as the innovations themselves.

In contrast to federalism, the argument for having a more unitary government is to reduce areas for political conflict. By being able to impose solutions more uniformly, unitary government may avoid beggar-thy-neighbor behaviors among political subunits. Advocates of federalism, however, point out that having fewer administrative areas for conflict does not result in more effective environmental policy. Ultimately, the terms of the dispute tend to make the impact of more federal or more centralized political institutions largely indeterminate a priori.

When it comes to distinguishing empirically between "federal" and more "unitary" systems for the purposes of comparison, the issues are more complex than they first appear. The defining feature of federalism is guaranteed division of responsibility between central and regional governments, often with some concurrent powers. Most political scientists classify Canada, Germany, Switzerland, and the United States as strongly federal; Austria and Belgium as weakly federal. The other eleven countries considered here are typically categorized as unitary states. Among countries in either group, however, there tends to be a great deal of variation in how much day-to-day power subunits have.

Lijphart (1999) looks beyond constitutional differences and attempts to take elements of de facto subnational governmental power into account when evaluating federalism in a comparative context (also see Castles 1999). For instance, he incorporates the degree of subnational control over taxation. Powers like taxation are important because they provide practical constraints on the true independence of subnational government. Because his characterization more closely resembles the institutional processes likely to matter for environmental policy, I use his ranking of countries (see column 4 of Table 6.1).

This measure presents a nuanced picture of federalism. For instance, unitary Belgium and the Netherlands are classified as semifederal due to the important degree of political and economic power delegated to religious and ideological groups in "social" areas like education, health care, and culture.[7] The Scandinavian countries, along with Japan, are classified as primarily unitary but with some degree of informally decentralized institutional practices.

Do these results more accurately reflect the administration of environmental policies in the respective countries? To a large degree, they do (cf. OECD 1977a, 1977b, 1993a, 1993b, 1994a, 1994b, 1995a, 1995b, 1995c, 1996, 1997b). For example, despite the characterization of government in Scandinavia and Japan as centralized, the administration and implementation of environmental policy tends to be decentralized.[8] Similarly, although the United States is characterized as having a centralized environmental policy due to the presence of a strong Environmental Protection Agency, most of its regulations are in fact implemented by the states (Rosenbaum 1998; Lowery 1992). Conversely, responsibility for environmental policy implementation is considered centralized in unitary countries like France and the United Kingdom.

Proportional and Plurality Electoral Representation

Two other political institutional arrangements that can be expected to influence environmental policy outcomes are electoral and party systems. Both have a significant influence on the capabilities of political systems to represent diffuse interests such as environmental regulation. The major dimension along which one can expect such institutions to matter is the degree of proportional representation (PR) in the electoral system. Generally speaking, proportional representation systems offer good opportunities for access by environmental interests to the political arena. This is so for two reasons.

First, PR makes it easier to form parties that represent intensive environmental interests. "Proportional representation presents relatively low

---

[7] Belgium became a formally federal state after 1993 but is considered semifederal here because the change is unlikely to affect changes in environmental outcomes in the 1975–95 period.

[8] Relying on the more traditional formal assessment of "unified government" would imply that Scandinavian countries had environmental administrations as centralized as even Britain or France.

barriers to the formation and parliamentary representation of small parties. Thus it offers diffuse interests a different path to access – establishment of a distinct party" (Vogel 1993). In contrast, plurality systems limit the entry of new parties. To the extent that environmental issues are not highly salient to many voters and do not represent a dimension distinct from other policy issues, environmental issues may have a hard time gaining prominence in such settings.

By presenting more credible prospects of stimulating the formation of a separate environmental party, proportional representation is also likely to encourage established parties to take the environment more seriously and gives voters a clearer, policy-based notion of what they are voting for. As we saw in Chapter 4, only PR systems have environmental parties of any appreciable electoral significance.

The second way that PR encourages the effective representation of diffuse interests (as opposed to plurality voting laws) is by discouraging a "localist" bias among individual legislators. Parties (and candidates) under plurality voting rules can solidify their power by allowing individual party MPs to become favorites in their districts by providing particularistic favors in government. Simultaneously, such representatives can claim to be less accountable for generic policy developments because they are only one member of a large legislature. The end result may be greater emphasis on particular benefits (what an individual member can control and deliver to local constituents) and less attention to national policy as such.

By contrast, in multimember districts under proportional rules of representation legislators (or even parties) are less likely to have a sole claim on particularistic benefits in a district (e.g., another legislator or even party may also represent the district). Moreover, parties in PR systems with the power to win particularistic benefits in the legislature are less able to shirk responsibility for overall policy outcomes, particularly when legislative and executive power are combined, as in unitary systems. Both factors – less clear claim to loyalty via patronage and less ability to shirk responsibility for general policy outcomes – reinforce the pursuit of public, diffuse benefits rather than narrow constituency-specific interests (Noll 1983).[9]

---

[9] The implication is *not* an absence of patronage in PR systems, simply that the institutional basis for them is less pervasive. To return to the logic of the provision of public goods, parties in PR systems have fewer incentives to pursue policies that are geographically redistributive than do representatives in single-member districts.

The extent to which generic appeals are favored over particularistic ones will also depend on the relative size of the district. If, as in the case of the Netherlands, there is only one district (the entire country), party appeals will tend toward more generic policies. Where the relative district size is smaller, there may be more opportunity to develop parties based on regional particularities.

Despite the name, proportional representation systems are not precisely proportional. Beyond the technical limits to proportionality (in the limit, legislatures must have as many members as are citizens in the electorate to *guarantee* proportionality), proportionality is limited through the number of seats in a district, counting rules, or by establishing an electoral threshold: the proportion of the vote a party must receive to get any representatives. For example, Sweden requires a minimum of 4 percent of the vote for a party in order for it to gain seats.

To account for these differences, I use a measure of proportionality that provides the "effective" percentage of the vote a party needs for representation: effective threshold (Lijphart 1994). A higher threshold implies higher entry barriers for new parties (see column 5 of Table 6.1). Consistent with expectations, all of the plurality electoral systems have high effective thresholds. (Japan and Ireland have distinctive voting rules but high electoral thresholds.)[10] Countries with typical list-PR systems tend to have greater proportionality, as expected. That proportionality is linked to the strength of environmental parties can be seen in comparing thresholds with the average vote of environmental–left–libertarian parties between 1975 and 1995, discussed in Chapter 4. The correlation is −.63.[11]

Political Correlates of Environmental Performance

As we have seen, hypotheses about the relationship between political institutions and environmental outcomes are often diametrically opposed. Some maintain that one type of institution tends to promote better environmental outcomes, whereas others maintain that the opposite arrangement does so. This sometimes leads to the suggestion that political institutions

---

[10] Recent changes in Japanese electoral rules have no impact on the period under consideration and are thus not evaluated.

[11] This correlation is high even if one controls for postmaterialism, income, or even the share of the service economy. In other words, the correlation is not due to other alleged causes of high environmental party vote shares.

are incapable of helping us explain variation in environmental policy and performance. Seldom, however, do tests of such hypotheses go beyond the consideration of two or three countries or a (sometimes misleading) classification of countries.

In this section, I examine the relationship between each of the political institutional factors discussed in the previous section and indicators of environmental performance. I first examine bivariate correlations and turn to a multivariate analysis that controls for other explanations of environmental performance. At the end of this discussion, I also combine the five political variables discussed earlier into two distinctive institutional configurations that we might expect to explain variations in environmental performance. The findings show limited evidence for an effect of unified governmental institutions on environmental outcomes.

Figure 6.1 breaks down environmental performance based on the extent to which governments tend to be formed by a single party or in coalition. It suggests that greater single-party dominance is, if anything, associated with worse environmental performance. The correlation is modest at best −.34 (p < .18). Three of the six best performing countries always had coalition governments in the period (Germany, the Netherlands, and

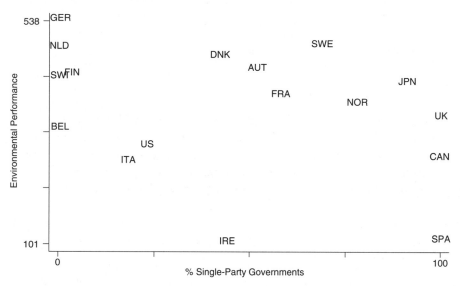

Figure 6.1   Single-Party Government and Environmental Performance

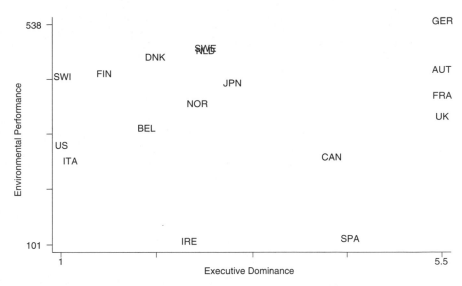

Figure 6.2 Executive Dominance and Environmental Performance

Switzerland).[12] The evidence only weakly supports the idea that having multiple parties in a government increases environmental performance.

To test for the impact of separation of powers *within* national government, I look at the bivariate evidence for executive dominance and the cameral structure of the legislature. Figure 6.2 demonstrates that there is also no systematic relationship between the strength of the executive and environmental performance. The correlation is .09, effectively zero. For bicameralism there is likewise very weak evidence of any relationship. Figure 6.3 shows that unicameral Finland, Sweden, and Denmark have enjoyed good environmental performance, while more bicameral Canada, Italy, and Spain have enjoyed lackluster performance. However, unicameral Ireland and strongly bicameral Germany and Switzerland deviate from the pattern substantially. Ireland has a highly asymmetrical bicameral system and very poor environmental performance, whereas the strong bicameralism in Germany and Switzerland has not prevented good environmental performance since the 1970s. The overall correlation is −.13.

Federalism also has no systematic impact on environmental performance. As Figure 6.4 demonstrates, good performers have both high

---

[12] Although it may appear that Spain and Ireland are outliers, the correlation is actually somewhat closer to zero (−.25) if they are excluded.

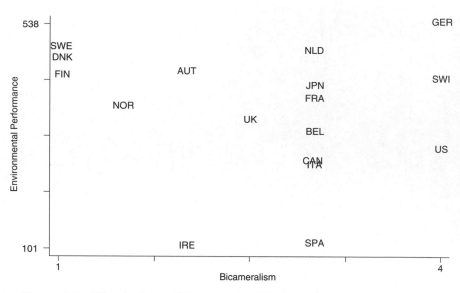

Figure 6.3   Bicameralism and Environmental Performance

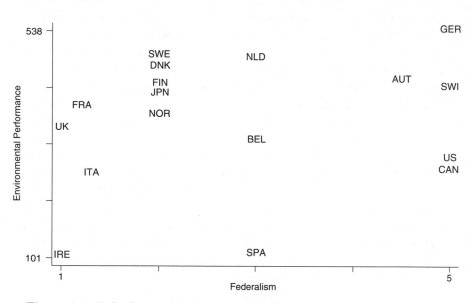

Figure 6.4   Federalism and Environmental Performance

180

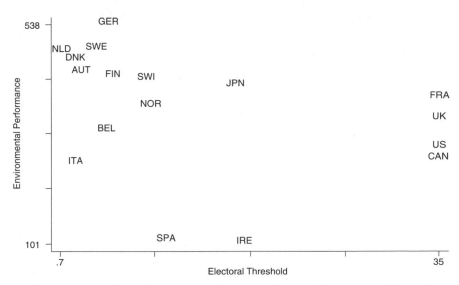

Figure 6.5   Effective Electoral Threshold and Environmental Performance

(Switzerland and Germany) and low (Sweden and Finland) levels of federalism, as do poor performers (Canada and the United States, and Ireland and Italy, respectively). Thus, while there are certainly disputed advantages and disadvantages of federal systems for achieving good environmental results, there is no systematic evidence favoring one general arrangement among the seventeen advanced democracies in this study.

Next, I examine the relationship between PR electoral systems and performance in two ways. First, I directly examine environmental performance under the assumption that better representation of diffuse environmental interests translates into better outcomes. Figure 6.5 shows that the lower barriers to entry for new parties are, the higher is environmental performance. There is a weak overall association between electoral system threshold and environmental performance. ($-.34$, p < .18). If one excludes the plurality electoral systems, the relationship between electoral threshold and performance among the PR systems is considerably higher ($r = -.53$, p < .06). All four plurality electoral systems, in contrast, score below the median. There are several deviations from the pattern. Italy has a proportional electoral system, but poor performance; Belgium combines a proportional electoral system with at best moderate environmental performance; and Japan combines a relatively high electoral threshold and moderate performance.

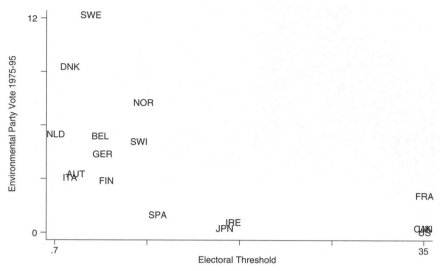

Figure 6.6   Electoral Threshold and Environmental Party Support

Thus, it appears that proportional representation is influential in promoting better environmental outcomes. Given the correlation between electoral threshold and environmental party vote seen in Figure 6.6 and vote and performance, there is a reason to suspect that effects of proportional electoral systems are manifested in the support for environmental parties. It is not clear whether this relationship will hold up in multivariate analysis. Moreover, it is hard to say from simple correlations exactly how proportionality assists environmental performance – that is, whether through creating "space" for the representation of environmental parties or by enhancing the pursuit of collective goods by virtue of the fact that politicians in PR systems are less tied to a narrow local constituency.

In addition to considering the effects of political institutions separately, an alternative approach is to combine the measures in a way that captures meaningful conceptual and empirical distinctions among countries. This approach will be necessary to reduce the number of explanatory variables, because there are only seventeen cases. As in previous chapters, my approach to reducing the data is based on criteria (following from the discussion in the previous section) for what variables should theoretically go together.[13]

---

[13] This contrasts with Lijphart's use of factor analysis to combine variables without clear underlying theoretical reasons. As a search for patterns in democracy, this may not be problematic (though compare Lijphart 1984), but when those patterns are used to help explain economic and social outcomes, it is not clear what those "factors" represent. This

Federal-unitary government is logically grouped with the previously combined executive dominance and bicameralism to define a country's institutional Veto Structure (or separation of powers). This concept of veto structure is similar to one provided in the literature on the political economy of the social policy (Huber, Ragin, and Stephens 1993, 1997; Huber and Stephens 2001; Immergut 1992). The extent of coalition government and the electoral threshold comprise a second combined measure that I refer to as the degree of Multiparty Politics. Both of these variables affect the likelihood of having environmental issues prominently represented within the chambers of political power.

The combined (and standardized) scores for both combined variables are presented in the last two columns of Table 6.1. The bivariate correlation between environmental performance and both of these measures results in what one would expect. A higher Multiparty Politics score – more proportional representation and larger proportion of coalition governments – is negatively correlated with environmental performance ($-.40$) as expected. There is no correlation between Veto Structure and performance ($-.01$).[14]

In summary, the bivariate evidence suggests that only two of the main dimensions of difference in democratic political institutions have much impact on environmental performance. More frequent coalition government and a higher degree of proportional representation are both associated with better cross-national environmental performance. There is an even stronger correlation if these two features coexist.[15]

Multivariate Analysis

This section examines the impact of the political institutions previously discussed in multivariate regression models. This permits controls for different political institutions simultaneously, as well as variables identified in previous chapters as having potential impacts on environmental performance. The models build on those from previous chapters and thus

---

makes it difficult to accept his correlation analyses – say, between economic performance and the "parties" dimension – as a satisfactory causal explanation.

[14] The party government correlation is negative because a higher score on both Electoral Threshold and Coalition Government implies less proportionality.

[15] Although there may be a conceptual affinity between these two features of party politics, there is not one in fact. First, among PR systems there are variations in the extent of minority versus coalition government; single-party minority governments are classified as single-party. Second, among plurality systems, presidentialism (France and the United States) provides an opportunity for de facto coalition government that is absent in nonpresidential systems. For this reason, there is independent variation along both institutional dimensions.

test the validity of previous findings with the independent impact of political institutions.

Recall from the previous chapter that the model of performance to this point includes measures of income (and its square), geographical advantage, environmental mobilization, and measures of the prevailing patterns of interest group coordination and policy-making concertation in each of our seventeen countries. Table 6.2 presents results from this model adding the political institutional measures separately. For ease of exposition (and because the results are similar for the other measures), I report only the results using Siaroff's Integration score as a measure of corporatism. I also dropped the environmental mobilization term, because the estimates are imprecise (and counterintuitive) and there is no value for Switzerland. I present estimates with and without the income-squared term.

For only one of the *individual* political institutional variables is there an impact on environmental performance that is distinguishable statistically from zero: Executive Dominance. That result provides some support to the hypothesis that a more unified government leads to better results. The sign of the estimates for Federalism is also consistent with the claim that more unified governments (i.e., those with fewer veto points) have better environmental performance. The estimates for Bicameralism and Single-Party Government are (respectively) negative and positive, although the signs of each coefficient changes when the income-squared term is included in the model. On balance, this provides additional (albeit somewhat weaker) support for the hypothesis that unified and accountable governments have enjoyed better environmental performance than have more divided government.

The stark difference between the multivariate and bivariate results for Single-Party Government and Electoral Threshold demonstrates how including controls can affect inferences in small samples. The sign of Electoral Threshold estimates, once controls are introduced, is the *opposite* of what the bivariate correlation suggests. The critical control in this case appears to be corporatism.[16] Indeed, if we ignore the higher standard error, the

---

[16] Although the two variables are correlated ($r = -.77$), the addition of Corporatism variables reverses the sign of the point estimates for Electoral Threshold. Collinearity does not bias point estimates; it simply inflates standard errors. However, omitting an important variable (such as Corporatism) from the model does introduce bias. Further analysis suggests that the collinearity between Corporatism and Electoral Threshold does inflate the errors for the latter, but not substantially (2.47 vs. 2.68). Indeed, the standard error for Electoral Threshold is stable (2.30 to 2.68) in alternative specifications.

Table 6.2. Regression Results: Political Institutions and Environmental Performance

Independent Variables	Baseline		Single-Party Government		Executive Dominance		Bicameralism		Federalism		Proportionality/Electoral Threshold	
Political institution			−.06 (.52)	.37 (.61)	15.4 (10.4)	25.0** (9.9)	5.6 (22.8)	−10.7 (27.3)	−3.5 (13.3)	−13.0 (15.5)	2.7 (2.1)	3.6 (2.6)
Integration	49.6** (16.5)	65.2*** (19.5)	49.1** (17.9)	67.4*** (20.3)	57.5*** (16.7)	70.9*** (16.5)	52.9** (21.9)	58.1* (27.1)	50.2** (17.4)	65.9*** (19.7)	75.1** (25.7)	97.9*** (30.0)
Geographic advantage	9.6 (10.8)	16.4 (13.1)	8.9 (12.9)	20.3 (14.8)	11.9 (10.4)	17.0 (11.0)	7.5 (14.2)	20.2 (16.6)	9.8 (11.2)	16.5 (13.3)	12.4 (10.7)	19.6 (12.9)
Income (1975)	21.7*** (6.6)	3.0** (1.0)	21.9*** (7.1)	3.2** (1.1)	16.7** (7.1)	3.4*** (.01)	22.0*** (6.9)	3.3* (1.3)	21.3*** (7.0)	3.5** (1.2)	19.8*** (6.6)	2.3* (1.1)
Income squared	−.00094** (.00033)		.00096** (.00036)		−.00068* (.00036)		−.00097** (.00036)		−.00092** (.00036)		−.00088** (.00033)	
Constant	−987*** (304)	−148 (106)	991*** (320)	−197 (134)	−837** (307)	−290** (105)	−1019** (343)	−126 (124)	−970*** (324)	−170 (110)	−994*** (297)	−235* (120)
Observations	17	17	17	17	17	17	17	17	17	17	17	17
Adjusted R^2	.77	.64	.75	.62	.75	.75	.75	.62	.75	.63	.78	.66
Turning point	11,543		11,406		12,279		11,340		11,576		11,250	

Note: Standard errors in parentheses.

* $p < .10$; ** $p < .05$; *** $p < .01$.

Table 6.3. *Regression Results: Separation of Powers, Party Government, and Environmental Performance*

Veto structure	−11.3	−23.5**		
	(11.9)	(10.6)		
Party government			6.9	17.4
			(14.1)	(16.2)
Integration	47.8**	53.9**	56.2**	79.7***
	(16.7)	(17.9)	(21.7)	(23.6)
Geographic advantage	15.3	25.0*	12.3	22.2
	12.4	(12.1)	(12.4)	(14.1)
Income (1975)	18.1**	4.5***	20.7**	0.03**
	(.076)	(1.2)	(.071)	(.010)
Income squared	−.00073*		−.00089**	
	(.00040)		(.00036)	
Constant	−850**	−266**	−962**	−200
	(338)	(107)	(319)	(116)
Observations	17	17	17	17
Adjusted R^2	0.77	0.72	0.75	0.64
Turning point	12,397		11,629	

Note: Standard errors in parentheses.

* $p < .10$; ** $p < .05$; ***$p < .01$.

estimated improvement in environmental performance from moving from the highest (35.0) to the lowest (.7) score for Electoral Threshold falls from about +110 points (+80 if the income squared term is included) to −110 (−90) points when Corporatism is added.

The effect of more Single-Party Government changes from positive to negative when the income-squared term is added. The marginal (negative) bivariate relationship also disappears once controls are introduced. In this case, entering any of the other variables (i.e., income, geography, corporatism, or environmental mobilization) alone or in combination renders the estimate of Single-Party Governments substantively and statistically insignificant.

Table 6.3 reports regression results using the two combined measures, Multiparty Politics and Veto Structure. As before, estimates are reported both with and without the income-squared term, and Environmental Mobilization is excluded to preserve degrees of freedom. Again, including it in the models does not significantly alter the reported coefficient estimates themselves, which suggests that omitting it does not bias estimates. The results in the table differ considerably from the bivariate results in the last section. First, the estimated effect of the party government dimension of political institutions has no significant effect. Estimates for the other variables are largely unchanged when the Multiparty Politics variable is added, suggesting that this variable adds no new information.

Second, the estimated effect of Veto Structure – the combined degree of federalism, bicameralism, and executive dominance over the legislature – does systematically impact environmental performance, *but only if the income-squared term is excluded from the analysis*. This contrasts with the weak bivariate correlation but is consistent with the findings in Table 6.2. Holding other variables constant, going from the most divided and "veto-prone" institutional arrangement (executive legislative balance, strong federalism, and strong bicameralism) to the most unified arrangement (dominant executive, unicameralism, and unitary government) improves environmental performance by almost 160 points. If both income-squared and Veto Structure are included (column 1), the former is statistically significant at $p < .10$, but the latter is not significant. Because the two variables are correlated (.59), we would expect the standard errors of both to be higher.

Income and Environmental Performance Reconsidered

Because income and veto structure are significant if the other is excluded from the model, which should be excluded? The argument in favor of accepting a "separation-of-powers effect" over the "income-squared effect" is ultimately more compelling. As mentioned in Chapter 3, most economists looking at the relationship between income and environmental performance empirically have dismissed the income-squared effect as being the product of a few "anomalous" cases.[17] A greater separation of powers "explains" the anomaly of poorer performance in those very rich countries – United States, Canada, and Switzerland (the only countries with incomes over the estimated turning points in *any* of the models estimated) – that do more poorly than their income, geography, and other factors predict. In other words, lower environmental performance in these three countries is due to the fact that their very decentralized political institutions make it more difficult to deal with diffuse benefit-concentrated

---

[17] The significance of the income-squared term in the more fully specified model depends critically on two extreme cases, Ireland and the United States. For reasons discussed at greater length in the next chapter, this further justifies accepting the political explanation over the "income-squared" one.

cost problems like environmental protection, not that they are "too rich."

Advocates of "limits to growth" might insist that beyond a certain point more income leads to worse environmental performance and that income is as good an explanation of performance as political institutions. There are several problems with such an argument, however. First, many of the existing empirical and theoretical accounts reject this conclusion. Second, it does not provide a compelling reason to draw the line between Sweden or Germany and Switzerland or the United States. Without any clear reason to believe that the income of the latter countries crosses the line between "sustainable abundance" and "unsustainable abundance," the estimates here (and in the EKC literature more generally) are perhaps anomalous. Third, the political institutional explanation helps to account for one other outlying case in addition to Switzerland, Canada, and the United States. Belgium, which is otherwise expected to have a high environmental performance score, is a highly fragmented political system.

A problem for giving precedence to the institutional explanation (Veto Structure) is that its effect is sensitive to which other variables are included in the model. This implies that the estimates are not very robust, and such results warrant caution. As for the robustness of the "income-squared effect," we have seen previously that it is quite robust empirically.

In summary, separation of powers (i.e., the Veto Structure variable) receives fair, though somewhat ambiguous, empirical support as an explanation of environmental performance. Given the thin theoretical reed that supports the competing explanation – that Canada, Switzerland, and the United States are simply too rich – it seems more reasonable to favor the institutional explanation.

Conclusion

This chapter has examined the role of political institutions and their effects on national environmental performance. Although scholars differ about the impact of most of these institutions on performance, the analysis here found only one systematic relationship between political institutions and performance. Political democracies in which political power is more unified tend to have, all else equal, better environmental performance than those in which power is more divided. As suggested in the first section of this chapter, the main reason to expect more unified political power to be effective in promoting environmental performance is that unity allows democratic governments to provide public goods, such as environmental protection, that have diffuse benefits and concentrated costs. This logic is similar to that suggested in the previous chapter.

For some, these results may not come as a surprise. In many domains, political scientists have suggested that the concentration of power better enables democratic regimes to regulate powerful interests in the public interest than does an arrangement providing for more balance between branches or levels of government. Indeed, some of the early work following the emergence of the limits-to-growth debate suggested that a more Hobbesian state might be necessary to curb environmental problems (Ophuls 1977; Heilbroner 1980). Unlike previous work in comparative environmental policy, the current study provides the first rigorous statistical support (weak though it may be) for this contention in the area of environmental policy. Although the results rest on a limited number of observations and are subject to some important qualifications, they are consistent with this set of institutional arguments. On the other hand, the results of this chapter show that there is little evidence for the effect of other differences in political institutions that have often been emphasized in the literature on environmental protection. Some of these findings may be surprising or controversial given the importance sometimes attributed to such differences.

The results and analysis here may shed some light on why competing claims have been either highly disputed or indeterminate. First, competing claims often analyze the effects of particular institutional arrangements (federalism *or* dominant executives). This chapter suggests that, considered singly, individual attributes of divided power (such as federalism) are *not* correlated with environmental performance. However, when one considers *configurations* of individual institutions that are commonly thought to divide or concentrate power within countries, the more general impact of having divided or unified political power emerges more clearly.

Another consideration suggested here is the importance of controlling for alternative explanations of environmental policy performance in multivariate models. Environmental outcomes are complex phenomena, undoubtedly with multiple partial explanations; this implies the need for multivariate analysis. The results here clearly demonstrate that looking at bivariate relationships alone can be quite misleading.

Although some might interpret these results as undermining the utility of political decentralization, such a conclusion would still be premature. The results do point to a dilemma in environmental policy that is common in

189

politics, but support for concentrated power should not be exaggerated. Left to their own devices, larger groups of "independent" actors tend to have greater difficulties coordinating their actions (even if they are internally well organized) to avoid environmental problems. This problem was widely recognized even by Coase (1960), who is often considered an advocate of "decentralized" solutions to externality problems. Overcoming "diffuse benefit, concentrated cost" problems can often be facilitated by centralized institutions, provided that they can effectively aggregate general interests, compel compliance, or otherwise help actors to coordinate their behavior in mutually beneficial ways (Taylor 1987). There is not always a guarantee that they will. The necessity of centralization for the solution of collective action problems remains a central question in political theory and is certainly not answered here.

7

Checking the Robustness of the Results

All too often, the results of statistical tests turn out to be fragile. That is, when one or two minor changes are made in the data or the variables in the model, originally compelling results turn out to be much less so. This issue is particularly critical in a comparative study such as this one, which relies on statistical analysis and a limited number of observations (Bernhard 1998; Bollen and Jackman 1985; Granato, Inglehart, and Leblang 1996; Jackman 1986; Western 1995). The previous chapter touched on one such problem in trying to adjudicate between competing empirically valid explanations for the same phenomenon. Given the general problems of measurement error in the concepts studied here and some of the particular problems with the environmental outcome data discussed in Chapter 2, demonstrating that the overall findings are "robust" lends them further validity.

Diagnosing Influential Observations

Bollen and Jackman note at the beginning of their article on influential cases in statistical analysis:

Regression analysis is a powerful tool in social research because it helps to identify and summarize relations between variables. The emphasis on generalization is critical: Among the many assumptions that statistical analysis involves is the idea that a minority of observations does not determine the obtained results. We are justly skeptical of empirical results that are unduly sensitive to one case (or a very small number of observations). (1985: 510–11)

To illustrate how this can happen, consider the following example. Figure 7.1 is a scatterplot of two variables. An OLS regression, similar to

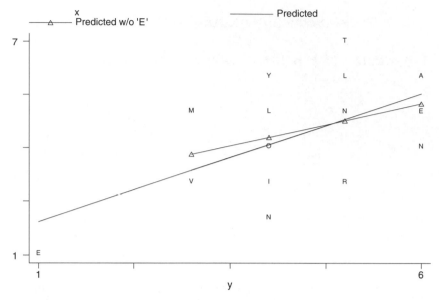

Figure 7.1   Statistical Effect of an Influential Observation

that employed in the preceding chapters, suggests that there is a statistically significant, positive relationship between X and Y. A point change is Y associated with a .72 point change in X, and the estimated interval is statistically different from zero. Furthermore, knowing Y helps to explain about 30 percent of the variation in X. As may be obvious, this statistical relationship is the result of a single influential value E. If we omitted that observation and recomputed the results, the estimated effect of Y on X is less than .5, the estimate is not statistically different from zero, and knowing Y explains almost no variation in X. Thus, a single piece of information has moved us from "something" to "nothing."

Because one of the main arguments of this book is that our understanding of environmental policy can benefit from more of a "large-n" comparative analysis, heeding this caution is important. At various points in the book, I have attempted to point out instances where a statistical correlation (or its absence) was due to outlying observations.[1] I have also attempted to bolster my main argument with more detailed information

---

[1] Bollen and Jackman (1985) assert that the term "outlier" refers to observations that are somewhat distinct from the other observations in a data set. This does not necessarily mean that results are unduly influenced by that observation.

about particular cases. Here I look a bit more formally at the results once all of the main explanatory factors (structural, cultural, and institutional) are specified.

Bollen and Jackman suggest several diagnostic tools for determining if there are influential cases. Table 7.1 provides information on several of the tests they describe. Each test shows the relevant statistic for each observation; the statistic can be evaluated against the "critical value" in Table 7.1 to determine if the data point is an "outlier," justifying further inspection to ascertain how it affects the results.

Given the ubiquity of these procedures in statistical software packages, which, like Bollen and Jackman, discuss the underlying math, I do not provide a technical discussion here. However, it is worth briefly mentioning what these tests mean. The "hat matrix" provides an estimate of the impact of each individual country observation on the dependent variable. In other words, it tests for the presence of observations that have high "leverage" on the statistical estimates. (In the example provided in Figure 7.1, point E has a hat matrix value of .51, almost two times the cut-off value of .27.) The studentized residuals show the error associated with each observation. An error beyond two standard deviations is considered "large," and the effect of such an error is to reduce the "fit" of the model or an individual paramter. The *Dfits* test, in essence, multiplies the first two tests in a summary measure of influence. Finally, the *DFBeta* test examines the influence of each observation on each of the individual coefficients estimated in the regression. This test can thus identify an observation that has a large impact on a particular coefficient, even if it has a limited impact on the power of the model as a whole. Table 7.1 provides scores on these tests using the "final model" from Chapter 6." That model is

Environmental Performance $= \beta_0 + \beta_1$ Income (1975)
$+ \beta_2$ Geographic Advantage
$+ \beta_3$ Veto Structure $+ \beta_4$ Income
$+ \beta_5$ Corporatist Integration $+$ Error

The tests suggest three potentially influential or outlying cases: Ireland, Germany, and Belgium.

Of course, identifying potential statistical outliers does not tell us what to do with them. On the principle that one should be conservative in rejecting a null hypothesis, outliers are a problem when they reduce or inflate parameter estimates (i.e., have undue *leverage*), as observation "E" does in Figure 7.1. In addition, by "making exception" for a case that has *a large*

Table 7.1. *Test Statistics for Influential Cases*

Statistic	Description	Critical Value	Cases Exceeding Critical[a]		
			Corporatism	Concertation	Integration
Diagonal of "hat matrix"	Influence that observation i has on the predicted value of dependent variable	$3p/n$ (.71)	None	None	None
Studentized residuals	Influence that the error variance of observation i has on the total error variance	t-score (1.96)	Germany (2.75)	Germany (2.81)	Germany (2.67)
Dfits	Combined influence exerted by effects of A and B	$2\,(p/n)^{1/2}$ (1.08)	None	Ireland (−1.21)	Belgium (−1.10) Germany (1.08)
DFBetas	For each variable (x), the impact of removing i on the value of x	1.00	None	None	None

[a] Country (score) is identified where critical value is exceeded.

residual, we might find more statistical support for a hypothesis than we otherwise would.

Germany and Belgium both increase the *error* in the model; they also have a modest effect on two of the individual coefficient estimates – Veto Structure and Geographical Advantage, respectively. Germany has a decentralized political system but, as we know, had the highest environmental performance. If Germany is excluded from the calculations, the Veto Structure estimate is much more pronounced (and more precisely estimated). This is shown in the results reported in Table 7.2. Germany's good environmental performance, despite its formal system of separated power, is notable for one other reason as well. If Germany is excluded, Veto Structure has a much stronger negative impact on environmental performance than does Income Squared (results not shown). This reinforces the decision in the previous chapter to accept the theoretically driven political explanation over the more empirically based U-shaped income effect.

In contrast to Germany, Belgium is an outlier primarily because its environmental performance is uncharacteristically poor for a small and densely populated country. Indeed, the size and precision of the Geographic Advantage estimate is much greater if Belgium is excluded from the estimation. Notably, Belgium is a marginal outlying case. It exceeds the critical values of the test statistics only when integration is used as the proxy for corporatism.

If both Germany and Belgium are removed from the integration model estimation, the results are even more impressive. All estimates are now significant at better than $p < .01$, and the model explains almost 85 percent of the variance (adjusted). Of course, this better fit follows directly from the fact that both observations were poorly estimated by the model.

Ireland, which is also influential only in one version of the final model (Corporatist Concertation), has a combination of moderate influence and a large negative residual. Like Belgium, it performs somewhat worse than predicted by the model. As the results in Table 7.2 show, removing Ireland reduces the magnitude of the *income* coefficient considerably and also reduces the magnitude of the coefficients for Veto Structure and Geographic Advantage. Although neither of the latter terms are statistically significant at conventional levels when Ireland is excluded, both estimates are in the expected direction and different from zero at $p < .25$. The estimate for Concertation, on the other hand, is somewhat higher when Ireland is excluded. This is again not that surprising because Ireland has a low performance level and a moderate degree of concertation.

Table 7.2. *Regression Results: Predictors of Environmental Performance Dropping Influential Cases*

Independent Variables	Economic Integration (Siaroff)				Corporatism (Lijphart & Crepaz)		Corporatist Concertation (Lehmbruch)			
	All Cases	Without Germany	Without Belgium	Without Germany & Belgium	All Cases	Without Germany	All Cases	Without Germany	Without Ireland	Without Germany & Ireland
Income	4.5	4.8***	4.6***	4.8***	4.7***	4.9***	5.2***	5.3***	3.9**	4.2***
	(1.2)	(.01)	(1.0)	(.9)	(1.2)	(1.0)	(1.3)	(1.0)	(1.5)	(1.1)
Geographic advantage	25*	24.5**	33.3**	31.3***	28.5**	26.9**	27.2*	24.5*	20.9	19.0
	(12.1)	(9.9)	(11.8)	(9.6)	(12.7)	(10.2)	(14.6)	(11.7)	(14.5)	(11.2)
Veto structure	−23.5**	−28.6***	−21.3**	−26.3***	−21.1*	−26.6**	−20.7	−25.9**	−15.9	−21.4*
	(10.6)	(8.9)	(9.7)	(8.1)	(11.8)	(9.7)	(13.1)	(10.6)	(12.9)	(10.1*)
Corporatism	53.9**	46.9***	52.4***	46.5***	54.0**	48.4**	49.3*	46.9**	54.9**	51.9**
	(17.9)	(14.8)	(16.2)	(13.3)	(21.3)	(17.3)	(24.6)	(19.6)	(23.7)	(18.2)
Constant	266**	−278***	−260**	−272	109	140	−246*	−265**	−122	153
	(107)	(87)	(97)	(79)	(123)	(99)	(123)	(98)	(143)	(110)
Adjusted R²	0.72	0.80	0.79	0.85	0.68	0.78	0.64	0.75	0.57	0.72
Observations	17	16	16	15	17	16	17	16	16	15

Note: Standard errors in parentheses.
* p < .10; ** p < .05; *** p < .01.

Robustness of the Results

Table 7.3. *Regression Results: OLS and Robust Estimates*

Independent Variables	OLS	Boot-strapped Residuals (1,000 reps)	Bounded Influence	Biweight/ Robust Regression
Income (1975)	4.5***	4.5**	4.4***	4.6***
	(1.2)	(1.5)	(.9)	(1.2)
Geographic advantage	25.0*	25.0	25.3**	25.7*
	(12.1)	(14.9)	(9.4)	(13.1)
Veto structure	−23.5**	−23.5**	−22.2**	−25.2**
	(10.6)	(10.6)	(8.4)	(11.5)
Integration	53.9**	53.9**	54.6***	50.9**
	(17.9*)	(21.7)	(13.5)	(19.3)
Constant	−266**	−81	−249	−271**
	(107)	(193)	(93)	(116)
Adjusted R^2	0.72		.80	
Observations	17	17	17	17

Note: Standard errors in parentheses.
* $p < .10$; ** $p < .05$; *** $p < .01$.

Several studies point out that simply dropping observations that appear to be "deviant" is an extreme solution because it discards information. Although certain observations may appear to unduly influence statistical inferences under normal assumptions, this does not imply that they should be discarded. Such deviant cases can also be handled using less familiar "robust regression" techniques. Alternative methods for calculating estimates are discussed in Granato et al. (1996) and Western (1995). Table 7.3 reports the traditional OLS, Welsch's bounded influence, biweight (robust) regression, and bootstrapped residual estimates and standard errors. The results indicate that all estimated parameters (with the possible exception of Geographic Advantage) are robust.[2]

Do the Results Hold in Europe Only?

Most of the countries (fourteen) included in the analysis in this book are in Western Europe. In addition to their grographical proximity, these countries are notably different from the three other countries in the sample – the United States, Canada, and Japan. For instance, all of the Western European

---

[2] With the exception of veto structure, model parameters in equations using alternative measures of corporatism are also robust to these alternative estimation procedures.

Table 7.4. *Regression Results for Western European Countries Only*

Independent Variables	OLS	Boot-strapped Residuals (1,000 reps)	Bounded Influence	Biweight/ Robust Regression
Integration	51.8**	53.9**	51.8	49.4*
	(22.6)	(33.4)	(16.8)	(23.7)
Income (1975)	4.9***	4.9***	5.1***	5.0***
	(1.4)	(1.5)	(1.3)	(1.5)
Geographic advantage	22.5	22.5	23.4*	23.7
	(17)	(21.1)	(12.9)	(17.8)
Veto structure	−24.4	−24.4	−20.2	−27.5*
	(13.7)	(22.1)	(12.4)	(14.4)
Constant	−295**		−308***	−302
	(118)		(101)	(124)
Adjusted R^2	0.72		0.82	
Observations	14	14	14	14

Note: Standard errors in parentheses.
* $p < .10$; ** $p < .05$; *** $p < .01$.

countries are comparatively small and (with the exception of Switzerland) had much lower incomes in the 1970s than did the United States. This raises a potential objection that, although no individual cases influence the results, unique features of the non-European countries (particularly Canada and the United States) collectively influence the results considerably. To see, I estimated the Integration model with only the European countries included.[3] The results, reported in Table 7.4, reinforce the findings in the full set of countries. Comparing the results with Table 7.3, for example, the estimates and errors are quite similar. The overall (adjusted) variance explained is the same as it is in the full model. The only real discrepancy among individual coiefficients is for per capita income: its estimated impact is *larger* in Europe alone than in the entire sample. This is not too surprising, however, because two of the three excluded countries combine poor performance and high wealth, while the third (Japan) combines a low starting period income level with moderate environmental performance.

[3] Given that the Integration variable is the only one of the three to take explicitly into consideration changes during the later 1980s and 1990s, it could be considered a more accurate indicator of corporatism over the period as a whole. The other measures of corporatism produce consistent but slightly weaker results, particularly for Geographic Advantage and Veto Structure.

Robustness of the Results

Revisiting the Environmental Performance Indicator

As a final check on the robustness of the results, we turn to the measures used in defining the dependent variable. Applying the same logic as we just did to the analysis of influential observations, we can also investigate the possibility that our model for explaining environmental performance is based on the influence of one of the components of the environmental performance index. Just as we would not want to make a generalization about a statistical relationship that is due to a single observation, we would not want to conclude that our model explains environmental performance if our results depend critically on the precise variables in the index. This possibility is checked in two ways. First, each of the six measures is eliminated; second, the model is tested against two measures of environmental performance developed elsewhere, one with a similar methodology to the one used for this study, and another using a considerably different design.

Table 7.5 shows the results of the model when each component of the index is excluded. For each excluded item there are three sets of estimates. The first set is the OLS coefficients. The second set shows the standardized coefficients, reported to provide some basis for comparing the impact of each excluded variable.[4] The third set of results shows the estimates using the Welsch bounded influence procedure. This approach is preferred over the other two methods just reported in Table 7.4 because it limits the impact of large "outlying" and "influential" observations on the estimates.

Ideally, varying the components in the analysis should have little to no impact on the coefficients. However, given the small number of cases analyzed and the limited number of available environmental performance components, more variation is possible. The estimates in Table 7.5 do suggest some variation, but the results are very robust. All estimates in the OLS models are in the direction previously found. Save one (the effect of Veto Structure if water treatment coverage is excluded), all are also significantly different from zero at least at the 10 percent level. The bounded influence results are even more compelling. All of these estimates are in the expected direction and (save one) are estimated within a 95 percent confidence interval.

---

[4] Dropping a component of the performance index changes the mean, range, and standard deviations of the dependent variable. The degree of change depends on which performance component is dropped. This makes it impossible to compare the nonstandardized estimates in the table. Because the independent variables are unchanged across the estimates, the betas for a given variable do have a meaningful comparative interpretation from one set of results to another.

Table 7.5. *Results Dropping Individual Environmental Performance Index Measures*

Independent Variables	Baseline b	Baseline Beta	Baseline Bounded Influence b	SO_x Excluded OLS	SO_x Excluded Beta	SO_x Excluded Bounded Influence b	NO_x Excluded OLS	NO_x Excluded Beta	NO_x Excluded Bounded Influence b	Waste Excluded OLS	Waste Excluded Beta	Waste Excluded Bounded Influence b	Recycling Excluded OLS	Recycling Excluded Beta	Recycling Excluded Bounded Influence b	Fertilizer Excluded OLS	Fertilizer Excluded Beta	Fertilizer Excluded Bounded Influence b	Water Treatment Excluded OLS	Water Treatment Excluded Beta	Water Treatment Excluded Bounded Influence b
Income (1975)	4.5*** (1.2)	.72	4.4*** (.9)	3.6*** (1.0)	.72	3.7*** (.7)	3.8*** (1.1)	.66	3.6*** (.7)	3.6*** (.9)	.66	3.3*** (.7)	4.3*** (1.1)	.81	4.1 (.9)	3.8*** (1.0)	.78	3.8*** (.8)	0.037 (.011***)	.66	3.5*** (1.0)
Geographic advantage	25.0* (12.1)	.35	26.2** (9.4)	20.6* (10.5)	.35	23.2** (7.7)	20.3* (11.0)	.26	20** (7.9)	24.5** (8.9)	.36	24.1*** (6.8)	25.2** (11.4)	.41	24.7** (9.0)	17.9 (11.0)	.32	22.0** (7.9)	22.2* (12.1)	.34	20.3** (9.0)
Veto structure	−23.5** (10.6)	−.37	−22.2** (8.4)	−18.1* (9.1)	−.35	−17.8** (6.9)	−18.7* (10.3)	−.38	−20.6*** (3.0)	−12.6 (8.3)	−.29	−13.9** (6.1)	−24.6** (10.0)	−.46	−23.3** (7.9)	−19.0* (9.7)	−.38	−18.8** (7.2)	−18.4 (10.6)	−.32	−17.4* (8.7)
Integration	53.9* (17.9)	.48	54.6*** (13.5)	41.6** (15.4)	.46	42.9*** (11.2)	55.1** (18.6)	.56	54.5*** (11.0)	58.6*** (14.9)	.55	51.6*** (10.5)	33.2* (16.8)	.35	31.6** (12.7)	35.2** (16.2)	.40	32.3** (11.2)	50.8** (17.8)	.50	50.0*** (13.2)
Adjusted R²	.72		.80	.69		.82	.69		.85	.79		.86	.66		.71	.63		.73	.67		.73
Observations	17		17	17		17	17		17	17		17	17		17	17		17	17		17

Note: Standard errors in parentheses.

* $p < .10$; ** $p < .05$; *** $p < .01$.

The other test of the robustness estimates the same model using two independently derived measures of environmental performance as dependent variables. The first, developed by Jahn (1999), evaluates performance on several pollution measures over the period 1980–90. Some pollution problems used in this measure are similar to the ones used in this study, though most are not. For instance, he includes several items for which there are not comparable data for the 1970s, like hazardous waste, or no measure of change over time.

The second measure is the Environmental Sustainability Index (ESI), developed by the World Economic Forum, Yale Center for Environmental Law and Policy, and Center for International Earth Science Information Network (2001). It combines measures of current environmental systems, stresses on those systems, human vulnerability to such disturbances, capacity to respond to environmental problems, and global stewardship. Unlike Jahn's measure and my own, the ESI does not measure change over time. The data coverage in the ESI is much spottier than Jahn's or my own index.[5] Finally, it includes many "environmental" indicators – the portion of GDP devoted to *any type* of R&D, infant mortality, the prevalence of infectious disease, deaths from natural disasters – that might be considered tangential to national environmental performance (or sustainability) per se. For this reason, I use both the overall index and a subindex, composed of measures closer to those used here.[6]

Although, for a variety of reasons, neither of these measures constitutes as good a measure of comparative environmental performance in the modern environmental era as the index developed for this study, they do serve as independent confirmation that my results are not an artifact of my particular construction of the dependent variable. We would generally expect results (with the exception of Geographic Advantage for reasons to be explained) to be consistent with the findings presented thus far.

Table 7.6 presents the regression results and associated betas. Two facts should be kept in mind when interpreting the results. First, Jahn's index is inverted: good performers receive a low (not a high) score. Thus, we would expect all estimates to have the opposite sign compared to our measure.

---

[5] Because the ESI has a global frame of reference, the data issues that they confront are enormous. But even for countries in my sample, there are serious problems. For instance, all data for the *entire* water quality component of their index are missing for six of the seventeen countries.

[6] I used the average scores for the environmental system, environmental stress, and global stewardship items of the ESI.

Table 7.6. *Regression Estimates with Alternative Performance Indicators*

Independent Variables	Jahn (1999)[a]	Beta	ESI (2001)	Beta	SSG Components Only	Beta
Income (1975)	−.20	−.27	1.4	.31	.07	0.14
	(0.12)		(1.1)		(.11)	
Geographic advantage	−3.97***	−.46	−3.54**	−.68	−5.09***	−0.82
	(1.24)		(1.20)		(1.20)	
Veto structure	1.45	.19	−1.21	−.25	−1.16	0.21
	(1.08)		(1.05)		(1.05)	
Integration	−8.15***	−.61	3.97**	.47	5.16**	0.53
	(1.82)		(1.76)		(1.77)	
Constant	117.0***		39.2***		30.9**	
	(11)		(10.6)		(10.6)	
Adjusted R^2	.80		.52		.63	
Observations	17		17		17	

[a] Jahn's measure is inverted (100 = worst performance).
* $p < .10$; ** $p < .05$; *** $p < .01$.

Second, the range of these dependent variables is considerably lower than my environmental performance index. (Jahn's index ranges between 53 and 100, while the ESI Index ranges only between 44 and 80.5.) Because of this, we would expect the coefficient estimates to be lower.

Despite the limitations of these alternative indices of performance, the results in the table suggest that the model performs well. Using Jahn's measure, both the Corporatism and Geographic Advantage are precisely estimated ($p < .01$) and their substantive impact is substantial.[7] Going from the least to most corporatist country results in a predicted decrease in Jahn's index of about 24 points which is about half of the observed range of the dependent variable. The corresponding prediction for Geographical Advantage is just about the same; for income it is 16 points, and the estimate is almost significant at $p = .10$. Veto Structure does not have a strong substantive effect and is the least precise estimate in the model.

For ESI and the System, Stress, and Global (SSG) subindex of the ESI, the results, though weaker, are also reasonably good, particularly for neocorporatist institutions. The sign for Geographic Advantage is the opposite

---

[7] Estimates restricting the sample to only European countries are similar to these. The results using the ESI resemble the OLS estimates, although they are weaker for reasons discussed earlier.

of what we found using the other two dependent variables. That is, all else equal, small densely populated countries score lower on the ESI (SSG), and the effect is significant. Going from the most advantaged to the most disadvantaged results in a predicted effect of about 21 (30) points of the range of the index; this is more than half (three-quarters) of the observed variance.

The reversal in sign for Geographic Advantage does not, in fact, contradict my earlier findings due to the particular way the ESI is constructed. The authors of the ESI get many of their sustainability measures by dividing pollution by land area and measuring at a single point in time (the late 1990s). All else equal, this implies that their measure will likely report a lower sustainability score in smaller, more crowded jurisdictions. Moreover, the logic behind the argument that population density and limited geographic area result in better performance over time is based on the presumption that such countries have more intensely felt problems. The negative coefficient in the estimate is consistent with a greater intensity of problems within a smaller country. The negative coefficient for my (and Jahn's index) show that this problem is more likely to be mitigated over time.

Conclusion

The validity of statistical results conducted on a limited number of cases – a common problem in the comparative politics – is sometimes undermined by the influence of one or two "outlying" cases or deviations from assumptions of normality.[8] This study, a cross-national comparison of seventeen countries, is certainly vulnerable to such problems. This chapter has demonstrated that the positive empirical results obtained are not generally attributable to "rogue observations" or the specific items included in our measure of the environmental performance. The results for the positive impact of corporatist institutions are particularly robust. Countries characterized by more encompassing producer interests and consensus-based policy making are generally associated with better environmental performance, whereas countries with more pluralist forms of economic interest organization and policy making are robustly associated with poorer performance. The positive association between environmental performance and smaller country size and higher population density is less robust. Even in this case, however, the evidence points suggestively in that direction.

---

[8] The impact of environmental mobilization (conditional on the other variables in the model) is not robust if included in these models; the estimates typically retain a negative sign but are generally not statistically different from zero at any reasonable cutoff point.

8

Conclusion

The paucity of studies in the comparative political economy literature that address environmental problems is somewhat surprising. First environmental protection is an important political issue. Since before the oil shocks of the 1970s, it has been one of the three most important social issues, often polling ahead of the traditional items of economic performance – growth, unemployment, and inflation. Second, environmental quality is a collective good that simultaneously affects human well-being and is intimately associated with economic production. The provision of collective economic "goods" (growth, low prices, full employment, etc.) is a common subject in comparative political economy, making the lack of attention to environmental outcomes all the more exceptional. Finally, the physical environment is a fundamental component of social risk that is a critical issue around which politics and economics interact.

Why does this oversight persist? There are several explanations. First, there has been a tendency to treat "environmental politics" (by both traditional political economists and by environmental policy specialists) as something that is fundamentally different from traditional political economy subject matter. The intellectual roots of environmental politics challenge much of the materialist and distributional consensus that is taken for granted in the study of contemporary political economy. For this reason, environmental policy has been consigned to a realm that is not very relevant to material welfare.

A second reason for the lack of attention to environmental issues comes from more serious and reasoned objections to the theories that placed environmental issues on the intellectual map. Most notable are the debates about value change and the debate over "limits to growth," both of which have been central elements in the development of the environmental issue.

204

Conclusion

For instance, most political economists tend to reject or ignore Inglehart's (and others) cultural explanations of political change. While the objections have merit, this should not diminish the importance of environmental pollution as a pressing policy issue worthy of closer study. Comparative political economy should be making stronger efforts to address environmental protection as a new issue among traditional mainstays of production and distribution.

A third reason for the lack of attention may be (or may have been) data. There has been relatively little available empirical data with which even to talk about "national" environmental performance in the same way as one can talk about the economic or political performance of nation-states. This may have placed limits on research historically, but since at least the 1980s, the available data have increased considerably. Although it remains true that many of these data are hard to use in systematic comparison, there is a growing body of cross-nationally comparable data at the disposal of social scientists. The OECD data used here are perhaps the most comprehensive, though far from being perfect or perfectly comprehensive.

A major purpose of this study has been to assess empirically how well many of the existing explanations of cross-national variations in structures, attitudes, and institutions account for differences in actual environmental outcomes. Given the various hypotheses (implicit and explicit) about the determinants of environmental performance, this study has drawn from a diverse array of the existing literature. It cannot claim to have produced a complete synthesis. However, it does constitute some progress, which may be summarized in the following six main findings.

First, *advanced democracies experienced a range of success in reducing major types of environmental pollution during the first two and a half decades of the environmental era.* Although there are signs of improvement in many areas and in most countries, there has not been the convergence often predicted in the environmental policy literature. Moreover, countries that do relatively well in one area of pollution control also tend to do relatively well in other areas. This suggests that good (bad) environmental performance may well be attributable to factors that extend beyond the idiosyncrasies of a particular pollutant, making it meaningful to speak of national environmental performance and its determinants.

Second, *an important and significant explanation for variations in national environmental performance is per capita income.* Among the wealthy nations analyzed in this study, higher national per capita income is associated with better environmental performance. However, the specific mechanisms through which higher income has been alleged to produce better performance – for example, reductions in some sources of pollution via economic structural change – are not as clearly associated with cross-national differences in performance. Thus, the prevailing (mostly) economic theories specifying why income should matter tend to do poorly in statistical models. (Of course, this does not mean that such changes are irrelevant altogether.) On the other hand, income does appear to be somewhat correlated with higher demand for environmental protection, although perhaps much less mechanically than economists sometimes assume. Finally, the empirical results suggest that, even if income is independently important, there are other important factors involved in explaining cross-national variations in environmental performance. For instance, we found in Chapter 3 that higher income is not by itself linearly associated with environmental progress. Indeed, the richest countries in the OECD have had worse performance than more middle income countries. And we found in Chapter 4 that, although per capita income did correspond to higher levels of mobilization (based on a variety of indicators), it explained no more than one-third of aggregate variation across advanced democracies. In other words, generating higher national wealth is not the simple answer to better environmental performance, but neither is limiting economic development per se.

Third, *differences in the political geography of countries also have an impact on environmental performance.* Larger size and lower population density make it easier to "avoid" dealing with some pollution problems, either because they can be "hidden" or because they were less acutely felt to begin with. Differences in "geographical advantage" help to account for why large and sparsely populated countries such as Canada and the United States have performed so poorly in the last two and a half decades, whereas smaller and more densely populated countries such as the Netherlands stand perhaps as world leaders in environmental performance. On the other hand, some relatively large and sparsely populated countries (e.g., Sweden) have good performance, and some small, densely populated countries, such as Belgium, do comparatively poorly.

Fourth, *there is little evidence that variations in public opinion or cultural attitudes – which are widely associated with environmental values – are robustly associated with differences in national environmental performance.* Although some measures of values and opinions are moderately correlated with performance in a bivariate analysis, these results do not stand up to more demanding multivariate tests. Indeed, most of the multivariate statistical models suggest that, all else equal, more mobilization is worse for performance.

Conclusion

These findings are important in light of the fact that the dominant political theories of environmental reform politics stress the importance of citizen opinion and attitudes, and the mobilization of environmental opinion in obtaining environmental reforms. Although the results should not be taken to mean that public opinion has a negative effect on performance (mobilization rose between the 1970s and 1990s in all countries considered here, and performance in all countries improved to some extent), it does strongly suggest public demand per se is far from sufficient in accounting for results.

In light of the effects of political and social institutions, one might be tempted to argue that public opinion has affected outcomes via institutional change. However, the institutional arrangements discussed in Chapters 5 and 6 were established in all cases before a marked rise in environmental awareness and for reasons that were quite independent of such opinion. Neocorporatist institutions were established to deal with macroeconomic problems and existed quite independently of environmental concern. (Indeed, Chapter 5 explained how many view such institutions as antithetical to environmental protection.) The formal political institutions discussed later in this chapter and in Chapter 6 were established well before environmental concerns were an issue. Thus, it is difficult to argue that public opinion about the environment causes the important institutional effect identified here. At the same time, it is worth stressing that, although the institutional arrangements found to be important here tend to predate environmental mobilization, this does not imply actors operating within these institutions would have taken up environmental issues in the absence of the general growth in environmental awareness and concern in advanced democracies since the 1970s.

The fifth main finding is that *the organization of economic interests and the relationship between such interests and the government is systematically associated with environmental performance.* This relationship holds true for a variety of alternative measures of the same underlying concept. Performance in countries with a combination of organized and encompassing economic interest groups as well as high levels of consensual policy making and implementation between companies, workers, and governments (and to varying degrees environmentalists) was much better than performance in those countries where interest groups were weakly organized, fragmented, and more confrontational.

The means by which such institutions produce better performance are complex. However, they work via the cooperative nature of firms' interaction with each other and their workers, cultivated amiable relations between business associations and government, generalized systems of compensation, information sharing, the incorporation of environmental groups interests, and, finally, interest group encompassingness. These factors interact to help reduce cheating among firms, reduce compliance costs, compensate potential losers, and permit the government to have somewhat more ambitious (and efficient) regulatory policy. Although cooperation does not imply the absence of conflicting objectives or emphases among groups, it is a mode of resolution of such conflicts that appears to promote rather than hinder progress over time.

This result stands in contrast to assumptions of many in the environmental community and in the environmental literature who suggest that cooperation in economics and regulatory policy ensures that the public good will be sacrificed in the pursuit of particularistic interests due to the hegemonic status of antienvironmental ideas. Yet it also contrasts with a widely held view among businesses that environmental regulation is best resisted until imposed. The contrast between my findings and the environmental literature is all the more stark when one considers that the neocorporatist style of politics has also been reasonably successful in generating relatively good economic performance even into the 1990s. Thus, neocorporatism appears to be conducive to both economic and environmental success.

Finally, the study suggests that *more centralized, democratic political institutions produce better environmental outcomes than do institutions that fragment constitutional political authority*. This lends credence to arguments that strong, centralized democratic authority facilitates both the pursuit of diffuse benefits as well as the imposition of concentrated costs. Both are often essential in environmental regulation. As with the good results for corporatist institutions, this finding also tends to diverge from some of the environmental politics literature, which argues for greater decentralization of political authority as essential to environmental progress. It is worth reiterating that this finding is less robust than most of the others.

These six main findings, coupled with the theoretical arguments as to why certain institutions will promote the pursuit of collective goods better than others, demonstrate the substantive importance of institutions in affecting substantive social outcomes, even when the original purpose of those institutions was to deal with somewhat different problems. Thus, the beneficial effects of neocorporatism and centralized political structures represent an example of the unintended consequences of institutions. In contrast to many examples of unintended consequences, these appear to be fortuitous (at least from a social perspective).

In addition to the implications for institutionalism, this study and its results make several other contributions to the study of comparative politics. First, as alluded to at the beginning of the chapter, this study begins to bring environmental performance into discussions of the comparative political economy of democratic performance. Given the growing importance of the environment to human welfare, processes of production, and the scope of government intervention into the economy, comparing macroenvironmental performance is as important as traditional forms of macroeconomic performance. Second, this study sets some new challenges and/or questions for neomodernization theories. They need to provide more thorough explanations for why public opinion, economic structural change, or postmaterialism seems to make little difference for environmental performance.

Finally, the results of this study further the case for adopting corporatist-style social institutions. Adopting institutions solely for consequences that are tangential to their direct function – regulating relations between businesses, labor, and government – is probably ill-advised. However, the ability of such institutions also to help deliver good environmental performance should be seen as another merit for reform in that direction. The argument that neocorporatist institutions might be strengthened in the context of environmental policy is perhaps provocative and leads to a discussion of some of the limitations of this study, as well as potential objections to its applicability in different areas or time periods.

The first objection pertains to the absence of detailed case studies that link specific institutional features represented in the statistical analysis to actual decisions (public or private) that lead to improved performance. Although this objection was part of the motivation for including the "country profiles" in Appendix II and for including a variety of controls, alternative specifications, and hypotheses in the statistical analysis in Chapter 5, neither truly answers this objection. Such case studies would involve a more extensive investigation into the relationship at various levels of the dense network of institutions. Some strong evidence of environmental corporatism that produces the effects that I expect might include consensual yet stringent environmental standards that were generally complied with; evidence that firms actively shared information relevant to pollution-related matters with others in the association and/or received such information from others; signs that associations (or those within the firm itself) would

209

crack down on cheaters (or that firms at least believed that they would and governments knew that they would); and evidence that these relationships and processes made firms more willing to accept environmental protection and adopt more proactive environmental policies.[1]

The second and third objections have to do with the continued viability and advantage of neocorporatist institutions (or centralized, democratic political institutions) in the face of European integration and economic globalization more generally. One might argue that the process of globalization and regional integration (particularly in Europe) eliminates all but the most trivial differences in the ways that countries can react to environmental issues. The EU has, in the 1990s at least, taken a much more proactive approach to environmental policy. The British have perhaps bristled more than any other country at the thought of making policy European-style, but environmental policies have undoubtedly been affected in both environmentally progressive (Germany, the Netherlands, Sweden, Denmark) and laggard countries (Spain, Italy). According to this argument, the largest source of variation in the institutional features of advanced democracies may gradually disappear as the EU comes to dominate environmental policy.

While European integration will undoubtedly lead to pressures for convergent policies (countries must adopt an increasing number of EU directives into law), the effects in terms of policy styles and outcomes have been appreciable and should remain so. This trend is reinforced by the importance attached to subsidiarity in the EU, which helps to preserve different arrangements. In addition, most neocorporatist countries have had open economic systems and have tended to adapt their economies toward sustainability without resorting to protectionism. Thus, at least the broader economic changes of integration that could undermine cooperative aspects of these systems (competition from countries with lower standards or wages) should be manageable, while preserving distinctive differences of implementation. Moreover, it is possible that the corporatist approach could diffuse more readily as a result of integration. Although this trend might eventually reduce the variation in national practices, such a move

[1] Wilson (2002) reports that one effort to develop neocorporatist style institutions for environmental policy at the state level in the United States involved fact-finding trips to Germany and the Netherlands to gain firsthand experience of such institutions in action. Although the fact that these two countries were used as models of environmental neocorporatism does not prove that such institutions work, it is strongly suggestive of how those policy-making arrangements and their efficacy are viewed internationally.

Conclusion

would nevertheless suggest convergence toward institutions that produce better, rather than worse, outcomes.

A related objection to integration is that the economic pressures of the globalization of finance and production (among other things) have undermined the ability to maintain viable neocorporatist networks (Kurzer 1993; Rodrik 1997). If these broader forces undermine the economic viability of neocorporatism, then there may be reason to expect this effective approach to environmental policy to crumble along with it. There are two reasons to be more sanguine, however. First, the evidence that globalization has fundamentally undermined corporatist institutions in these countries may be overstated (Kitschelt et al. 1999; Hall and Soskice 2001). Corporatist policy approaches appear to be surviving, despite some setbacks (Blom-Hansen 2001; Christiansen 1996). For example, much of the decline in corporatist boards in Scandinavian countries can be traced to streamlining and reorganizing the public sector, not with the power of peak interests per se, particularly when it comes to implementation (Christiansen and Rommetvedt 1999: 199–201; Blom-Hansen 2001). The case of corporatist decline attracting the most fanfare – Sweden – has been shown to be slightly exaggerated (Stephens 2000; Lundqvist 2000; Pestoff 1999).[2]

A second reason to be more optimistic is that the success of corporatist environmental policy may make it feasible on its own terms. Consensus seeking, extensive involvement of major groups at the policy-making stages, and shared responsibility by associations of regulated actors in the outcomes of government policy may be conducive to effective environmental policies independent of economic policy. Some countries, such as the United States, appear to be taking steps in environmental policy to emulate the consensus building and cooperative approach of corporatist countries (Caldart and Ashford 1999).

At the same time, it is important to stress the point that the success of "environmental corporatism" and consensus policy making and implementation are predicated on institutions that mediate the relationship between economic and social actors and governments. Thus, my results should not be taken to suggest that granting more flexibility to individual businesses in the area of environmental regulation in the name of a greater consensual policy making (as some, for example, have suggested in the United States)

[2] For instance, the legislation "undoing" corporatism replaced "official group" representatives with "individual" ones from the same sectors of society. In the case of employers, the confederation supplied information to the members and debriefed them.

constitutes a neocorporatist policy solution. As I have argued in this book, a more consensual approach to policy making more generally is essential to promoting cooperation and effective environmental progress. For example, promoting encompassing interest organizations among employers, workers, and environmental or consumer groups; the ability to strike broad "compensation" agreements; and a regulatory environment that is less hostile to negotiated outcomes would all be important (Spence and Gopalakrishnan 2000).[3] Such reforms might start with simply putting environmental, labor, business, and government officials in a room together, but must entail much more than that. Whatever the future holds, a major implication of the analysis in this study is that it is incorrect to make the desire to improve environmental policy a reason for getting rid of corporatist institutions.

A fourth objection to the results in this study is that the results are unique to the time period and environmental problems considered. For instance, once the time scale is extended to cover, say, 1970–2010, then the relative performance of corporatist countries will look less compelling, if for no other reason than that some countries will attain very low levels of pollution while other countries will slowly catch up. Similarly, objections might be made that the data considered cover only traditional, end-of-pipe environmental problems. In many respects, these are empirical questions. For the data up to 1995, there is not much of an argument that looking at say 1970–90 or 1980–95 makes a difference (Jahn 1998; Scruggs 1999, 2001). Whether the argument will remain true in, say, 2020 is hard to judge.

Using different performance measures of pollution could also matter. Ultimately, this type of empirical objection is difficult to answer, as it can be made about any data set or scientific claim; but I have attempted to do so. As discussed in Chapter 2, the types of pollution considered in this study cover all environmental media and are broad (i.e., not simply the traditional "point-source" problems); and my performance indicator is correlated with results elsewhere. Moreover, other evidence (admittedly more anecdotal) suggests that "source reduction" methods of reducing pollution

---

[3] Spence (1995) argues that the regulatory regime in the United States is based on the assumption that public support for environmental protection generally is poor. To the extent that an inefficient regulatory system increases the cost of regulation, the system can be a self-fulfilling prophecy because it produces more resistance (on economic-cost grounds) than it needs to. Spence's argument provides a greater place for environmental mobilization than indicated here, suggesting that the U.S. environmental movement is in part responsible for growth in public environmentalism.

are most advanced in precisely those countries with more consensual policy making and highly organized and encompassing economic groups (i.e., corporatist countries) – for example, Sweden, Denmark, and, to a lesser extent, Germany. Finally, the results at the end of Chapter 7 using alternative environmental performance indicators are consistent with my own.

In addition to the future avenues of further research I have already discussed, there are two, perhaps more ambitious, questions to be asked about environmental performance . The first is to determine the actual costs and benefits of pollution reduction across countries. Such a study would take a giant step forward in seeking to integrate the demand for environmental protection with broader elements of the political economy. It might also help to ascertain if environmental protection is actually cheaper under more consensual-corporatist institutions. This remains a popular claim among advocates of more consensual policy making, but one that has not really been tested.

In the past three decades, environmental issues have gone from being of minor concern to becoming one of the dominant topics of academic and policy discussion. A major reason is the growing realization that in the struggle to subdue the natural world – a project that has dominated Western society (if not all of humankind) – we have failed to consider some of the implications of success. Reconciling human well-being with continued environmental well-being remains an incomplete challenge. The results of this study suggest that, given certain institutional arrangements, the two appear to be more easily reconciled.

Estimated Measures of Environmental Performance

The purpose of this appendix is to explain how particular missing endpoint values were estimated in Tables 2.1–2.6.

NO_x and SO_x

Missing values in 1975 were estimated based on average changes in the other countries in the period 1970–75 or 1975–80 (-1.9% for SO_x in 1975 and -15.7% in 1970 and 18.7% for NO_x). Missing values for 1970 were not considered for NO_x because there were a large number of missing values (six) and no country (with data) experienced a decline in the period.

Waste

Values for Canada, Finland, and the Netherlands in 1975 were estimated based on the per capita growth in private consumption between 1975 and 1980 (Christiansen and Fischer 1999).

Denmark Data reported by the OECD for Danish waste generation in 1995 (560 kg/person) are based on a new estimation methodology and appear higher than the level reported for 1985 (480 kg/person). However, studies based on the new methodology (Andersen 1999a) indicate that waste generation fell considerably between 1987 and 1996 (due in part to a new waste tax enacted in the late 1980s and expanded in the early 1990s). The waste level reported for 1995 in Table 2.3 uses the old series (1985 value) as the base and the index of change (1987–96) calculated by Andersen. This produces a value for 1995 that is consistent with the rest of the series.

United Kingdom   The United Kingdom introduced both a new method of counting waste *and* a new aggregation unit in 1995. Prior to 1995, reported figures included only England and Wales. From 1995, reports included all of the United Kingdom. The new method of counting is not comparable with the old series. Unlike the Danish case, there are no time series estimates (e.g., between 1990 and 1995) based on the new formula. To get a consistent series, I estimated the 1995 waste generation level from the 1990 value and an index of per capita private consumption growth for 1990–95. This follows the method in Christiansen and Fischer (1999) mentioned earlier.

United States   Fischer and Crew's criteria for cross-sectionally comparable waste streams correspond (more or less) to three categories of waste reported by the EPA (1999): nondurables, container and packaging, and food and yard waste. Those figures (in thousands of tons) for 1996 in the United States were 55,500, 69,050, and 49,770, respectively. The total (174,320) is approximately 83 percent of the reported total waste generated.

Recycling

Estimates for 1980 for glass recycling in Spain, Norway, and Sweden are based on trends among their neighbors – Finland and Denmark for Sweden and Norway, France, and Italy for Spain. The comparative recycling scores generated from Equation 2 are not sensitive to whatever estimate is used for these countries because of the magnitude of gains between 1985 and 1995.

Wastewater Treatment

Information from national sources (in the Netherlands, the United States, and Canada) and the fact that a range of plausible estimates does not significantly affect the scores in Ireland and Spain suggest that the scores provided are reasonably accurate.

Canada   The 1970 coverage rate was estimated to be 30 percent, reflecting trends in the United States and policies in place (which resemble the U.S. program) to expand treatment coverage. Modern expansion of sewage treatment accelerated with government financial support to municipalities between 1961 and 1978. This and other information from officials at Environment Canada suggest that coverage increased from the mid- to late 1960s. Nevertheless, large portions of the population, particularly in Quebec, were apparently not covered through the late 1970s. For instance, Canadian data suggest that Montreal, Canada's largest city and metropolitan area, had no major municipal treatment facility until the 1980s.

Ireland I assumed coverage in 1970 to be half of what was reported in 1980. Alternative estimates for 1970 have only a marginal impact on country scores due to a lower bound of zero and extensive growth after 1980.

Italy I added 10 to the 1990 score to estimate the 1995 score. This is consistent with expansion efforts to upgrade treatment due to EU directives.

Netherlands Officials at the Dutch environment ministry (VROM) indicate that coverage improvements from 1970 to 1975 were negligible. I used 50 percent as an estimate. In any case, the marked improvements since 1975 make its score insensitive to the 1970 estimate.

Spain As with Ireland, I assumed coverage in 1970 to be half of what was reported in 1980. Alternative estimates for 1970 have only a marginal impact on country scores due to a lower bound of zero and extensive growth after 1975.

United Kingdom The coverage rate in 1970 is estimated to be 60 percent, thus resembling the levels and patterns in Germany and Sweden as well as other advanced Northern European countries. Alterations in this estimating assumption do not change the results significantly.

United States The 1995 value was estimated using secondary-tertiary coverage data, plus the difference between the figures for total and secondary-tertiary coverage in 1990 (EPA 1999: 26).

Fertilizer

The 1995 figure for Germany is based on West German data in 1989 and index of change from unified Germany statistics for 1991–95. (Estimates for West Germany alone are not available after 1990.) The change from the united Germany from 1990–91 is omitted in order not to overstate change in West Germany. The overuse of fertilizers was infamous in Eastern Europe generally and market liberalization and economic restructuring make it likely that consumption reductions in the East would explain more of the total declines in the first couple of years after unification. (Data for 1990 suggest that declines were much more rapid in the East.) Most of the West German declines in fertilizer use (> 90 percent of them) occurred between 1970 and 1990, years with separate statistics for West Germany.

Institutions for Environmental Policy Making in Fourteen Countries

This appendix briefly characterizes the degree of corporatism in environmental policy-making institutions that was summarized in Table 5.1. These descriptions should be taken as evidence demonstrating that national approaches to environmental policy resemble traditional approaches to policy making. Countries included in the environmental performance measures that do not have entries here are not covered due to a lack of data on their environmental policy institutions.

Austria (strong)

Austria has a long tradition of consensual policy making based on tripartite bargaining between peak economic interest organizations and the government in most major policy matters. The prevailing approach to environmental policy has also been one of cooperation and consensus seeking between the industry and labor confederations and the state. In its review of Austrian environmental performance, the OECD (1995a) noted that the regulatory instruments upon which Austrian environmental policy was constructed in the 1970s and 1980s were extensively negotiated with these social partners. There was also close cooperation between public authorities at all levels (federal, state, and local) and the private sector. Business and labor interests participate in official discussions in legislative process and in the chambers of commerce. A recent project report, the Joint Environmental Policy-Making Project, characterized Austria as having a "corporatist" policy-making style (JEP 1998).

One problem area in Austria has been the limited formal participation of environmental groups. The OECD, for example, suggested that such groups have been influential in particular cases but mainly as a result of protest rather than full incorporation into the process. There was an abortive discussion to creating an Environment Chamber to mirror the Chambers of Labor and Industry. Thus, while Austrian corporatist institutions are less successful at integrating environmental interests fully, the country is still considered to have "strong" corporatist environmental policy-making institutions.

Canada (very weak)

Canada has been strongly influenced by the U.S. experience and approach to environmental regulation (Hoberg 1991). Although there is some evidence of consultation with major interest groups during the drafting of the more recent Green Plan in Canada, such cooperation was notably absent historically (OECD 1995b). There is not a high level of trust and cooperation between business and regulators (Webb 1988; Thompson 1980). Moreover, Canadian economic interests are not highly centralized, there is no participation by more "pro-environmental" interests (environmental or consumer groups or unions), and there is little tradition of corporatist policy-making institutions in other areas of Canadian social regulation.

Harrison (1995) does suggest that there are some elements of regulatory enforcement that are more "cooperative" than in the United States, for example, limited sanctioning of violations and more flexibility. Her description emphasizes, however, that the institutional conditions spelled out for a concerted-consensual approach to environmental regulation fall well short of deserving a "corporatist" label.

Denmark (very strong)

The Danish policy style in some ways resembles the Austrian approach: consensus seeking among major economic interests (again, unions and industry, but also agriculture) throughout most of the postwar era. (Membership in Danish economic peak associations – the Danish Confederation of Trade Unions and Danish Confederation of Industry is widespread but not, as in Austria, compulsory.) That this approach carries over into the area of environmental regulation in Denmark is also noted by various studies (Blom-Hansen 2001; Anderson 1997; Moe 1995; Wallace 1995). Pollution control has been negotiated with the centralized industry association since the early 1970s; and labor organizations are also involved in the creation of regulations. Environmental groups are integrated into the policy-making and implementation process as well (JEP 1998). Finally, regulations are designed with the participation of the powerful National Association of Local Authorities. Moe (1995) suggests that the municipalities are particularly powerful in environmental matters because they operate many pollution creating and abatement facilities (waste retrieval and disposal, energy production facilities, and wastewater treatment centers).

Unlike other corporatist countries, the Danes do not generally use official advisory boards for general environmental issues. However, the use of an administrative court of appeal on environmental matters is borrowed from the Danish tradition of extensive use of administrative courts. The court is composed of representatives from the interested parties. The environmental appeal board was a concession to industry, which wanted an independent final arbiter rather than arbitration by the Ministry of Pollution. This board, composed of representatives of industry, the environmental ministry, and legal experts, has at times acted to restrain an "overzealous" Environmental Protection Agency. According to Wallace, the board of appeal was a compromise with industry groups and "was a powerful symbol of the government's willingness to listen to the concerns of industry.... With hindsight, this early concession may be seen as a pointer to the level of trust which was subsequently to be built up between the two parties" (1995: 26).

Finland (very strong)

Although Finland is typically characterized as being somewhat of a late adopter of neocorporatist institutions, from at least the 1970s, Finnish pollution control policy has been generally characterized as following a corporatist environmental policy (Joas 1997: 133–34). Moreover,

In both fields of water and air pollution, the public governing mode has been based on legal state regulation, but in a manner of negotiative problem-solving [*sic*]. One of the basic principles of the consensual style has been the continuous pursuit of a common framework of understanding for policy making. This kind of policy style has also been called *negotiated rule-making* in contrast to *command-and-control regulation*. (Sairinen 2000: 148–49)

Government commissions, working groups, and committees have been quite important in the Finnish system of environmental policy, providing a forum for conflict resolution and consensus building early in the process. The importance of such groups, as well as the representation of various stakeholders, has increased considerably since the 1970. Moreover, as in most other strong corporatist countries, the central interest group confederations (economic *and* environmental) are important shapers of public opinion on environmental issues.

France (weak)

France's approach to policy making has typically been interpreted as highly centralized and *dirigiste*. A small coterie of commonly and professionally trained bureaucrats is influential in the control of policy making as well. This approach shows up in many aspects of environmental policy. There is no formal procedure for consulting with industry groups (which are not highly organized), although the process of consulting with the powerful Industry Ministry might be considered a substitute of sorts for negotiations with a peak corporatist body because the ministry enjoys a close relationship with firms. The code of environmental laws is comprehensive, to the point of being overly complex, but is often not well enforced. Implementation occurs under the authority of different levels of government, but there is little coordination-negotiation between central and local governments. This contrasts with corporatist countries, such as Denmark, where coordination and negotiation between levels of government are extensive.

Economic and environmental decision making are relatively well integrated at the industry level. This is due in part to "the existence of a corps of government inspectors who thoroughly review permit applications and inspect licensed facilities; and partly to the fact that urban planning and civil protection regulations are taken into account from the outset of the licensing process" (OECD 1997b: 28). There is not, however, much evidence of consultation with other affected parties – local, environmental, consumer, or worker organizations (all poorly organized) – in the drafting or implementation of environmental legislation or regulations. Thus, the level of "corporatism" in French environmental protection can be considered weak overall.

Western Germany (strong/very strong)

The German system of environmental protection embodies many aspects of the corporatist model, including a prominent role for associations in making and implementing policy. Weidner (1996) explicitly characterizes the structure of environmental policy making as "ecological neocorporatism" (cited in Lenschow 1997), due to its policy progressiveness *cum* the relative exclusion of public interest groups in more "technical matters" (Pehle 1997). Policy making tends to rely on a consultation and advisory process drawing information from experts, from within industry and without. The tradition of cooperation between firms and the state has a long history in Germany, and the institutionalization of associational representation is so great that ministries tend to tell firms to communicate with them through their associations (Streeck 1983).

In areas like pollution emission controls, "the dominance of the implementation stage by experts from . . . the government and the firms has in practice come close to self-regulation" (Paterson 1989, cited in Aguilar Fernandez 1994). However, this "self-regulation" exists under the shadow of stringent standards. This institutionalized relationship was established in the environmental arena during the late 1960s to facilitate the new Social Democratic coalition's ambitious environmental program and in line with the party's explicitly cooperative approach to policy making. In their discussion of modern environmental policy in Germany, Weale, O'Riordan, and Kramme note how environmental policy was created within the framework of the general approach to governmental policy in other areas: cooperation in environmental policy "fitted the ideology of economic management prevalent at the time in West Germany. A social market economy could not be managed without cooperation between government and industry, and industry had long been expected to realize its responsibility for matters of social and public concern" (1990: 115).

Germany has been criticized for having a network of policy making that, in contrast to the Nordic countries and the Netherlands, is more exclusionary of public interest groups (i.e., the ecology movement), relying instead on more technical environmental expertise drawn, for instance, from universities. Recent changes suggest that the system is becoming more open to environmental groups. Nevertheless, as with Austria, limited representation of environmental interest groups throughout the period makes it hard to classify Germany with the Nordic countries.

Italy (weak)

The Italian political economy is characterized by a split personality. A huge divide separates the North, which often looks rather "corporatist" (at least at a local level) and the impoverished South. The Italian policy-making system is extremely fragmented and is often characterized as "process oriented" rather than "results oriented," involving little consensus seeking or the development of trust between interested groups (OECD 1994a: 87). Indeed, it develops in part from a large degree of mutual distrust between regulator (state) and regulated (industry) parties. This resembles the situation in the United States.

The predominant mode of resolving environmental policy issues has been closer to the statist models of policy imposition. While the de facto approach is more cooperative, this cooperation tends to be confined to the local level, driven by a desire to keep national-level bureaucrats out. Very recently, the Italian system has enjoyed more cooperative efforts at environmental policy making between employer, worker, and environmental groups (OECD 1994a: 98). These efforts exist at such an early stage, however, that they do not reflect the history of environmental policy making or the general policy style in the period considered here.

Japan (strong)

Japan has hybrid policy-making institutions wherein major elements of policy are negotiated between industry associations and government ministries, sometimes with, sometime without worker involvement. This has sometimes been referred to as "corporatism without labor." Like France, Japan has also often been considered to have a statist system of policy making. Unlike in France, however, industrial associations have a much greater and more autonomous voice in Japan. These industry groups have been involved in environmental policy making and within their own associations have environmental departments (Imura 1997). Thus, Japan can be considered to have stronger corporatist institutions in the area of environmental regulation than does France.

Within the "corporatism without labor" framework, the government has worked in a stringent but flexible manner with industry, and both have taken a highly "macro" and strategic approach to the relationship between the environment and the economy. This not only includes intensive efforts to develop "green technologies," but the Japanese government and industry also have consciously attempted to shift the economy out of a mode that had very high environmental impacts (at least in production) to one with a "greener" environmental profile (Moore and Miller 1994: chap. 2). The absence of a prominent labor element in Japanese-style corporatism, coupled with a very weak organizational presence of environmental groups, has probably prevented greater "social" pressure on industry and government.

The Netherlands (very strong)

The Netherlands has historically been considered a model of consociational-consensus democracy, whereby consensus seeking among associational leaders (in Catholic and Protestant communities) was firmly implanted (Lijphart 1968). Despite the collapse of religious pillarizaton in the late 1960s, economic associations of employers and unions participate on official advisory boards in charge of environmental policy, and consultation is extensive. This includes not only policy areas in the main environmental ministry (Ministry of Health and Environmental Protection) but also in the other ministries with authority over policies with significant environmental components (Bressers and Plattenburg 1997). Since the 1970s, the government has overtly subsidized independent environmental organizations.

There is a high degree of trust between business, labor, government, and even environmental groups, which have become integral parts of the process in the Netherlands, especially since the early 1980s (Cramer 1989; JEP 1998).

Major NGO's [nongovernmental organizations] are consulted on a number of issues and are invited by VROM [environment ministry] to meetings every other month. The government supports the activities of major NGO's by providing some Gld 15 million in annual support and additional resources for specific projects. NGO's and other organizations participate in several covenants with the government. There is even a covenant between Friends of the Earth and potato farmers. (OECD 1995c:131)

This practice has been adopted to reduce divisiveness (but not conflict) between opposing forces and is a clear extension of past consensual practice for dealing with new "conflicts" in society (Tellegen 1981).

Norway (very strong)

The historic approach to environmental policy making in Norway is characteristic of other Nordic countries and of the historic practice in other areas (Peters 1984: 157–70; Christiansen and Lundquvist 1996). Interest groups are given official sanction in the process of decision making, the process is consensual, and the role of peak associations of major economic actors (unions and employers) and subunits of government is extensive. This procedure of consensual bargaining among peak groups has extended to environmental policy making, where environmentalists, scientists, labor

225

groups, officials, and industry consult and negotiate environmental policy (Dalal-Clayton 1996; OECD 1993b; Sveen 1996).

Spain (very weak)

Similar in many ways to France and other countries in Southern Europe, the defining feature of regulation in Spain is statism. The role of interest groups in the public sphere is marginal at best. Aguilar Fernandez (1994: 44) reports that there has been no institutionalized relationship, or formal cooperation, between industry and public officials in the formation of environmental policy. Relationships with the administration operate primarily through a clientilist rather than an associational "collective action" mode. Although there is a closer role between industry and government in the *implementation* of policy, this appears to have been primarily to "collude" in not enforcing policy measures. Industry is generally unable to receive assistance for compliance and is unable to monitor environmental policy developments in the government (Aguilar 1993).

Sweden (very strong)

The Swedish institutional system is often held as the model of liberal corporatism, in which recognized interest groups participate extensively in public policy matters, often on advisory boards or similar types of arrangements; and policy is subject to ongoing negotiations among the affected parties and decided by consensus. Several detailed studies of the Swedish regulatory process have demonstrated that this process has been relied on extensively in the area of environmental regulation and related areas (Lundqvist 1980, 1997; Kelman 1981; Sahr 1985).

The role of peak industry and labor groups in these governing bodies was, until the 1990s at least, extensive. Moreover, Sweden extended the scope of consensus building extensively in the 1970s to include environmentalists (Ruin 1982). In many respects the effort to incorporate new groups into "legitimate" policy discussions mirrors the approach taken in the Netherlands.

United Kingdom (weak)

Traditionally, Britain has had cooperative relations between the industry and government, including in the enforcement of environmental policy. However, this relationship takes place in a context of highly fragmented interest group organizations and an abortive history of social partnership between government and major social interest groups. The close relationship between particular polluters and regulators has been shrouded in secrecy in most aspects of the regulatory process:

Because the regulatory inspectorates not only set means, but also targets, they possessed a high degree of pragmatic flexibility in pollution control, making it extremely difficult to ensure consistency of treatment and fairness of regulatory requirements.... Ashby and Anderson (1981) pinpointed the apparent failings of the inspectorate, its passion for confidentiality, its apparent arrogance and aloofness, its notorious unwillingness to prosecute and the seeming inconsistency of its highly flexible and discretionary procedures of regulation. (Weale et al. 1990: 147)

In the mid-1970s Britain had arguably moved in the direction of a more neocorporatist model of cooperation between interest organizations of workers, industry, and government. This approach was reflected in the establishment of advisory boards in a number of policy areas, including areas of environmental policy. In some respects, this process mirrored the approach taken in Germany, and for many of the same reasons. However, these institutions were short-lived. Weale et al. note that in the late 1970s, the Confederation of British Industry was unwilling to take on a self-policing role in the area and was happy to be provided with an opportunity to distance itself from tripartite corporatist bodies. The institutions were soon completely discredited by the Thatcher government. Policy making reverted back to more of an insular form.

Thus, while relations between business and regulators may be described as cooperative, it is hard to think of them as neocorporatist either in the sense that they are in Japan or France or, even less so, in the Netherlands or Sweden. There is a vital distinction between a relationship with minimal influence from nonproducer interests (even the "shadow of the law") and what we find in a corporatist institutional system.

In some respects, Britain may typify a pattern of co-optation or capture that many environmentalists fear: a regulatory agency with wide discretion, no appeal, and interacting overwhelmingly (if not exclusively) with a single-faceted constituency (industry) that is generally resistant to greater environmental regulation.

United States (very weak)

The typical characterization of the United States as the personification of the "pluralist" model in environmental policy making is generally appropriate. The U.S. policy system is probably the most contentious and rigid

227

in policy and result of all of the countries surveyed here. Part of the contentiousness is intentionally built into environmental legislation due to the lingering distrust not only of industry but also of government and any close relationship between the two (Buller, Lowe, and Flynn 1993; Hoberg 1991; Kelman 1981; Scholz 1991).

In some respects, the U.S. system might be considered progressive for a "pluralist" country because its regulatory structure has prevented some of the "industry dominance" that is more apparent in other pluralist countries like Canada and Britain. Nevertheless, the U.S. approach rejects consensus. Efforts in recent years to promote consensus building between regulators, environmentalists, and industry have been hampered by the competition to represent members, and the fragmented nature of producer groups (or, for that matter, environmentalists) tends to result in pressure to resist (at least initially) compromise (Andrews 1999: chap. 13; Spence and Gopalakrishnan 2000).

References

Abramson, Paul, and Ronald Inglehart. 1994. "Economic Security and Value Change." *American Political Science Review* 88: 336–54.

Aguilar, Susana. 1993. "Corporatist and Statist Designs in Environmental Policy: The Contrasting Roles of Germany and Spain in the European Community Scenario." *Environmental Politics* 2: 223–47.

Aguilar Fernandez, Susana. 1994. "Convergence in Environmental Policy? The Resilience of National Institutional Designs in Spain and Germany." *Journal of Public Policy* 14: 39–56.

Alt, James, and Alec Chrystal. 1983. *Political Economics*. Berkeley: University of California Press.

Andersen, Mikael Skou. 1994. *Governance by Green Taxes*. Manchester: Manchester University Press.

———. 1997. "Denmark." In Martin Jänicke and Helmut Weidner, eds., *National Environmental Policies: A Comparative Study in Capacity Building*, 157–74. New York: Springer-Verlag.

———. 1999a. "The Waste Tax 1987–1996: An Ex-post Evaluation of Incentives and Environmental Effects." Working report no. 18, Copenhagen: Danish Environmental Protection Agency.

———. 1999b. "Ecological Modernization Capacity: Finding Patterns in the Mosaic of Case Studies." In Ann-Sofie Hermanson and Marko Joas, eds., *Nordic Environments: Comparing Political Administrative and Policy Aspects*, 15–46. Aldershot: Ashgate.

Andersen, Mikael Skou, and Duncan Liefferink, eds. 1997. *European Environmental Policy: The Pioneers*. Manchester: Manchester University Press.

Andrews, Richard. 1999. *Managing the Environment, Managing Ourselves: A History of American Environmental Policy*. New Haven: Yale University Press.

Arrow, Kenneth, et al. 1995. "Economic Growth, Carrying Capacity and the Environment." *Science* 268: 520–21.

Arthur, W. Brian. 1994. *Increasing Returns and Path Dependence in the Economy*. Ann Arbor: University of Michigan Press.

229

Ashby, Eric, and Mary Anderson. 1981. *The Politics of Clean Air*. Oxford: Clarendon Press.

Aspen Berlin Conference. 1979. *Air Pollution Control: National and International Perspectives*. Selected readings prepared in conjunction with Aspen Berlin Conference, April 8–11, 1979. Washington, DC: American Bar Association.

Badaracco, Joseph. 1985. *Loading the Dice: A Five-Country Study of Vinyl Chloride Regulation*. Cambridge, MA: Harvard Business School Press.

Baumol, William, and Wallace Oates. 1988. *The Theory of Environmental Policy*. Cambridge: Cambridge University Press.

Beckerman, W. 1992. "Economic Growth and the Environment: Whose Growth? Whose Environment?" *World Development* 20: 481–96.

Bernhard, William. 1998. "A Political Explanation of Central Bank Independence." *American Political Science Review* 92: 311–27.

Blom-Hansen, Jens. 2000. "Still Corporatism in Scandinavia? A Survey of Recent Empirical Findings." *Scandinavian Political Studies* 23: 157–79.

    2001. "Organized Interests and the State: A Disintegrating Relationship? Evidence from Denmark." *European Journal of Political Research* 31: 391–416.

Boehmer-Christiansen, Sonja. 1995. *The Politics of Reducing Vehicle Emissions in Britain and Germany*. London: Pinter.

Bollen, Kenneth, and Robert Jackman. 1985. "Regression Diagnostics: An Expositor Treatment of Outliers and Influential Observations." *Sociological Methods and Research* 13: 510–42.

Boulding, Kenneth. 1966. "Environmental Quality in a Growing Economy." In H. Jarrett, ed., *Essays from the Sixth RFF Forum*. Baltimore: Johns Hopkins University Press.

Bressers, Hans, and Loret Plettenberg. 1997. "Netherlands." In Martin Jänicke and Helmut Weidner, eds., *National Environmental Policies: A Comparative Study in Capacity Building*, 109–32. New York: Springer-Verlag.

Brickman, Robert, Shiela Jasanoff, Thomas Ilgen. 1985. *Controlling Chemicals: The Politics of Regulation in Europe and the United States*. Ithaca: Cornell University Press.

Buller, Henry, Philip Lowe, and Andrew Flynn. 1993. "National Responses to the Europeanisation of Environmental Policy: A Selective Review of the Literature." In J. Liefferink, P. Lowe, and A. Mol, eds., *European Integration and Environmental Policy*, 175–95. London: Bellhaven.

Buttel, Frederick. 1987. "New Directions in Environmental Sociology." *Annual Review of Sociology* 13: 465–88.

Caldart, Charles, and Nicholas Ashford. 1999. "Negotiation as a Means of Developing and Implementing Environmental Policy." *Harvard Environmental Law Review* 23: 141–202.

Caldwell, Lynton. 1996. *International Environmental Policy*. Durham, NC: Duke University Press.

Castles, Francis. 1999. "De-centralization and the Post-War Political Economy." *European Journal of Political Research* 36: 27–53.

References

Christiansen, Kim, and Christian Fischer. 1999. *Baseline Projections of Selected Waste Streams: Development of a Methodology*. European Environment Agency Technical Report no. 28, September. <http://reports.eea.eu.int/TEC28/en>, June 5, 2002.

Christiansen, Peter Munk. 1996. "Business as Usual? Organized Interests in Danish Environmental Politics." Paper presented at Nordic Political Science Association Conference, Helsingfors, August 15–17.

Christiansen, Peter Munk, and Lennart Lundqvist. 1996. "Conclusions: A Nordic Environmental Policy Model?" In Peter Munk Christiansen and Lennart Lundqvist, eds., *Governing the Environment: Politics, Policy and Organization in the Nordic Countries*, 337–63. Copenhagen: Nordic Council of Ministers.

Christiansen, Peter Munk, and Hilmar Rommetvedt. 1999. "From Corporatism to Lobbyism? Parliaments, Executives and Organized Interests in Denmark and Norway." *Scandinavian Political Studies* 22: 195–220.

Church, Thomas, and Robert Nakamura. 1994. "Beyond Superfund: Hazardous Waste Cleanup in Europe and the United States." *Georgetown International Environmental Law Review* 7: 15–57.

Clarke, Harold, Allan Kornberg, Chris McIntyre, Petra Bauer-Kaase, and Max Kaase. 1999. "The Effect of Economic Priorities on the Measurement of Value Change: New Experimental Evidence." *American Political Science Review* 93: 637–47.

Coase, Ronald H. 1960. "The Problem of Social Cost." *Journal of Law and Economics* 3: 1–44.

Commoner, Barry. 1963. *Science and Survival*. New York: Viking.

Council on Environmental Quality. 1982. *The Global 2000 Report to the President: Entering the Twenty-first Century*. New York: Penguin.

Cramer, Jacqueline. 1989. "The Rise and Fall of New Knowledge Interests in the Dutch Environmental Movement." *Environmentalist* 9 (2): 101–20.

Crepaz, Markus. 1995. "Explaining National Variations of Air Pollution Levels: Political Institutions and Their Impact on Environmental Policy-Making." *Environmental Politics* 4: 391–414.

Cropper, Maureen, and Charles Griffiths. 1994. "The Interaction of Population Growth and Environmental Quality." *American Economic Review* 84: 250–54.

Crouch, Colin. 1993. *Industrial Relations and European State Traditions*. Oxford: Clarendon Press.

Dahl, Robert. 1956. *Preface to Democratic Theory*. Chicago: University of Chicago Press.

Dalal-Clayton, 1996. *Getting to Grips with Green Plans: National Level Experience in Industrial Countries*. London: Earthscan.

Dalton, Russell. 1994. *The Green Rainbow: Environmental Groups in Western Europe*. New Haven: Yale University Press.

Dalton, Russell, and Kai Hildebrandt. 1977. "Die Neue Politik: Politischer Wandel oder Schonwetterpolitik." *Politische Vierteljahresschrift* 18: 230–56.

Dalton, Russell, and Manfried Kuechler, eds. 1990. *Challenging the Political Order: New Social and Political Movements in Western Democracies.* New York: Oxford University Press.

Daly, Herman. 1991. "Elements of Environmental Macroeconomics." In Robert Constanza, ed., *Ecological Economics,* 32–46. New York: Columbia University Press.

Davies, J. Clarence, and Jan Mazurek. 1998. *Pollution Control in the United States: Evaluating the System.* Washington, DC: Resources for the Future.

Dearing, Michelle. 1992. "EC Vehicle Emissions." *Trade and Environmental Database Case Studies.* Case Study No. 21. <http://www.american.edu/projects/mandala/TED/eccar.htm>, September 18, 2001.

DeCanio, Stephan. 1993. "Barriers within Firms to Energy-Efficient Investments." *Energy Policy* 21: 906–14.

Doern, G. Bruce, and Thomas Conway. 1994. *The Greening of Canada: Federal Institutions and Decisions.* Toronto: University of Toronto Press.

Douglas, Mary, and Aaron Wildavsky. 1982. *Risk and Culture: An Essay on the Selection of Technological and Environmental Dangers.* Berkeley: University of California Press.

Downing, Paul, and Kenneth Hanf, eds. 1983. *International Comparisons in Implementing Pollution Laws.* Boston: Kluwer-Nijhoff.

Dunlap, Riley. 1995. "Public Opinion and Environmental Policy." In James Lester, ed., *Environmental Politics and Policy,* 63–113. Durham, NC: Duke University Press.

Dunlap, Riley, and Angela Mertig. 1995. "Global Concern for the Environment: Is Affluence a Prerequisite?" *Journal of Social Issues* 51: 121–37.

Dunlap, Riley, and Richard Scarce. 1991. "The Polls–Poll Trends: Environmental Problems and Protection." *Public Opinion Quarterly* 55: 651–72.

Edelman, Murray. 1964. *The Symbolic Uses of Politics.* Urbana: University of Illinois Press.

Ellis, Richard J., and Fred Thompson. 1997. "Culture and the Environment in the Pacific Northwest." *American Political Science Review* 91: 885–98.

Enloe, Cynthia. 1975. *The Politics of Pollution in a Comparative Perspective: Ecology and Power in Four Nations.* New York: David McKay.

Environment and Developmental Economics 1 (1996): 102–4.

EPA. 1998. *National Water Quality Inventory. 1998 Report to Congress.* <http://www.epa.gov/305b/98report/index.html>, June 5, 2002.

——— 1999. Summary of the 2000 Budget. EPA205-S-99-001, January. <http://www.epa.gov/ocfopage/budget/2000/2000bib.pdf>, November 15, 2000.

——— 2000. Municipal Solid Waste Management: Basic Facts. <http://www.epa.gov/epaoswer/non-hw/muncpl/facts.htm>, November 8, 2000.

Erskine, Hazel. 1972. "The Polls: Pollution and Its Costs." *Public Opinion Quarterly* 36: 120–35.

Esping-Andersen, Gosta. 1990. *The Three Worlds of Welfare Capitalism.* Princeton: Princeton University Press.

References

1999. *The Social Foundations of Postindustrial Societies.* New York: Oxford University Press.

European Environmental Agency. 1998. *Environmental Data Base.* <http://warehouse.eea.eu.int/>, October 20, 2000.

Finnish Ministry of Environment. 2000. *Signs of Sustainability: Finland's Indicators of Sustainable Development 2000.* Helsinki: Ministry of Environment. <www.vyh.fi/eng/environ/sustdev/indicat/inds2000.htm>, November 9, 2000.

Fischer, Christian, and Matthew Crew. 2000. *Household and Municipal Waste: Comparability of Data in EEA Member* countries. European Environment Agency Topic report no. 3/2000. <http://reports.eea.eu.int/Topic_report_No_32000/en>, June 5, 2002.

Food and Agriculture Organization. 2001. FAOStat Agriculture Database. <http://apps.fao.org/>, January 3, 2002.

Garrett, Geoffrey. 1998. *Partisan Politics in the Global Economy.* Cambridge: Cambridge University Press.

Garrett, Geoffrey, and Peter Lange. 1996. "Internationalization, Institutions and Political Change." In Robert Keohane and Helen Milner, eds., *Internationalization and Domestic Politics*, 48–75. Cambridge: Cambridge University Press.

General Social Survey. 1999. Cumulative Data File, 1972–1999. <http://www.icpsr.umich.edu/GSS/>, January 3, 2002.

Gilroy, John, and Robert Shapiro. 1986. "The Polls: Environmental Protection." *Public Opinion Quarterly* 50: 270–79.

Goodstein, Eban. 1994. "Jobs and the Environment: The Myth of a National Tradeoff." Economic Policy Institute, Washington, DC. Mimeographed.

1995. *Economics and the Environment.* Englewood Cliffs, NJ: Prentice Hall.

Granato, James, Ronald Inglehart, and David Leblang. 1996. "The Effect of Cultural Values on Economic Development." *American Journal of Political Science* 40: 607–31.

Grilli, Vittorio, Donato Masciandaro, and Guido Tabellini. 1991. "Political and Monetary Institutions and Public Financial Policies in the Industrial Countries." *Economic Policy* 13: 342–92.

Grossman Gene, and Alan Krueger. 1989. "Environmental Impacts of a North American Free Trade Agreement." In P. Garber, ed., *The US-Mexico Free Trade Agreement*, 13–56. Cambridge, MA: MIT Press.

1995. "Economic Growth and the Environment." *Quarterly Journal of Economics* 112: 353–78.

Hall, Peter. 1986. *Governing the Economy: The Politics of State Intervention in Britain and France.* New York: Oxford University Press.

Hall, Peter, and David Soskice, eds. 2001. *Varieties of Capitalism: The Institutional Foundations of Comparative Advantage.* New York: Oxford University Press.

Hammond, Allan, et al. 1995. *Environmental Indicators: A Systematic Approach to Measuring and Reporting on Environmental Policy Performance in the Context of Sustainable Development.* Washington, DC: World Resources Institute.

Harbaugh, William, Arik Levinson, and David Wilson. 2002. "Reexamining the Evidence for an Environmental Kuznets Curve." *Review of Economics and Statistics* 84 (2).

Hardin, Russell. 1982. *Collective Action*. Baltimore: Johns Hopkins University Press.

Harrington, Wintson, Richard Morgenstern, and Peter Nelson. 1999. "On the Accuracy of Regulatory Cost Estimates." Resources for the Future Discussion Paper 99-18. Washington, DC.

Harrison, Kathryn. 1995. "Is Cooperation the Answer? Canadian Environmental Enforcement in Comparative Context." *Journal of Policy Analysis and Management* 14: 221–44.

Heilbroner, Robert. 1980. *An Inquiry into the Human Prospect*. New York: Norton.

Hettige, Hemamala, Robert Lucas, and David Wheeler. 1992. "The Toxic Intensity of Industrial Production: Global Patterns, Trends, and Trade Policy." *American Economic Review* 82: 478–81.

Hettige, Hemamala, Muthukumara Mani, and David Wheeler. 1998. "Industrial Pollution in Economic Development: Kuznets Revisited." World Bank Policy Research Working Paper 1876. Washington, DC.

Hicks, Alexander. 1999. *Social Democracy and Welfare Capitalism: A Century of Income Security Politics*. Ithaca: Cornell University Press.

Hildebrandt, Eckart. 1994. *Industrial Relations and Environmental Protection in Europe*. Dublin: European Foundation for Living and Working Conditions.

Hoberg, George. 1986. "Technology, Political Structure and Social Regulation: A Cross-National Analysis." *Comparative Politics* 18 (3): 357–76.

———. 1991. "Sleeping with an Elephant: The American Influence on Canadian Environmental Regulation." *Journal of Public Policy* 11: 107–32.

Hofrichter, Jurgen, and Karlheinz Reif. 1990. "Evolution of Environmental Attitudes in the European Community." *Scandinavian Political Studies* 13 (2): 119–46.

Holland, Kenneth, F. Morton, and Brian Gilligan, eds. 1996. *Federalism and the Environment*. Westport, CT: Greenwood Press.

Huber, Evelyn, Charles Ragin, and John Stephens. 1993. "Social Democracy, Christian Democracy, Constitutional Structure and the Welfare State." *American Journal of Sociology* 99 (3): 711–49.

———. 1997. *Comparative Welfare States Data Set*. Northwestern University and University of North Carolina. <http://lissy.ceps.lu/compwsp.htm>, October 2, 1998.

Huber, Evelyn, and John Stephens. 2001. *Development and Crisis of the Welfare State*. Chicago: University of Chicago Press.

Hukkinen, Janne. 1995. "Corporatism as an Impediment to Ecological Sustenance: The Case of Finnish Waste Management." *Ecological Economics* 15: 59–75.

Immergut, Ellen. 1992. *The Political Construction of Interests: National Health Insurance Politics in Switzerland, France and Sweden, 1930–1970*. Cambridge: Cambridge University Press.

234

References

Imura, Hidefumi. 1997. "Japan." In Martin Jänicke and Helmut Weidner, eds., *National Environmental Policies: A Comparative Study in Capacity Building*, 73–88. New York: Springer-Verlag.

Inglehart, Ronald. 1977. *The Silent Revolution*. Princeton: Princeton University Press.

——— 1990. *Culture Shift in Advanced Industrial Democracies*. Princeton: Princeton University Press.

——— 1995. "Public Support for Environmental Protection: Objective Problems and Subjective Values in 43 Societies." *PS: Political Science and Politics* 28: 57–72.

——— 1997. *Modernization and Postmodernization*. Princeton: Princeton University Press.

Jackman, Robert. 1986. "The Politics of Economic Growth." *Journal of Politics* 49: 202–12.

Jaffe, Adam, and Karen Palmer. 1996. "Environmental Regulation and Innovation: A Panel Data Study." Resources for the Future Discussion Paper 95-03REV. Washington, DC.

Jaffe, Adam, Steven Peterson, Paul Portney, and Robert Stavins. 1995. "Environmental Regulation and the Competitiveness of U.S. Manufacturing: What Does the Evidence Tell Us?" *Journal of Economic Literature* 33: 132–63.

Jahn, Detlef. 1993. *New Politics in Trade Unions: Applying Organizational Theory to the Ecological Discourse on Nuclear Energy in Sweden and Germany*. Brookfield, Vt.: Dartmouth.

——— 1998. "Environmental Performance and Policy Regimes: Explaining Variations in 18 OECD-Countries." *Policy Sciences* 31: 107–31.

——— 1999. "The Social Paradigms of Environmental Performance. The Nordic Countries in an International Perspective." In Ann-Sofie Hermanson and Marko Joas, eds., *Nordic Environments: Comparing Political, Administrative and Policy Apsects*, 111–31. Aldershot: Ashgate.

Jamison, Andrew, Ron Eyerman, and Jacqueline Cramer. 1990. *The Making of the New Environmental Consciousness: A Comparative Study of Environmental Movements in Sweden, Denmark and the Netherlands*. Edinburgh: Edinburgh University Press.

Jänicke, Martin. 1992. "Conditions for Environmental Policy Success." In M. Jachtenfuchs and M. Strübel, eds., *Environmental Policy in Europe*, 71–97. Baden-Baden: Nomos.

Jänicke, Martin, H. Mönch, and M. Binder. 1993. Ecological Aspects of Structural Change. *Intereconomics* 28: 159–69.

Jänicke, Martin, Harald Mönch, Thomas Ranneberg, and Udo Simonis. 1989. "Structural Change and Environmental Impact." *Intereconomics* 24: 24–35.

Jänicke, Martin, and Helmut Weidner, eds. 1997. *National Environmental Policies: A Comparative Study in Capacity Building*. New York: Springer-Verlag.

JEP. 1998. *Joint Environmental Policy-Making: New Interactive Approcahes in the EU and Selected Member States, Final Report*. Wageningen Agricultural University, the Netherlands, October.

Joas, Marko. 1997. "Finland: From Local to Global Politics." In M. S. Andersen and D. Liefferink, eds., *European Environmental Policy: The Pioneers*, 119–60. Manchester: Manchester University Press.

Kamieniecki, Sheldon, and Eliz Sanasarian. 1990. "Conducting Comparative Environmental Research." *Natural Resources Journal* 30: 321–39.

Katzenstein, Peter. 1985. *Small States in World Markets: Industrial Policy in Europe*. Ithaca: Cornell University Press.

Kelman, Steven. 1981. *Regulating America, Regulating Sweden: A Comparative Study of Occupational Health and Safety Policy*. Cambridge, MA: MIT Press.

1992. "Adversary and Cooperationist Institutions for Conflict Resolution in Public Policymaking." *Journal of Policy Analysis and Management* 11: 178–206.

Kitschelt, Herbert. 1986. "Political Opportunity Structures and Political Protest: Anti-nuclear Movements in Four Democracies." *British Journal of Political Science* 16: 58–95.

1988. "Left Libertarian Parties: Explaining Innovation in Competitive Party Systems." *World Politics* 40: 194–234.

1989. "Explaining Contemporary Social Movements: An Exploration in the Comparison of Theories." Paper presented at the annual meeting of the American Political Science Association, Atlanta, August 31–September 3.

1994. *The Transformation of European Social Democracy*. New York: Cambridge University Press.

Kitschelt, Herbert, Peter Lange, Gary Marks, and John Stephens, eds. 1999. *Continuity and Change in Contemporary Capitalism*. Cambridge: Cambridge University Press.

Knight, Jack. 1992. *Institutions and Social Conflict*. Cambridge: Cambridge University Press.

Knoepfel, Peter, Lennart Lundqvist, Rémy Prud' homme, and Peter Wagner. 1987. "Comparing Environmental Policies: Different Styles, Similar Content." In M. Dierkes, H. Weiler, and A. Antal, eds., *Comparative Policy Research: Learning from Experience*, 171–185. London: Gower, Aldershot.

Knoepfel, Peter, and Helmut Weidner. 1986. "Explaining Differences in the Performance of Clean Air Policies: An International and Interregional Comparative Study." *Policy and Politics* 14: 71–91.

1983. "Implementing Air Quality Control Programs in Europe: Some Results of a Comparative Study." In Paul Downing and Ken Hanf, eds., *International Comparisons in Implementing Pollution Laws*, 191–211. Boston: Kluwer-Nijhoff.

Kopp, Raymond, Paul Portney, and Diane DeWitt. 1990. "International Comparisons of Environmental Regulation." Resources for the Future Discussion Paper QE90-22-REV. Washington, DC.

Kurzer, Paulette. 1993. *Business and Banking: Political Change and Economic Integration in Western Europe*. Ithaca: Cornell University Press.

Kuznets, Simon. 1955. "Economic Growth and Income Inequality." *American Economic Review* 45: 1–28.

References

Lane, J., and P. Ersson. 1999. *Politics and Society in Western Europe*. 4th ed. Beverly Hills, CA: Sage.

Lange, Peter, and Geoffrey Garrett. 1985. "The Politics of Growth: Strategic Interaction and Economic Performance in the Advanced Industrial Democracies." *Journal of Politics* 47: 792–827.

Laver, Michael, and W. Ben Hunt. 1992. *Policy and Party Competition*. New York: Routledge.

Lehmbruch, G. 1984. "Concertation and the Structure of Corporatist Networks." In J. Goldthorpe, ed., *Order and Conflict in Contemporary Capitalism*, 60–80. Oxford: Clarendon Press.

Lenschow, Andrea. 1997. "Transformation of European Environmental Governance." EUI Working Paper 97/61. Florence: European University Institute.

Levy, Marc. 1993. "The Power of Tote-Board Diplomacy." In Peter M. Haas, Robert O. Keohane, and Marc A. Levy, eds., *Institutions for the Earth: Sources of Effective International Environmental Protection*, 75–132. Cambridge, MA: MIT Press.

Lichbach, Mark, and Alan Zuckerman, eds. 1997. *Comparative Politics: Rationality, Culture and Structure*. Cambridge: Cambridge University Press.

Liefferink, Duncan. 1996. *Environment and the Nation State – the Netherlands, the EU and Acid Rain*. Manchester: Manchester University Press.

Lijphart, Arend. 1968. *The Politics of Accommodation: Pluralism and Democracy in the Netherlands*. Berkeley: University of California Press.

————. 1971. "Comparative Politics and Comparative Method." *American Political Science Review* 65: 682–93.

————. 1984. *Democracies: Patterns of Majoritarian and Consensus Government in Twenty-one Countries*. New Haven: Yale University Press.

————. 1992. *Parliamentary versus Presidential Government*. Oxford: Oxford University Press.

————. 1994. *Electoral Systems and Party Systems: A Study of Twenty-seven Democracies, 1945–1990*. New York: Oxford University Press.

————. 1999. *Patterns of Democracy*. New Haven: Yale University Press.

Lijphart, Arend, and Markus Crepaz. 1991. "Corporatism and Consensus Democracy in Eighteen Countries: Conceptual and Empirical Linkages." *British Journal of Political Science* 21: 235–56.

Lindblom, Charles. 1977. *Politics and Markets: The World's Political-Economic Systems*. New York: Basic Books.

Lowe, Philip, and Wolfgang Rüdig. 1986. "Political Ecology and the Social Sciences – The State of the Art." *British Journal of Political Science* 16: 513–50.

Lowery, William. 1992. *The Dimensions of Federalism: State Governments and Pollution Control Policies*. Durham, NC: Duke University Press.

Lundqvist, Lennart. 1974. "Do Political Structures Matter in Environmental Politics? *Canadian Public Administration* 17: 119–41.

————. 1980. *The Hare and the Tortoise: Clean Air Policies in the United States and Sweden*. Ann Arbor: University of Michigan Press.

237

1997. "Sweden." In Martin Jänicke and Helmut Weidner, eds., *National Environmental Policies: A Comparative Study in Capacity Building*, pp. 45–72. New York: Springer-Verlag.

2000. "Capacity-Building or Social Construction? Explaining Sweden's Shift towards Ecological Modernization." *GeoForum* 31: 20–32.

Mangun, William. 1988. "A Comparative Analysis of Hazardous Waste Management Policy in Western Europe." In Charles Davis and James Lester, eds., *Dimensions of Hazardous Waste Politics and Policy*, 205–21. Westport, CT: Greenwood.

Markovits, Andrei. 1986. *The Politics of West German Trade Unions*. Cambridge: Cambridge University Press.

Meadows, Dennis. 1972. *Limits to Growth: A Report for the Club of Rome's Project on the Predicament of Mankind*. New York: Universe Books.

Meadows, Donella, Dennis Meadows, and Jorgen Randers. 1992. *Beyond the Limits*. Post Mills, Vt.: Chelsea Green.

Milbrath, Lester. 1984. *Environmentalists: Vanguard for a New Society*. Albany: State University of New York Press.

Miliband, Ralph. 1969. *The State in Capitalist Society*. London: Basic Books.

Moe, Mogens. 1995. *Environmental Administartion in Denmark*. Copenhagen: Danish Ministry of Environment and Energy. <http://www.mst.dk/udgiv/Publications/1995/87-7944-324-9/html/contents.htm>, June 11, 2002.

Moore, Curtis, and Alan Miller. 1994. *Green Gold: Japan, Germany, the United States and the Race for Environmental Technology*. Boston: Beacon Press.

Morgenstern, Richard, William Pizer, and Jhih-Shyang Shih. 1997. "Are We Overstating the Real Economic Costs of Environmental Protection?" Resources for the Future Discussion Paper 97-36-REV. Washington, DC.

2000. "Jobs versus the Environment: An Industry-Level Perspective." Resources for the Future Discussion Paper 99-01-REV. Washington, DC.

Motavalli, Jim. 1997. "The Producer Pays." *E: the Environemntal Magazine* 8: 36–41.

Mueller Rommel, F., ed. 1989. *New Politics in Western Europe: The Rise and the Success of Green and Alternative Lists*. Boulder: Westview Press.

Noll, Roger. 1983. "The Political Foundations of Regulatory Policy." *Zeitschrift für Staatswissenschaft* 139: 37–404.

OECD. 1977a. *Environmental Policies in Japan*. Paris: OECD.

1977b. *Environmental Policy in Sweden*. Paris: OECD.

1978. *Employment and Environment*. Paris: OECD.

1991. *Environmental Data Compendium*. Paris: OECD.

1993a. *Environmental Performance Review: Germany*. Paris: OECD.

1993b. *Environmental Performance Review: Norway*. Paris: OECD.

1994a. *Environmental Performance Review: Italy*. Paris: OECD.

1994b. *Environmental Performance Review: Japan*. Paris: OECD.

1995a. *Environmental Performance Review: Austria*. Paris: OECD.

1995b. *Environmental Performance Review: Canada*. Paris: OECD.

1995c. *Environmental Performance Review: Netherlands*. Paris: OECD.

References

1996. *Environmental Performance Review: Sweden*. Paris: OECD.

1997a. *Environmental Data Compendium*. Paris: OECD.

1997b. *Environmental Performance Review: France*. Paris: OECD.

1998a. *Towards Sustainable Development: Environmental Indicators*. Paris: OECD

1998b. *Waste Minimization Profiles of OECD Member Countries*. Paris: OECD Environment Directorate, May.

1999. *Environmental Data Compendium*. Paris: OECD.

Olson, Mancur. 1965. *The Logic of Collective Action*. Cambridge, MA: Harvard University Press.

1982. *The Rise and Decline of Nations*. New Haven: Yale University Press.

Ophuls, William. 1977. *Ecology and the Politics of Scarcity: Prologue to the Political Theory of the Steady State*. San Francisco: W. H. Freeman.

O'Riordan, Timothy. 1979. "The Role of Environmental Quality Objectives in the Politics of Pollution Control." In T. O'Riordan and R. D'Arge, eds., *Progress in Resource Management and Environmental Planning*, vol. 1. New York: John Wiley.

Paehlke, Robert. 1989. *Environmentalism and the Future of Progressive Politics*. New Haven: Yale University Press.

1997. "Environmental Values and Public Policy." In Norman Vig and Michael Kraft, eds., *Environmental Policy in the 1990s*, 75–94. Washington, DC: Congressional Quarterly Press.

Page, Benjamin, and Robert Shapiro. 1983. "Effects of Public Opinion on Policy." *American Political Science Review* 77: 175–90.

Panatoyou, T. 1993. "Empirical Tests and Policy Analysis of Environmental Degradation at Different Stages of Economic Development." Working Paper WP238, Technology and Employment Program. Geneva: ILO.

Parties and Elections in Europe. 2001. <http//www.parties-and-elections.de/indexe.html>, October 3.

Paterson, W. 1989. "Environmental Protection, the German Chemical Industry and Government: Self-Regulation under Pressure." In S. Bulmer, ed., *The Changing Agenda of West German Public Policy*. Aldershot: Dartmouth.

Pearce, David, Anil Markandya, and Edward Barbier. 1989. *Blueprint for a Green Economy*. London: Earthscan.

Pehle, Heinrich. 1997. "Domestic Obstacles to an International Forerunner." In M. S. Andersen and D. Liefferink, eds., *European Environmental Policy: The Pioneers*, 161–209. Manchester: Manchester University Press.

Persson, Torsten, and Guido Tabellini. 2000. *Political Economics: Explaining Economic Policy*. Cambridge, MA: MIT Press.

Pestoff, Victor. 1999. "The Disappearance of Social Partnership in Sweden during the 1990s and Its Sudden Reappearance in Late 1998." Paper presented at the European Consortium for Political Research Joint Session. Mannheim, Germany March 26–31. <http://www.essex.ac.uk/ecpr/jointsessions/Manpapers/w19/pestoff.pdf>, June 10, 2002.

Peters, B. Guy. 1984. *The Politics of Bureaucracy*. 2nd ed. New York: Longman.

1991. *European Politics Reconsidered*. New York: Holmes Meier.

Piasecki, Bruce, and Gary Davis. 1987. *America's Future in Toxic Waste Management: Lessons from Europe.* Westport, CT: Greenwood.

Porter, Michael. 1990. *The Comparative Advantage of Nations.* New York: Free Press.

Portney, Paul. 2000. "Environmental Problems and Policy, 2000–2050." *Journal of Economic Perspectives* 14: 199–206.

Powell, G. Bingham. 1982. *Contemporary Democracies: Participation, Stability and Violence.* Cambridge, MA: Harvard University Press.

Przeworski, Adam, and Fernando Limongi. 1997. "Modernization: Theories and Facts." *World Politics* 49: 155–83.

Rathje, William, and Cullen Murphy. 1992. *Rubbish! The Archeology of Garbage.* New York: Harper Collins.

Reece, C. 1983. *Deregulation and Environmental Quality: The Use of Tax Policy to Control Pollution in North America and Western Europe.* Westport, CT: Quorum Books.

Richardson, Dick, and Chris Rootes, eds. 1995. *The Green Challenge: The Development of Green Parties in Europe.* New York: Routledge.

Richardson, J. J., ed. 1982. *Policy Styles in Western Europe.* London: Allen and Unwin.

Ringquist, Evan. 1993. *Environmental Protection at the State Level.* Armonk, NY: M. E. Sharpe.

Rodrik. Dani. 1997. *Has Globalization Gone Too Far?* Washington, DC: Institute for International Economics.

Rohrschneider, Robert. 1988. "Citizens' Attitudes toward Environmental Issues: Selfish or Selfless." *Comparative Political Studies* 21: 347–67.

1990. "The Roots of Public Opinion toward New Social Movements: An Empirical Test of Competing Explanations." *American Journal of Political Science* 34: 1–30.

Rose-Ackerman, Cynthia. 1995. *Controlling Environmental Policy: The Limits of Public Law in the United States and Germany.* New Haven: Yale University Press.

Rosenbaum, Walter. 1998. *Environmental Politics and Policy.* Washington, DC: Congressional Quarterly Press.

Ruin, O. 1982. "Sweden." In Jeremy Richardson, ed., *Policy Styles in Western Europe.* Boston: Allen and Unwin.

Sabatier Paul, and David Mazmanian. 1981. "Implementing Coastal Zone Management Laws in California and France." In Paul Downing and Kenneth Hanf, eds., *International Comparisons in Implementing Pollution Laws.* Boston: Kluwer-Nijhoff.

Sahr, R. 1985. *The Politics of Energy Policy Change in Sweden.* Ann Arbor: University of Michigan Press.

Sairinen, Rauno. 2000. *Regulatory Reform of Finnish Environmental Policy.* Ph.D. dissertation, Helsinki University of Technology, Center for Urban and Regional Studies.

Sbargia, Alberto. 1996. "Environmental Policy." In Hellen Wallace and William Wallace, eds., *Policy-Making in the European Union,* 235–56. Oxford: Oxford University Press.

Schattschneider, E. E. 1960. *The Semi-Sovereign People.* Hinsdale, IL: Dryden Press.

References

Scholz, John. 1991. "Cooperative Regulatory Enforcement and the Politics of Administrative Effectiveness." *American Political Science Review* 85: 115–36.

Schroll, Markus, and Erich Staudt. 1999. "Mandatory Recycling but at What Cost?" *Waste Age* 30: 20–21.

Scruggs, Lyle. 1999. "Institutions and Environmental Performance in Seventeen Industrial Democracies." *British Journal of Political Science* 29: 1–31.

——— 2001. "Is There Really a Link between Neo-Corporatism and Environmental Performance? Evidence for the 1990's." *British Journal of Political Science* 31 (4): 686–92.

Seldon, T., and D. Song. 1994. "Environmental Quality and Development: Is There a Kuznets Curve for Air Pollution." *Journal of Environmental Economics and Management* 27: 147–62.

Sen, Amarta, 1970. *Collective Choice and Social Welfare*. San Francisco: Holden-Day.

Shafik, Nemat. 1994. "Economic Development and Environmental Quality: An Econometric Analysis." *Oxford Economic Papers* 46: 757–73.

Shafik, Nemat, and Sushenjit Bandyopadhyay. 1992. "Economic Growth and Environmental Quality: Time Series and Cross-Country Evidence." Background Paper for the World Development Report 1992. Washington, DC: World Bank.

Shugart, Matthew S., and John Carey. 1992. *Presidents and Assemblies: Constitutional Design and Electoral Dynamics*. Cambridge: Cambridge University Press.

Siaroff, Alan. 1999. "Corporation in 24 Industrial Democracies: Meaning and Measurement." *European Journal of Political Research* 36: 175–205.

Simon, Julian, and Herman Kahn. 1984. *The Resourceful Earth*. New York: Blackwell.

Solesbury, William. 1976. "Issues and Innovations in Environmental Policy in Britain, West Germany and California." *Policy Analysis* 3: 1–32.

Soskice, David. 1999. "Divergent Production Regimes: Co-ordinated and Uncoordinated Market Economies in the 1980's and 1990's." In Herbert Kitschelt, Peter Lange, Gary Marks, and John D. Stephens, eds., *Continuity and Change in Contemporary Capitalism*. Cambridge: Cambridge University Press.

Soysal, Yasemin. 1994. *The Limits of Citizenship: Migrants and Postnational Membership in Europe*. Chicago: University of Chicago Press.

——— 1997. *Limits of Citizenship*. Chicago: University of Chicago Press.

Spence, David. 1995. "Paradox Lost: Logic, Morality, and the Foundations of Environmental Law in the 21st Century." *Columbia Journal of Environmental Law* 20: 145–82.

Spence, David, and Lekha Gopalakrishnan. 2000. "Bargaining Theory and Regulatory Reform: The Political Logic of Inefficient Regulation." *Vanderbilt Law Review* 53: 599.

Stephens, John. 2000. "Is Swedish Corporatism Dead? Thoughts on Its Supposed Demise in the Light of the Abortive 'Alliance for Growth' in 1998." Paper presented at the 12th International Conference of Europeanists, Council of European Studies, Chicago, March 30–April 1.

Stern, D., M. Common, and E. Barbier. 1996. "Economic Growth and Environmental Degradation: The Environmental Kuznets Curve and Sustainable Development." *World Development* 24: 1151–60.

Stimson, James, Michael MacKuen, and Robert Erikson. 1995. "Dynamic Representation." *American Political Science Review* 89: 543–65.

Streeck, Wolfgang. 1983. "Between Pluralism and Corporatism: German Business Associations and the State." *Journal of Public Policy* 3: 3–23.

Strom, Kaare, and Steve Swindell. 1993. "Political Parties, Institutions and Environmental Reform." University of California Center for German and European Studies Working Paper 2.17. Berkeley.

Summers, Robert, and Alan Heston. 1991. "The Penn World Table (Mark 5): An Expanded Set of International Comparisons, 1950–1988." *Quarterly Journal of Economics* 106: 327–68.

Sween, Björn. 1996. "Industry's Responses to Comply with Environmental Laws and Regulations." *Industry and Environment* 19 (1): 23–24.

Taylor, Michael. 1987. *The Possibility of Cooperation.* Cambridge: Cambridge University Press, 1987.

Tellegen, Egbert. 1981. "The Environmental Movement in the Netherlands." *Progress in Resource Management and Environmental Planning* 3: 1–32.

Thompson, Andrew. 1980. *Environmental Regulation in Canada: An Assessment of the Process.* Vancouver: Westwater Research Center.

Tokar, Brian. 1997. *Earth for Sale: Reclaiming Ecology in the Age of Corporate Greenwash.* Boston: South End Press.

TUC (Trade Union Congress). 1996. "Trade Unions and the Environment: A Multi-Stakeholder Initiative." Background Report for the TUC Environment Symposium. Chatham House, London, November 22.

Vail, David, Knut Per Hasund, and Lars Drake. 1994. *The Greening of Agricultural Policy in Industrial Societies.* Ithaca: Cornell University Press.

Vogel, David. 1986. *National Styles of Regulation: Environmental Policy in Great Britain and the United States.* Ithaca: Cornell University Press.

——— 1993. "Representing Diffuse Interests in Environmental Policymaking." In K. Weaver and B. Rockman, eds., *Do Institutions Matter?*, 237–71. Washington, DC: Brookings Institution.

——— 1995. *Trading Up: Consumer and Environmental Regulation in a Global Economy.* Cambridge. MA: Harvard University Press.

Vogel, David, and Veronica Kun. 1987. "The Comparative Study of Environmental Policy: A Review of the Literature." In Meinolf Dierkes, Hans Weiler, and Ariane Antal, eds., *Comparative Policy Research: Learning from Experience*, 99–170. Aldershot: Gower.

Wall, G. 1976. "National Coping Styles: Policies to Combat Environmental Problems." *International Journal of Environmental Studies* 9: 239–45.

Wallace, David. 1995. *Environmental Policy and Industrial Innovation: Strategies in Europe, the USA and Japan.* London: Earthscan Publications.

WCED (World Commission on Environment and Development). 1987. *Our Common Future.* New York: Oxford University Press.

References

Weale, Albert. 1992. *The New Politics of Pollution*. Manchester: Manchester University Press.

Weale, Albert, Timothy O'Riordan, and Louise Kramme. 1990. *Controlling Pollution in the Round*. London: Anglo German Foundation.

Weaver, Kent, and Bert Rockman, eds. 1993. *Do Institutions Matter?* Washington, DC: Brookings.

Webb, Kernaghan. 1988. *Pollution Control in Canada. The Regulatory Approach in the 1980's*. Ottowa: Law Reform Commission.

Weidner, Helmut. 1995. "25 Years of Modern Environmental Policy in Germany." WZB Discussion Paper, FSII 95(301). Wissenschaftszentrum Berlin, Berlin.

———. 1996. "Umweltkooperation and alternative Konfliktregelungsverfahren in Duetschland: Zu Entstehung eines neuen Politiknetzwerkes." WZB Schriftenreihe FII, Berlin: 96(302).

Westerlund, R. 1980. "Sweden." In *Air Pollution Control: National and International Perspectives*. Selected Readings Prepared in Conjunction with Aspen Berlin Conference, April 8–11, 1979. Washington, DC: American Bar Association.

Western, Bruce. 1995. "Concepts and Suggestions for Robust Regression Analysis." *American Journal of Political Science* 39: 786–817.

Wetstone Gregory, and Armin Rosencranz. 1983. *Acid Rain in Europe and North America: National Responses to an International Problem*. Washington, DC: Environmental Law Institute.

Wiarda, Howard. 1997. *Corporatism and Comparative Politics: The Other Great "Ism."* New York: M. E. Sharpe.

Wilson, Graham. 2002. "Imposing Cooperation." Paper presented at the annual meeting of the Midwest Political Science Association, Chicago, April.

World Economic Forum, Yale Center for Environmental Law and Policy, and Center for International Earth Science Information. 2001. *Environmental Sustainability Index*. <http://www.ciesin.columbia.edu/indicators/ESI>, January 1.

Index

acid rain, 29, 33
agency capture, 128, 147
agricultural policies, 47, 149
Aguilar Fernandez, S., 133, 226
air pollution, 127, 130, 147
ambient quality measures, 24–7, 59
Andersen, M. S., 3, 126, 215
Andrews, P., 87, 144, 228
associations. *See* industry associations
Australia, 17
Austria: economic growth and, 72t, 92t, 108, 149; federalism in, 166t, 174 ; fertilizer use in, 45t, 46–7; general environmental concern in, 85t; geographic advantage and, 74t; hazardous waste in, 52; income in, 67t, 68, 108; industrialization in, 67t, 68; interest groups in, 99t, 100, 101t; mobilization in, 112t; municipal waste generation in, 38t, 39; nitrogen oxide emissions in, 34, 35t; performance of, 51t, 52, 115; policy-making style in, 133, 134t, 155t, 219–20; political parties in, 104t; population density and, 74; postmaterialism in, 106t; recycling in, 40–1; separation of powers in, 170–1; single-party/coalition government in, 166t, 167; sulfur oxide emissions in, 30t; wastewater treatment in, 43; willingness to pay in, 92t, 95
automobile exhausts, 34–5, 52

Badaracco, J., 127
Belgium: economic growth/cycles in, 72t, 87–8, 91, 92t, 93–4, 107, 149; electoral systems in, 166t, 181; federalism in, 166t, 174–5; fertilizer use in, 45t, 46–7; general environmental concern in, 85t, 86; geographic advantage and, 74t, 76, 195,

206; income in, 67t; industrialization in, 67t; interest groups in, 99t, 100, 101t, 102; mobilization in, 112t; municipal waste generation in, 38t; nitrogen oxide emissions in, 34, 35t; performance of, 51t, 76, 181, 188; policy-making style in, 133, 155t; political parties in, 104t; postmaterialism in, 106t; recycling in, 41; separation of powers in, 170–1, 188; single-party/coalition government in, 165, 166t; as statistical outlier, 193, 195; sulfur oxide emissions in, 30t; unemployment in, 91, 107; wastewater treatment in, 43t, 44; willingness to pay in, 92t, 95, 102
bicameralism, 16, 166t, 170–1, 179, 183–4
Bollen, K., 191, 193
Brickman, R., 127
Britain. *See* United Kingdom

Canada: economic growth and, 71, 72t, 92t, 108; federalism in, 166t, 174, 181; fertilizer use in, 45t, 46–7, 49; general environmental concern in, 86; geographic advantage and, 73–4, 76, 206; income in, 61–2, 67t, 76, 108, 187–8; industrialization in, 67; interest groups in, 99t, 100, 101t, 102; mobilization in, 112t, 118–19; municipal waste generation in, 38t, 215; nitrogen oxide emissions in, 35t; performance of, 51t, 71, 76, 118–19, 181, 187–8; policy-making style in, 127, 133, 134t, 155t, 220; political parties in, 87n9, 104t, 105; population density and, 74, 77; postmaterialism in, 105, 106t; recycling in, 41; separation of powers in, 170–1, 179, 187–8; single-party/coalition government in, 165; sulfur oxide

Index

111–20; models of, 59–60, 193; political
institutions and, 177–87; postmaterialism
and, 116–17; in prior research, 124–31
Environmental Sustainability Index, 53,
201–2
Erikson, R., 11
Eurobarometer surveys, 83–4, 90–1, 96–7
European Union (EU): convergence and, 5,
22, 32–5, 47, 210; general environmental
concern in, 84–6; nitrogen oxide
emissions in, 34, 37; public opinion in,
88–93; sulfur oxide emissions in, 32–3. *See*
also individual member countries
executive dominance, 16, 166t, 169–70, 179,
183–4. *See also* separation of powers

federalism, 15–16, 163, 166t, 172–5,
179–81, 183–4
fertilizer use, 5, 23, 44–50, 217–18
Finland: economic growth and, 72t, 92t, 94;
federalism in, 166t, 181; fertilizer use in,
45t, 46–7; general environmental concern
in, 85t; geographic advantage and, 74t;
hazardous waste in, 52; income in, 67t;
industrialization in, 67t; interest groups
in, 99t, 101t, 102; mobilization in, 112t,
115–16, 118–19; municipal waste
generation in, 38t, 39, 215; nitrogen oxide
emissions in, 35t; performance of, 51t, 52,
115–17, 118–19, 181; policy-making style
in, 133, 134t, 155t, 221–2; political parties
in, 103n, 104t; population density and, 74;
postmaterialism in, 105, 106t, 117;
recycling in, 40–1; separation of powers
in, 169–71, 179; single-party/coalition
government in, 165, 166t; sulfur oxide
emissions in, 30t, 31; unemployment in,
107; wastewater treatment in, 43t;
willingness to pay in, 92t, 95
Food and Agriculture Organization, 46
France: automobile exhausts in, 37;
economic growth/cycles in, 72t, 87–8,
92t, 93–4, 107; federalism in, 166t, 175;
fertilizer use in, 45t; general
environmental concern in, 12, 85t, 86, 88;
geographic advantage and, 74t, 76;
income in, 67t, 107; industrialization in,
67t; interest groups in, 99t, 100, 101t;
mobilization in, 112t, 113, 118–19;
municipal waste generation in, 38t, 39;
nitrogen oxide emissions in, 34, 35t;
performance of, 51t, 118–19;
policy-making style in, 126, 133, 134t,
155t, 222; political parties in, 103n, 104t,
105; postmaterialism in, 106t; recycling

in, 41t; separation of powers in, 169–71;
single-party/coalition government in,
166t, 167; sulfur oxide emissions in, 30t;
unemployment in, 91, 107; wastewater
treatment in, 43, 126; willingness to pay
in, 92t, 95
free-rider problem, 14, 144, 148

Garrett, G., 122–3
geographic advantage, 9, 56, 72–7, 118–19,
159, 202–3, 206
Germany: automobile exhausts in, 37;
economic growth/cycles in, 72t, 88, 92t,
93–4; European integration and, 210;
federalism in, 166t, 172, 174, 181;
fertilizer use in, 45t, 46–7, 217–18;
general environmental concern in, 85t,
86–8; geographic advantage and, 74t, 76,
195; hazardous waste in, 52; income in,
67t, 76, 195; industrialization in, 67t,
68–9; interest groups in, 99–102, 112,
223; mobilization in, 112–13, 115;
municipal waste generation in, 38t,
39–40; nitrogen oxide emissions in, 34,
35t; nuclear power in, 172; performance
of, 51t, 52, 76, 115, 127, 156, 178, 180–1,
195; policy-making style in, 126, 133,
134t, 149, 155t, 156, 222–3; political
parties in, 87n9, 103n, 104t, 112, 164;
pollution dispersal methods in, 24;
population density and, 74;
postmaterialism in, 106t; recycling in, 41t;
separation of powers in, 170–1, 179;
single-party/coalition government in,
164–5, 166t, 178; as statistical outlier,
193, 195; sulfur oxide emissions in, 30t,
32; trade unions in, 138; veto structure
measures and, 166t, 195; wastewater
treatment in, 43t, 126; willingness to pay
in, 92t, 95
glass recycling, 5, 23, 40–1, 49–50
globalization, 122–3, 210–11
Granato, J., 197
Greece, 17, 85t, 92t, 99t, 100, 101t, 107–8,
112
greenhouse effect, 33
"green" marketing, 12
green parties. *See* political parties
Grossman, G., 57–9, 61

Hall, P., 124
Harbaugh, W., 61
Hardin, R., 132
Harrison, K., 127, 220
hat matrix tests, 193

Index

landfills, 37, 40
Lange, P., 122–3
left-libertarian parties. *See* political parties
legislatures. *See* bicameralism
Lehmbruch, G., 132–3, 154
Levinson, A., 61
Lichbach, M., 6n
Lijphart, A., 16, 154, 162, 165, 170–1, 174, 182n
limits-to-growth theories, 7, 9, 56–7, 188, 204
Long Range Transboundary Air Pollution Treaty (LRTAP), 29, 33–4
Lowe, P., 79
Lundqvist, L., 125, 127, 135, 143, 167–9
Luxembourg, 85t, 92t, 99–100, 101t, 108, 112

MacKuen, M., 11
markets and marketing, 1, 12, 57, 71, 82
Masurek, J., 53
Mertig, A., 121n
methodologies. *See* environmental performance, methodology of
mobilization. *See* environmental mobilization
modernization theories, 64, 130
Morgenstern, R., 137
multipartyism, 166t, 183, 186–7
municipal waste generation, 5, 23, 37–40, 48–50, 73, 215–16

nature protection groups, 97–8
negotiated rule-making, 221
neocorporatism, 13–15, 123, 184, 186; advantages of, 140–51; concertation and, 132–3; critiques of, 134–40; globalization and, 211; measurement of, 154–5. *See also* interest groups, environmental; policy-making styles
Netherlands: automobile exhausts in, 37; economic growth/cycles in, 72, 87–8, 92t, 93–4; electoral systems in, 166t, 177; European integration and, 210; federalism in, 166t, 175; fertilizer use in, 45t, 46–7; general environmental concern in, 85t, 86–8; geographic advantage and, 74t, 206; hazardous waste in, 52; income in, 67t; industrialization in, 67t; interest groups in, 99–103, 108, 110, 115, 140; mobilization in, 112t, 113, 115, 118–19, 159; municipal waste generation in, 38t, 39, 215; nitrogen oxide emissions in, 34, 35t; performance of, 51t, 52, 72, 76, 115, 118–19, 159, 178; policy-making style in,

126, 133, 134t, 140, 155t, 225; political parties in, 87n9, 103, 104t; population density and, 74, 77; postmaterialism in, 105, 106t; recycling in, 40–1; separation of powers in, 170–1; single-party/coalition government in, 165, 166t, 178; as statistical outlier, 102, 110; sulfur oxide emissions in, 30t; wastewater treatment in, 43t, 126, 216–17; willingness to pay in, 92t, 95, 102–3
"new environmental paradigm," 10–11, 80
new social movements, 87, 96
New Zealand, 17
nitrogen oxide emissions (NO_x), 4–5, 23, 33–7, 47, 49–50, 52, 215
nonpoint pollution, 42, 45
Norway: economic growth and, 71, 72t, 92t, 94; fertilizer use in, 45t, 46–7; general environmental concern in, 85t; geographic advantage and, 74t; hazardous waste in, 52; income in, 67t; industrialization in, 67t; interest groups in, 99t, 101t, 102; mobilization in, 112t; municipal waste generation in, 38t, 39; nitrogen oxide emissions in, 34, 35t; performance of, 51t, 71; policy-making style in, 133, 134t, 155t, 225–6; political parties in, 87n9, 104; postmaterialism in, 106t; recycling in, 41t, 216; separation of powers in, 170–1; single-party/coalition government in, 165, 166t; sulfur oxide emissions in, 30t; wastewater treatment in, 43t; willingness to pay in, 92t, 95, 102
nuclear power expansion, 172

oil crisis (1975–80), 29, 31
Olson, M., 14, 148, 168
Organization for Economic Cooperation and Development (OECD), 5, 19–20, 29, 38. *See also individual member countries*
O'Riordan, T., 223

packaging laws, 39
Panatoyou, T., 66
paper recycling, 40–1, 49–50
permit systems, 82, 126
Pizer, W., 137
pluralism, 13–15, 135, 141. *See also* policy-making styles
policy-making styles, 125–35, 152–60, 219–28; concertation and, 132–3, 136, 154; flexibility and, 146–7; incrementalism and, 132; information and, 141–6, 151; organization of interests and, 148–51, 207

Index

Anthony W. Marx, *Making Race, Making Nations: A Comparison of South Africa, the United States, and Brazil*

Joel S. Migdal, Atul Kohli, and Vivienne Shue, eds., *State Power and Social Forces: Domination and Transformation in the Third World*

Scott Morgenstern and Benito Nacif, eds., *Legislative Politics in Latin America*

Wolfgang C. Muller and Kaare Strom, *Policy, Office, or Votes?*

Maria Victoria Murillo, *Labor Unions, Partisan Coalitions, and Market Reforms in Latin America*

Ton Notermans, *Money, Markets, and the State: Social Democratic Economic Policies since 1918*

Paul Pierson, *Dismantling the Welfare State? Reagan, Thatcher, and the Politics of Retrenchment*

Simona Piattoni, ed., *Clientelism, Interests, and Democratic Representation*

Marino Regini, *Uncertain Boundaries: The Social and Political Construction of European Economies*

Jefferey M. Sellers, *Governing from Below: Urban Regions and the Global Economy*

Yossi Shain and Juan Linz, eds., *Interim Governments and Democratic Transitions*

Theda Skocpol, *Social Revolutions in the Modern World*

David Stark and László Bruszt, *Postsocialist Pathways: Transforming Politics and Property in East Central Europe*

Sven Steinmo, Kathleen Thelan, and Frank Longstreth, eds., *Structuring Politics: Historical Institutionalism in Comparative Analysis*

Susan C. Stokes, *Mandates and Democracy: Neoliberalism by Surprise in Latin America*

Susan C. Stokes, ed., *Public Support for Market Reforms in New Democracies*

Duane Swank, *Global Capital, Political Institutions, and Policy Change in Developed Welfare States*

Sidney Tarrow, *Power in Movement: Social Movements and Contentious Politics*

Ashutosh Varshney, *Democracy, Development, and the Countryside*

Elisabeth Jean Wood, *Forging Democracy from Below: Insurgent Transitions in South Africa and El Salvador*